The Good Idea:
Democracy and
Ancient Greece

*ESSAYS IN CELEBRATION
OF THE 2500TH ANNIVERSARY
OF ITS BIRTH IN ATHENS*

PUBLISHED UNDER THE AUSPICES OF THE
SPEROS BASIL VRYONIS CENTER FOR THE STUDY OF HELLENISM

This is the twenty-second volume in the series
Hellenism: Ancient, Mediæval, Modern

The Good Idea: Democracy and Ancient Greece

ESSAYS IN CELEBRATION

OF THE 2500TH ANNIVERSARY

OF ITS BIRTH IN ATHENS

Edited by
John A. Koumoulides

ΕΝΘΑ ΤΙΘΑΙΒΩΣΣΟΥΣΙ ΜΕΛΙΣΣΑΙ

Published by
Aristide D. Caratzas
New Rochelle, New York • Athens • Moscow

Copyright © 1995 by John A. Koumoulides

All rights reserved. No part of this book may be reproduced
in any form without the written permission of the publisher.
Copyright for " 'Ever in Process of Becoming:'
The Autochthony of the Greeks" held by
Colin Renfrew and is published by permission.

Published by
Aristide D. Caratzas, Publisher
Melissa Media Associates, Inc.
30 Church Street (P.O. Box 210)
New Rochelle, NY 10802

Library of Congress Cataloging-in-Publication Data

The good idea : democracy and ancient Greece : essays in celebration
    of the 2500th anniversary of its birth in Athens / edited by John A.
    Koumoulides.
        192 p. 23 cm
        Includes bibliographical references.
        ISBN 0-89241-562-2
        1. Democracy—Greece—Athens—History.
        2. Democracy—Greece—History.
        I. Koumoulides, John A., 1938–
JC79.A8G66 1995
320.438—dc20   95-18701
                                                            CIP

Contents

	Preface *John A. Koumoulides* Professor of History, Ball State University	**1**
1	**"Ever in Process of Becoming": The Autochthony of the Greeks** *Professor Lord Renfrew of Kaimsthorn, FBA* Disney Professor of Archaeology, University of Cambridge	**7**
2	**The School of Greece** *Professor Sir John Boardman, FBA* Lincoln Professor of Classical Archaeology, University of Oxford	**29**
3	**Liberty and the Ancient Greeks** *Oswyn Murray* Fellow, Balliol College, University of Oxford	**33**
4	**How Democratic Was Ancient Athens?** *Professor Robert Browning, FBA* University of London	**57**
5	**Cleisthenes and His Reforms** *Dr. Robin Lane Fox, FRSL* Reader in Ancient History, University of Oxford	**71**
6	**Aristotle's Ideals of Life** *Professor Sir Anthony Kenny, FBA* University of Oxford	**95**
7	**Democracy After 2,500 Years** *Sir David Hunt, KCMG, OBE*	**119**

Contents

8 Democracy: The First Twenty-Five Centuries   133
Dr. Leslie Lipson
Professor Emeritus of Political Science, University of California, Berkeley

9 Citizenship as a Form of Psycho-Social Identity   147
Professor Eli Sagan
New York School for Social Research

10 The Role of Cyprus in the Ancient Mediterranean and the Origins of Its Hellenization   161
Professor Vassos Karageorghis
University of Cyprus

Appendices   175
Α Constitutional Development of Athens: Key Terms and Dates, 175
Β Thucydides (460-400 B.C.) Pericles' Funeral Oration, 177
Γ Aristotle (384-322 B.C.) *Politics*, Book VI. ii, 181
Δ Law for the Protection of Democracy (337-336 B.C.), 182

The Contributors to this Volume   183

Index   187

This volume is dedicated to

†Angelos Th. Angelopoulos
and
Panayiotis Th. Angelopoulos

Ἀνδρί τοι χρεών μνήμην προσεῖναι,
τερπνόν εἴ τί που πάθοι.
If a man has received a kindness from another,
he ought ever to keep it in grateful remembrance.
—Sophocles

Preface

In 1992-1993, in a year-long birthday party, we celebrated the 2,500th anniversary of the world's first democracy. In Greece, where the seeds were planted for the free institutions to which every country in the world today aspires, and in the United States of America, where the miracle was reborn in the eighteenth century,[1] a plethora of activities commemorated the Athenian invention and secular miracle.[2]

If the ancient Greeks were concerned with good government, it was probably because they had seen so many examples of the bad kind, monarchy, tyranny and oligarchy not excepted. From 560 B.C. Athens was ruled by the tyrant/dictator, Pisistratus. Such rulers, who exploited local grievances to seize personal power, were a common Greek phenomenon of the sixth century, the age of tyrants. Tyranny, however, did not necessarily contain overtones of cruelty or oppression: indeed, Athens under Pisistratus was a prosperous and flourishing place. Tyranny ended in Athens in 510 B.C. In 508/7 B.C., after a brief period of aristocratic rule, Cleisthenes, a member of the aristocratic Alcmaeonidae family, instituted reforms and, as Herodotus wrote, democracy was invented.

Cleisthenes' reforms created the constitutional and social framework for the establishment of the first democracy in the world. The aristocrat *qua* democrat divided the citizens of Athens into ten tribes that cut across social and geographical boundaries. In doing so he broke up alliances among the old noble families and shifted political power from its previous aristocratic base to the Assembly of the people, the *Ekklesia*. Cleisthenes replaced the old tribal and religious structures of Attica with a new political entity, the *demos*, and gave equal political rights to all free citizens of Athens, regardless of their social and economic status.

Although many refinements were yet to come, Cleisthenes is thus credited with initiating democracy, a system by which political power is vested in the *demos*, the common people. Of course, it was not a perfect democracy. Women, slaves and aliens had no say, and men only reached adulthood at the age of thirty. From then on, decisions concerning the city were taken by the body of the *demos*, in this case the entire body of enfranchised Athenian males, gathered as the citizens' Assembly (*Ekklesia*), the sovereign authority, which decided by majority, and a citizens' Council (*Boule*). All government offices were held by the citizens themselves, who were chosen by lot.[3]

The main significance of Cleisthenes' reforms was that they freed man's spirit. Athenians developed a love of freedom and a critical and inquisitive attitude towards all human affairs. At its height under Pericles the Athenian democracy produced drama, art, architecture, political theory and philosophy of such power and excellence that they continue to shape Western civilization.

The anniversary of the birth of democracy comes at a crucial point in time. In the closing decade of the 20th century, against a background of earth-shaking events in the former Soviet Union and Eastern Europe and plans for European unity after centuries of conflict, the ancient word *demokratia* is invoked again and again as the ideal solution to all the problems of our complex modern world.[4] Indeed, the 2,500th anniversary of democracy offers us a unique opportunity to throw open the question of the importance and relevance of democracy to today's world and to our lives. In his work entitled *Ancient Greece*, Sir Stanley Casson observed:

It may be asked what we have in common with Ancient Greece. It will be sufficient to answer if we say that we have common ideals. The Greek strove, as we strive, to think clearly, to act justly, and to live freely. That he did not succeed completely in doing any of these things for long is the clear verdict of history, for Greek culture faded in the twilight of philosophic decadence, moral failure, and political subjection. But it is from the failures as well as from the successes of Greece that we can strive to establish the outlines of our own life. Complete success is a hard taskmaster just because it is hard to live up to. Partial success and the causes of failure provide better instructors to an imperfect world. From its imperfections we can get a hint of what the greatness of Greece might have been; from its perfections we can learn our own shortcomings.

What makes Greeks so unbounded a store of wealth for us to draw from is that the Greeks at the time of the height of their greatness never lost touch with humanity. Whatever they did or thought was judged by the one standard of mankind. 'Man is the measure of all things,' said their own proverb. And this greatness was the greatness of a national spirit, not of a party, a sect, or a dynasty.[5]

In the funeral oration (431 B.C.) of Pericles we have an eloquent summary of the Athenian vision of a democratic society:

Preface

XXXVII. We live under a form of government which does not emulate the institutions of our neighbours; on the contrary, we are ourselves a model which some follow, rather than the imitators of other peoples. It is true that our government is called a democracy, because its administration is in the hands, not of the few, but of the many; yet while as regards the law all men are on an equality for the settlement of their private disputes, as regards the value set on them it is as each man is in any way distinguished that he is preferred to public honours, not because he belongs to a particular class, but because of personal merits; nor, again, on the ground of poverty is a man barred from a public career by obscurity of rank if he but has it in him to do the state a service. And not only in our public life are we liberal, but also as regards our freedom from suspicion of one another in the pursuits of every-day life; for we do not feel resentment at our neighbour if he does as he likes, nor yet do we put on sour looks which, though harmless, are painful to behold. But while we thus avoid giving offence in our private intercourse, in our public life we are restrained from lawlessness chiefly through reverent fear, for we render obedience to those in authority and to the laws, and especially to those laws which are ordained for the succour of the oppressed and those which, though unwritten, bring upon the transgressor a disgrace which all men recognize.[6]

The heritage of Western civilization is a treasure-chest that each generation discovers anew. The 2,500th anniversary of the birth of democracy offers us all an opportunity to reconsider the world of ancient Greece and draw from "its unbounded store of wealth"[7] lessons to better understand our world, appreciate and defend democracy and our heritage, and devote our energies and means to the creation of a more humane, just and free world where we can all live in dignity, mutual respect and understanding.

During the academic year 1992-1993, under the auspices of Ball State University's Greek Studies Programme, a diverse group of scholars visited the university and participated in the year-long lecture series and other activities in commemoration of democracy's 2,500th birthday. The present volume is not a history of democracy and its development in ancient Athens. The book consists of the papers given at Ball State University during that academic year, together with the essays of Professor Sir John Boardman and Professor Leslie Lipson, especially written at the invitation of the editor. From Renfrew's autochthony of the Greeks, Murray's discussion of ancient democratic ideas and institutions, Fox's reforms of Cleisthenes, Lipson's analysis of the continuing importance of democracy, Sagan's profound social and political changes from an archaic agricultural society to a democratic and imperial society, to the influence of Greece on the world of Cyprus, the contributors have fulfilled the primary goal of the lecture series: trace the course of democracy from its ancient origins to its modern manifestations, discuss its significance for our own times and understand and appreciate the many contributions of Greece to Western civilization. The purpose of the book is to share the scholarship of our distinguished scholars with the greater public.

I am most grateful to both those who took part in the lecture series and those who kindly accepted my invitation to contribute essays for this publication. I wish to record my debt of gratitude to the Friends of the Greek Studies of Ball State University, for their twenty-five-year-long generous financial support and dedication to the programme. In particular, I wish to thank Dr. and Mrs. Philip Ball, Mr. and Mrs. Edmund F. Ball, Mr. and Mrs. Clell Douglass, Professor and Mrs. Richard Burkhardt, Dr. and Mrs. John J. Pruis, Mr. and Mrs. Jack Buckles, Mrs. Elizabeth Hinshaw, and Mrs. Joanna Meeks.

I am especially grateful to Professor John A. Crook, FBA, Emeritus Professor of Ancient History, St. John's College, University of Cambridge, who first suggested "the good idea" for the title. I am grateful to Viscount Norwich, Sir David and Lady Hunt, Professor and Mrs. Angelos Angelopoulos, Mr. and Mrs. Panayiotis Angelopoulos, Mr. and Mrs. Theodore Angelopoulos, Mr. and Mrs. John Bilimatsis, Mr. and Mrs. Angelos Canellopoulos, Mr. and Mrs. Ioannis Lainopoulos, Mr. and Mrs. Michael Jaharis, and Mr. and Mrs. Nikos Kefalidis. I am also grateful for the friendship and moral support of the Hon. Dr. John Brademas, President Emeritus of New York University, United States Senator Paul S. Sarbanes of the state of Maryland, United States Representative Lee H. Hamilton of the state of Indiana, as well as Mr. Peter N. Marudas, Mr. Marvin F. Moss and Mr. Wayne Vance. I owe a particular debt of gratitude to the President and members of the Board of the A. G. Leventis Foundation, Paris, France, the President and members of the Board of the Kosta and Eleni Ourani Foundation of the Academy of Athens, and the Jaharis Family Foundation, for generous subventions. Finally, I thank Professor Ray White, Chairman, Department of History, Ball State University, and Ms. Jan Dragoo for her assistance in typing the manuscript. I am most grateful to my editor, Mrs. Evanthia Allen, who did such excellent work on the typescript, and the publisher, Mr. Aristide D. Caratzas, Melissa Media Associates, Inc., for including this volume in his list of scholarly publications.

John A. Koumoulides

Preface

NOTES

[1] Richard, C. J., *The Founders and the Classics: Greece, Rome and the American Enlightenment* (Cambridge: Harvard University Press, 1994).

[2] Among the activities organized to celebrate 2,500 years since the birth of democracy in Greece, are the following: "The Archaeology of Democracy," an International Conference held under the aegis of the American School of Classical Studies at Athens, Athens, 4-6 December, 1992; "Commemorating the 2,500th Anniversary of the Birth of Democracy," under the auspices of The Society for the Preservation of the Greek Heritage, held in Washington, D. C. Spring 1993; "The Cradle of Democracy: Athens Then and Now," The Alexander S. Onassis Center for Hellenic Studies, New York University, 21-22 November, 1992; "Athenian Democracy," The University of California, Santa Cruz, 21 June-30 July, 1992, and numerous other activities. Also publications such as, Dunn, J. (ed.), *Democracy: The Unfinished Journey 508 B.C. to A.D. 1993 (Oxford: Oxford University Press, 1992).*

[3] Jones, P., "The Invention of Democracy," *Cambridge: The Magazine of the Cambridge Society*, Number 30 (Summer, 1992), 60-66; Hansen, M. H., "Kleisthenes and the Icons of Democracy," *History Today*, Volume 44 (1), (January, 1994), 14-21; Ober, J., "What Democracy meant to the Athenians," *ibid.*, 22-27; Kyrtatas, D., "The Athenian Democracy and its Slaves," *History Today*, Volume 44 (2), (February, 1994), 43-48. See also Hansen, M. H., *The Athenian Democracy and the Age of Demosthenes* (Oxford: B. Blackwell, 1991), and Davies, J. K., *Democracy and Classical Greece*, (Cambridge: Harvard University Press, 1993).

[4] When Chinese students occupied Tienanmen Square in 1989, they raised a statue and called it "The Goddess of Democracy." In 1979 their older siblings turned a length of Peking brick into "Democracy Wall," where freedom of expression briefly flourished. In both cases the name and spirit of democracy were summoned to oppose the geriatric tyrants of the Forbidden City. China still waits for democracy, but Tienanmen Square did much to make possible the 1989 revolutions in Eastern Europe. The crowds there likewise invoked democracy.

[5] Casson, S., *Ancient Greece: A Study* (London: Oxford University Press, 1992) p. 7.

[6] Thucydides, *History of the Peloponnesian War*, II. xxxvii. English translation by C. F. Smith. (Cambridge: Harvard University Press, 1980), 322-325.

[7] Casson, p.7

1

"Ever in Process of Becoming" The Autochthony of the Greeks

Colin Renfrew

On this occasion I should like to try something which may be rather daring, rather risky when undertaken by one who is certainly not a classical scholar. It is to examine again a question which can perhaps, in one sense, only be answered by a prehistorian. This is the question posed by a distinguished contemporary of Sir Arthur Evans, namely Sir John Myres, as the title of a most interesting book: *Who Were the Greeks?*[1]

The question is not an easy one, indeed it has proved to be more difficult than the Riddle of the Sphinx. For it is one of those trick questions without a definite answer. Or at least it can only be answered by asking rather carefully what it means.

Of course, we all know who the Greeks were. They defeated the Persians, fell into conflict in the Peloponnesian War, invented many of the arts and the sciences, accompanied Alexander in the conquest of the east, and although conquered politically by Rome, not only lived on in the Byzantine Empire, but also intellectually dominated the west. For as Horace acknowledges:

> *Graecia capta ferum victorem cepit et artis*
> *intulit agresti Latio.*[2]

But what was their origin? Where did they come from? How do we account for their remarkable abilities and achievements? In that sense, who were they?

It is now possible, I believe, to offer observations which augment in two ways those of Myres and his contemporaries. Let us, however, acknowledge at the outset that Myres reached the nub of the solution in the last paragraph of his book, with the observation: "The general conclusion is that the Greeks never wholly were 'one people,' but were ever in process of becoming."[3] The first contribution is methodological: to examine more carefully the concept of "ethnicity," of what it is to have an "ethnikotita," a "nationality," of what it means to have some kind of collective identity. From this examination we shall conclude, as others have before, that the full self-identity of "being Greek" as we think of it now only emerged in the fifth century B.C. in the aftermath of the Persian Wars. To be Greek had a more restricted meaning before that time, and before the seventh century B.C. a very restricted meaning indeed.

The second contribution arises from the great wealth of new data which allows us to think in terms of a series of continuities across the "Dark Ages" – continuities in population, culture, religion and language. We can now begin to see more clearly that what had emerged by the fifth century B.C. was the result of a series of transformations which we can trace back to the Mycenaeans and further back to the Minoans, to the first palaces, to the international spirit of the Early Bronze Age, back perhaps to the Neolithic period and the first farmers, and beyond to the first fishers and the first traders of the Aegean.

I shall argue that there was no "coming of the Greeks," that Greek culture, Greek beliefs and probably the Greek language developed here, within the land which we know as Greece today, that in that sense the Greeks were autochthonous and were "ever in the process of becoming."

Of course, such ideas are not entirely new. The Minoan-Mycenaean antecedents of Greek religion were brilliantly analysed by Martin Nilsson[4] many years ago. And several writers in recent years, not least my colleague in Cambridge, Anthony Snodgrass[5], have described the formation of Greek society in the Archaic period, increasingly well documented in recent excavations in such island cities as Naxos, Zagora on Andros, and Minoa on Amorgos. But these ideas are certainly not widely accepted. Many history books still offer a picture of three successive "waves" of invading Aeolians, Ionians and Dorians, based on what I feel is a misinterpretation of the account given by the classical authors. Victor Ehrenberg, for instance, opens his in many ways excellent book, *The Greek State* with the words: "When we speak of the Hellenic State we are thinking of the political forms that grew out of the age of Greek immigration into the Aegean."[6]

I would argue that, on the contrary, it is time to view "the glory that was Greece" as the creation and product of human beings who have lived in the Aegean for several millennia. We should undertake the analysis, the reconstruction, in terms of the material which we have, and not in terms of the importation or immigration of the key elements of our story. Certainly, Greek civilization formed here, in a long series of transformations, and we should investigate this remarkable process with the material before us, without appeal to a crucial role for outside agencies, unless there is good evidence for them.

ON ETHNICITY

Recently Ernest Gellner has shown with great clarity how the idea of the modern nation state is very much a recent creation of the past two centuries.[7] Personal identity is often represented today in terms of national identity, of the citizenship of a territorially defined nation state. But it was not always so. Ethnic awareness, the sense of belonging to a larger group has several ingredients. They were well summarized by the Father of History when the Athenians, addressing the Lacedaemonians, spoke of:

The kinship of all Greeks in blood and speech, and the shrines of gods and the sacrifices that we have in common, and the likeness of our way of life. Τὸ Ἑλληνικὸν ἐον ὅμαιμόν τε καὶ ὁμόγλωσσον, καί θεῶν ἱδρύματα τε κοινὰ καὶ θυσίαι ἤθεα τε ὁμότροπα.[8]

This implicit definition of ethnicity comes very close to that of the modern anthropologist:

Ethnos ... can be defined as a firm aggregate of people, historically established on a given territory, possessing in common relatively stable particularities of language and culture, and also recognising their unity and differences from other similar formations (self-awareness) and expressing this in a self-appointed name (ethnonym).[9]

That special self-identity shared by a large group of people – "ἐμεῖς οἱ Ἕλληνες,"[10] for example – is therefore based on several factors working together:

1. On a shared territory, or land
2. On common descent ('blood' as we, like the ancient Greeks, term it)
3. On a shared language
4. On a community of customs, or culture
5. On a community of beliefs, or religion
6. On a name, an ethnonym, to express the identity of the group
7. On self-awareness, self-identity: ethnicity is what people believe it to be. Part of that self-awareness is a perception of the "otherness" of the others, the outsiders, the barbarians or those who are not "us"
8. On a shared history, or myth of origin

It is now my claim that none of these things was imported into Greece, ready-made, as it were. Contrary to the traditional view, there was no "coming of the Greeks," when an incoming tribe, with its own customs, language, religion, shared descent and self-identity arrived in Greece. That used to be the prevailing view. It was first held that there was either a single coming of the Greeks at the end (or during) the Dark Ages, or at some point in the Bronze Age – perhaps at the beginning of the Middle Bronze Age, associated with a class of pottery known as Minyan ware.

This was sometimes elaborated, using special interpretations of the Classical historians, into three waves of invaders: Achaeans, Ionians and Dorians, which would conveniently account for the three principal dialects of the Greek language in Classical times.

Difficulty in finding any archaeological traces whatever for the "Dorian invasions" has led to a retreat from this position. Its latest version is that the coming of the Greeks might be set back in the Early Bronze Age, associated with events such as the end of the House of Tiles at Lerna, and the change in painted pottery in the Argolid, notably with Lerna IV[11] associated with the phase sometimes known as "Early Helladic III," around 2100 B.C. In fact, that painted pottery is probably a style developed within Greece, and its importance has been exaggerated.

I shall argue instead for a greater degree of continuity under each of the main headings which we have recognized, going right back in some cases to the origins of farming in Greece before 6000 B.C., and in a few respects perhaps further. At that time there was nowhere a Greek language, nor a Greek civilization, no Greek religion, no Greek ethnicity. And what I believe we can begin to trace is the gradual development of all these things, in a series of developments and transformations – some of them very large transformations – which took place on Greek soil, that is to say, within the territories of what we have later come to call Hellas.

It is not possible to give a very good account of these things yet. For some aspects such as language, it will never be possible to give a full account, since the nature of language before the practice of writing is to some extent unknowable. But I think we can set the framework, sketch the outlines, for further work. No one element of what I have to say is decisive. But I think we can see now that the old picture is an illusory one. We can see that, underlying the excellent work which scholars like Ian Morris[12] have been doing to broaden our understanding of the developments in Greek society in the period following the Dark Ages, we need comparable work in order to understand the nature of those still rather mysterious transformations which brought about the gradual evolution of what became Greek culture and Greek ethnicity.

"Ever in Process of Becoming"

1. *The Land*

To define rather better what we have in mind, I'll begin with some indications of the territories and communities of which we are speaking.

Starting with "man the measure of all things," in the most typical early Greek form, the *kouros*, a distribution map of find-spots of Greek *kouroi* begins to outline what a map of Doric temples might do even better, i.e. the extent of Greek religion and culture in the sixth century B.C. A second, purely archaeological map can fill out this impression: the distribution of city states issuing coinage around 500 B.C. For this emphasizes the complete separation between political power – very much divided – and Greekness (ethnicity) which is a fundamental feature of our story.[13]

A more complete picture of the extent of city life in Greece around 400 B.C. was compiled by Ernst Kirsten,[14] and is usefully supplemented in a reminder by Anthony Snodgrass,[15] referable to the archaic period some two centuries earlier, that the territories of Hellas extended well beyond the lands where the *polis* prevailed. For in much of mainland Greece there was no *polis* organization. The social unit was the *ethnos*, commonly translated as the "tribe." The *ethnos* had the same unity of language, religion and custom as the *polis*, and to some extent the self-identity, but it lacked the central urban focus, and in consequence it lacked city life. But the inhabitants of the *ethne* were as much Greeks as those of the *poleis*. And of course they had their own individual and local ethnicities.

The maps, then, give a geographical context for our enquiry. What were the origins of the ethnic unit which they demarcate?

In the first place, as Kirsten[16] illustrated, there is a very striking correlation between the extent of early Greek urbanism and that of the Mycenaean world some 800 years earlier. This gives a clear archaeological hint that there may be significant continuities here. It is one reinforced by more recent work which makes it clear that the term "Dark Age" for the two or three centuries between the decline of the Mycenaean world and the emergence of Greek culture in the Geometric age which preceded the full Archaic period is something of a misnomer.

Moreover, that Mycenaean distribution is itself anticipated some 1500 years earlier again, if we look at the "international spirit" which is so much a feature of the early Bronze Age of the Aegean around 2600 B.C. For although each area – the Cyclades, Crete, south Greece, the Troad – had its own "culture," already there were trading contacts, associated with the development of bronze metallurgy, which were bringing these areas together into a single functioning unit.[17] It is here, ultimately, that we must seek for the roots of the Aegean unity which developed into Greek ethnicity.

2. Genetic Unity

The issue of descent, in broad genetic terms, is one which need not detain us for long. The old attempts at determining "race" in terms of "craniometry" and measurements on long bones have largely been discredited. Genetic research is at present based largely on blood group studies (see Cavalli-Sforza *et al.*, 1994)[18], and increasingly molecular genetics, working directly with DNA is being used.[19]

In these circumstances it is safest to say that genetically the present inhabitants of Greece in the main resemble those of neighbouring lands. Ammerman and Cavalli-Sforza[20] have argued for a significant population input from Anatolia with the inception of farming in Greece. But it is probably true to say that the genetic evidence would not at present militate against a later immigration from the north (e.g. the Coming of the Greeks). It simply gives no good evidence for suggesting such a migration.

Genetic evidence with greater geographic detail will no doubt become available in due course. At this time it does little to help answer the question "Who were the Greeks?".

3. The Greek Language

The Greek language, as most scholars would unhesitatingly agree, belongs to the broader grouping of the Indo-European languages. Wherever the Greek language evolved, it must have done so, linguists agree, from an earlier Proto-Indo-European language.

John Chadwick has already anticipated part of what I have to say:

To ask when the Greeks reached Greece may well be a meaningless question. We have no evidence to prove that Greek existed as a separate language before its speakers were established in Greece, and some indications to the contrary. If we postulate a single invasion at the beginning of the Early Helladic III period, bringing an Indo-European idiom which, after influence by the surviving indigenous peoples, emerged as Greek, we have a more economical hypothesis and one which fits better the facts as at present known. The development of the dialects will then have taken place inside the southern Balkan area, and after 2100 B.C.[21]

I would agree with that view in every particular but one, namely the date of the arrival of individuals with Proto-Indo-European speech in Greece, which I would place far earlier than the date suggested by Chadwick.

But on a further issue I agree with him. He has proposed that, of the dialects,

"Ionic can be a later probably post-Myceanaean development, Aeolic may be equally late."[22] He goes on to suggest that in the Mycenaean world two dialects were simultaneously in use. The first, spoken by the elite, was a standard Mycenaean, closely related to late Arcadian and Cypriot. The second, "substandard" Mycenaean, spoken by the majority of Mycenaeans, was the source of West Greek (including the Doric dialect). After the collapse of the Mycenaean world, this "substandard" Greek came to be spoken in most of the Peloponnese, and it was transported to Crete (and the southern Aegean islands) by the Greeks who moved to Crete after the end of the Minoan palaces in the fifteenth century B.C.[23]

As for the initial arrival of the Proto-Indo-European language to Greece, I have suggested that Proto-Indo-European came to Greece and then to much of the rest of Europe with the first coming of farming from Anatolia.[24] The earliest Neolithic settlement of Greece seems to be in Thessaly and south Macedonia. Crete may have been settled at the same time, but by different groups of people, speaking a different dialect. From this early Proto-Indo-European language, in some regions of Greece (possibly Thessaly and lands to the south) an early form of Greek language would gradually have developed in the later Neolithic and Early Bronze age, probably from c. 5000 to c. 2000 B.C.

It should be remembered, however, that there are other words in Greek, including the place names ending in -inth- and in -ss- which cannot be regarded as Greek. They are frequently considered to be non-Indo-European[25] and certainly non-Greek.[26] How are they to be accounted for if Indo-European farmers had already arrived in Thessaly by 6000 B.C.?

I can see two alternative possibilities there. One is that the Greek language evolved first in Thessaly, while in other areas the evolution of the Proto-Indo-European was slower, so that it retained archaic features, including these place names. A more effective possibility, in my view is that for some time after the arrival of the Proto-Indo-European first farmers in Thessaly, there remained in other parts of Greece small numbers of hunter-gatherers speaking a non-Indo-European language, of which these place names would be a last remaining trace. Just as in other parts of Europe[27] the local "Mesolithic" languages sometimes survived the coming of farming as the hunter-gatherers adopted the new farming methods, so in parts of the Peloponnese and perhaps in Central Greece (Aetolia and Acharnania) the pre-Indo-European language survived for many centuries or millennia before becoming absorbed into the Greek language, perhaps in the Early Bronze Age.

The first alternative would follow the view that the pre-Greek language, with the place names, is nonetheless an early Indo-European language. The second assumes that it was a non-Indo-European language of the Upper Palaeolithic hunter-gatherers of mainland Greece and that these survived in some areas for many centuries after the coming of farming.

Common to both these views is the idea, as proposed by Chadwick, that the Greek language evolved in Greece from the basis of an earlier Proto-Indo-European language. There was no direct importation into Greece of a "Greek" language.

4. Customs and Culture

The formation of a unified culture, of a *koine*, where none previously existed, can only come about through long and persistent interactions. Fortunately, this is a process which the archaeological record allows us to document in some detail.

Already, from the very beginning of the early farming period, there was at least one commodity which was carried widely in ships, and then on land, over much of the Aegean. This was obsidian. Obsidian is a volcanic glass, found particularly on the Cycladic island of Melos, much valued for the manufacture of flake and blade tools. Trace-element analyses[28] have shown that the tools of obsidian found on early Neolithic sites throughout the Aegean are of Melian origin. We see here evidence for the first Aegean seafaring – evidence for which the Franchthi Cave extends back into Upper Palaeolithic times. Thus trade and commercial contact were already laying the foundations for the commerce which was to develop in later centuries.

By the Early Bronze Age, with the development of metallurgy, as we have seen, an international spirit had developed, with a widespread trade in metal objects. Both boat models and incised designs on Cycladic pottery vessels give us a graphic glimpse of the sea-going vesssels which were available for these trading enterprises. At this time fortified settlements developed quite widely. There is evidence too, notably at Sitagroi in Macedonia, for the domestication of the grape, and it has been argued that olive cultivation also developed in the third millennium[29] Certainly if we look at the distribution of Early Bronze Age fortified settlements and cemeteries in relation to regions of significant olive production[30] or of viticulture, we see a striking correlation.

Two factors were at work here, which fundamentally governed the settlement distribution of Minoan-Mycenaean society and the palace civilizations which it sustained. The first was maritime trade in the Aegean and beyond, as reflected in the trade in obsidian, and then in metal. The second was the Mediterranean climate and vegetation which, more than any other factor, governed the extent reached by the Minoan-Mycenaean civilization[31]

The subsistence base of the Minoan-Mycenaean world, like that of its Greek successor, was founded upon the Mediterranean triad of wheat (with barley), the olive and the vine. The commercial counterpart was founded upon Aegean maritime trade.

The maintenance and development of such commercial links as these can be seen continuing through Bronze Age times, first in the Cycladic pottery of the later Bronze Age[32] and then with the wide distribution of the "Marine Style" of pottery of the fifteenth century B.C.[33]

The most significant historical event of that time in the Aegean must certainly be the fall of the Minoan palaces, except Knossos, and the replacement at that site of one writing system (Minoan Linear A) by another (Linear B). For through the work of Ventris and Chadwick[34] we know the latter to be the system worked out probably in mainland Greece to record texts in the early form of the Greek language which we have come to call Mycenaean Greek. Whether the Minoan civilization collapsed or was overthrown, the aftermath entailed the occupation of Knossos by Mycenaeans and the eventual conversion of Crete to the Greek language. This took the form, as Chadwick has suggested, of the successor of "working class" Mycenaean: Doric Greek.

It was now that the Mycenaean *koine* reached its fullest extent, as documented by the distribution of pottery in the Late Helladic IIIA2-B styles. This distribution is in the first instance a documentation of trading links. The question of Mycenaean settlement is not precisely the same, and this may well be a case where "the flag follows trade." Certainly, the evidence for Mycenaean settlement in Cyprus comes from a later phase (Late Helladic IIIC1). But the question of Greek ethnicity in Cyprus is one which goes beyond the scope of the present paper.

5. Religion and Beliefs

The religious unity of the Greek world is prefigured already in the Neolithic and Early Bronze Age periods. But the story of the development of the Aegean religions is a complex one. And it is not at all a story of increasing uniformity in any straightforward way. Indeed there were divergences, so that it may not be quite accurate to use Martin Nilsson's term, the "Minoan-Mycenaean religion,"[35] until very late in the story, in the Late Helladic IIIC period. There were separate religions through most of the later Bronze Age, although they were related. But we can now begin to trace the series of transformations which resulted, ultimately, in the Olympic pantheon as we see it in Homer and in Hesiod.

1. In the Neolithic period we see elements of unity shared between Crete, the mainland and the Cyclades. Despite local variations, we see in each area the seated form – in marble in the Cyclades and the mainland, in terracotta in Crete – which suggests (if one accepts these figures as having some religious relevance) some elements of common belief which we may be able to trace back to the Neolithic of central Anatolia. It was suggested above that this was the original source area for the first farmers who brought with them to the Aegean their Proto-Indo-European language. In the early Neolithic at least, before divergences and transformations, there may also have been some common elements of belief.

2. It is in the Early Bronze Age of the Cyclades that we see one trajectory of development reach its peak. I am referring, of course, to the folded arm figures of marble which are such a frequent feature. The smaller ones have been found mainly in burials. It should be noted that this belief system, or aspects of it, extended to Crete, where such figures were imported and also made locally (the Koumasa variety). There are also relevant finds in Euboea and Attica, just a few in the Peloponnese and the mainland more widely.

Just a few larger figures are known, monumental figures, and I have suggested that these may have been used in more public cult places or sanctuaries, of which the sadly looted site at Dhaskaleio Kavos on Keros may be an example.

The very development of burial in cemeteries in the Cyclades at this time is another feature of importance when we consider the belief system.

In Crete, in addition to some comparable figures of marble, we see the development of the Minoan figurative tradition in terracotta in the important class of vessel figurines, which include the well-known example from Myrtos. Crete develops its own traditions of communal burial at this period.

3. With the Middle Bronze Age we enter upon the period of the Minoan first palaces. What was, perhaps, a local and popular religion is transformed, with the emergence of a state society, into a more standardized belief system, with the development of the Minoan peak sanctuaries. This change heralded the more organized link between peak sanctuaries and palaces during the Second Palace period.[36] The religious symbolism, for instance, of double axes, becomes more explicit. Human figures, in Kamares ware and in a few exceptional cases of faience, are found.

It is at this time that the temple at Aghia Irini was first established. We might try to see it as in some sense the successor, with its cult figures, of the large marble figures of the Cycladic Early Bronze Age (although the Kea figures apparently begin in the Late Bronze Age). But this was again a significant transformation. It is the differences as much as the similarities which impress us.

4. With the Second Palaces of Crete we are in the heyday of the Minoan religion, documented now at open-air sites (the later peak sanctuaries) and in areas within the palaces where splendidly carved stone vessels were used in ceremonies of libation. Although the frescoes of the Minoan palaces and of Akrotiri on Thera still offer abundant scope for debate, there can be little doubt that many of them have a religious significance. This is a sophisticated palatial religion.

5. That religion suffered a marked transformation with the end of the Minoan palaces. Many of its features were adopted on the mainland, but they were transformed in a way which we do not yet fully understand. Our earliest evidence of a well-appointed shrine comes from Mycenae, already nearly two centuries after the collapse of the Minoan palaces.

And it is after that collapse that in Crete we first encounter the little shrines of that distinctly post-palatial deity, the "Minoan Goddess with Upraised Arms." Although the ultimate origins of this divinity are undoubtedly Minoan, she seems to be a local adaptation of the Mycenaean figures such as we see them in Mycenae and on Phylakopi in Melos.

The urban shrine at Phylakopi dates from this time, drawing perhaps as much on Cycladic traditions (Kea) as on those of the mainland or of Crete.

6. It is at the very end of the Bronze Age, in the Late Helladic IIIC period, that we see further significant changes and signs of the beginning of a symbolic unity which may have a bearing upon the origins of Greek religion some three centuries later.

The shrine at Tiryns dates from this time. Like that of Mycenae it is not close to the palace proper, the *megaron*. But unlike the Mycenae shrine, it is post-palatial in date.

In Crete at this time we see some of the "stylised" animal figures, undoubtedly of Mycenaean inspiration, such as are well known from Amyklai, and so abundant in the "collapse" of the shrine at Phylakopi.[37] At just a few late Cretan sites (notably Phaistos and Aghia Triadha) we see too the small Mycenaean Phi and Psi figurines found also at Phylakopi and a few island sites, and at sites in the eastern parts of mainland Greece and the Peloponnese.[38] This is the time when the religious symbols used on Crete and the mainland converge, and it must be a crucial period for the transformations which are to follow.

It is at this period at Phylakopi that we find two examples of the "smiting god," bronze imports from the Levant that are almost the first representations of a male deity that we have from the Aegean. They find their successors in the early dedications of some of the sanctuaries founded two centuries later – at Delphi, Olympia, on Samos. Significantly, perhaps, such a figure occurs at the one site which shows undoubted religious continuity from the Bronze Age to the Iron Age: Delos (the Artemision deposit).

At Phylakopi also we find what are almost the only male figures of terracotta known from the Mycenaean world. They have a considerable significance in foreshadowing the artistic developments of a couple of centuries later. There is evidence in Crete (for instance from Kato Syme) to suggest continuity between the two periods. And indeed there are similarities in the painted decoration between one of the Phylakopi males[39] and the well-known centaur from Lefkandi[40], from a grave in the Protogeometric cemetery.

What I have tried to summarise here is what we can begin to perceive as a series of transformations, as the religious beliefs and the form of expression of those beliefs (which is what we see) changed radically in the course of a few hundred years on a number of occasions. The transformation across what we call the "Dark Ages" was only one of these and was not necessarily any more radical than any of the others.

Now where, in this sequence of events, is there clear evidence of religious inspiration from outside? The first Neolithic farmers are likely to have brought with them a system, or systems, of beliefs which we may be able to relate to beliefs and practices in the area whence the farming economy of Europe derived, Central Anatolia. But after that, it is doubtful whether there are very significant influences upon the Aegean. Certainly in the late Mycenaean period we have seen the importation into the Aegean in significant numbers of the bronze figures generally termed "smiting god." They come from the Levant and there had their own role within the local Levantine or Phoenician system of beliefs. It is not yet clear whether something of that context of meanings came with them, or whether they were simply convenient images to import. This is a field for further consideration.

In all of this, however, there seems no need to seek to "import" any of the deities of the Olympic pantheon. That there was a very early shared basis of belief along with the Proto-Indo-European language in each area may well be the case, but it may have been initially the beliefs of peasant farmers. The notion, so eloquently expressed by Georges Dumézil, that there was some developed and widely shared "Indo-European" religion seems to be a Dumézilian construction.[41]

Stefan Zimmer[42] has usefully listed and annotated the names of the Olympian deities (and their ancestors Uranos and Kronos) and here I quote him directly:

"Ever in Process of Becoming" 19

Uranos: Greek formation, perhaps "rainer" (OI *vars*); but not related to OI *Varuna*-!

Kronos: without etymology, the meaning "old man," occurring only in names, is based on the mythology or on popular etymology (:χρόνος).

Zeus: inherited as name of the god of "bright daylight sky," = OI *Dyaus* (*pita*), Hitt. *s°ius°* "god," L *dius* "day" (in *nudius tertius* "the day before yesterday").

Hera: without convincing etymology (hardly "goddess of the year"), probably pre-Greek < non-Indo-European.

Athene: unexplained, pre-Greek < non-Indo-European.

Aphrodite: of unknown origin, pre-Greek < non-Indo-European; the name may be altered by Greek popular etymology.

Hermes: of disputed origin; pre-Greek according to Schwyzer and Chantraine

Apollon: without acceptable etymology, probably of (non-Indo-European?) Anatolian origin, cf. Lydian *Pldans*, Luwian *Apulunas*, *Hitt.].ap-pa-li-u-na-as°*

Artemis: no convincing etymology known ("bear goddess"?); Lydian forms *Artimús, Artimul, Artimu-k*

Dionysos: perhaps a Thracian name "son (?) of Zeus;" but in fact without etymology

Poseidon: from an older (or perhaps even wrongly archaized?) name form Ποτειδάϝων, meaning "Lord (husband) of the Earth."

Ares: of unclear stem formation, probably belonging to ἀρή "damage, ruin." Not inherited from Proto-Indo-European!

Hephaistos: without etymology, pre-Greek, probably non-Indo-European

Demeter: Indo-European "Mother Earth," though the details of the first member of the compound are not clear. A probable parallel is found in the name of the Messapic goddess *damatura*

There is nothing here to suggest dependence on some common, earlier Indo-European pantheon of the sort adumbrated by Dumézil. We may accept that the terms for Zeus and Demeter have a very early origin. Perhaps the underlying concepts were already present in the cosmologies (whatever they were) of the first farmers in Greece. But, in general, the list is such as one might expect if, over the millennia, drawing both on Proto-Indo-European and non-Indo-European roots, the elements of a pantheon were constructed. (The "pre-Indo-European" may here be the language of the -nthos and -ssos place names, sometimes called "Pelasgian" by scholars).

I do not pretend to have explanations available here for the names and features of the Hellenic pantheon in the form set out, for instance, by Hesiod, and as depicted in monumental sculptures and in vase paintings of the sixth and fifth centuries B.C. My point is simply that there is nothing in them that was imported *in toto* in some significant intervention, some appearance of an alien *deus ex machi-*

na upon the Aegean stage.

Many aspects of Greek religion have Mycenaean antecedents. But perhaps the most important new feature was the establishment in the eighth and seventh centuries B.C. of important sanctuaries dedicated to individual deities. We have little evidence for open-air sanctuaries of this kind, remote from urban settlement, in the Mycenaean world (the peak sanctuaries of Crete are of a different kind). The few hypaethral sanctuaries which we have from Mycenaean times (such as the Amyklaion) do not become major cult sites in the Geometric period. Only Eleusis and Delos have good claims for significant continuities, and their nature in the Mycenaean period is far from clear. In Crete, Kato Syme is notable for the apparent continuity in its use.

It is perhaps of note that three of the greatest cult centers, those of Olympia, Dodona and Delphi, lie in regions of Greece where early *polis* formation did not take place. They lie in those more westerly areas where *ethne* prevailed. Now it is a feature of societies based upon the *ethnos* principle that while (by definition) they lack urban centers, the pattern of settlement being a more dispersed one, they do in general have periodic centers. Such centers have ritual and social functions. They are the centers of major periodic festivals at which the unity of the *ethnos* is affirmed and reinforced by appropriate ritual observations. One can readily imagine, therefore, how a major cult center, but one lacking urban pretensions, could emerge more easily in a region where *ethnos* organization prevailed, rather than in the self-contained environment of the *polis*, whose patron deity would be revered within the polis but in any neighboring *polis* would be ranked as secondary to its own tutelary god. This is a point to which we shall return below.

Meanwhile, it is appropriate to reassert that the Greek religion is something with a long and complex history, which developed as a result of a whole series of transformations. There is no ready source, whether Indo-European or otherwise, from which many of its salient features may be derived, other than the obvious one, the Mycenaean world which preceded it. Once this is realized, the very considerable scholarly project of studying how that religion came about can more appropriately be tackled. Fortunately, the task was initiated, with considerable success, half a century ago by Martin Nilsson and some of his contemporaries.

6. Ethnonym

The history of the word which the Greeks used to designate themselves (as they still do), Hellenes, is itself pertinent and of interest.

Here the relevant issue is that the earliest sources, notably Homer, do not yet use the term to describe that assemblage of people who were later termed Greeks.

This point was already definitively analyzed by Thucydides, in the fifth century B.C. in Book I, iii of his account of the Peloponnesian War:

Before the Trojan War, Hellas, as it appears to me, engaged in no enterprise in common. Indeed, it seems to me that as a whole it did not yet have this name, either, but that before the time of Hellen, the son of Deucalion, this title did not even exist . . . But when Hellen and his sons became strong in Phthiotis and were called in to the aid of other cities, the clans thenceforth came more and more by reason of this intercourse to be called Hellenes, though it was a long time before the name could prevail among them all. The best evidence of this is given by Homer; for though his time was much later than that of the Trojan War, he nowhere uses this name of all, or indeed of any of them except the followers of Achilles of Phthiotis, who were in fact the first Hellenes, but designates them in his poems as Danaans and Argives and Achaeans. And he has not used the term Barbarians either, for the reason it seems to me that the Hellenes on their part had not yet been separated off so as to acquire one common name by way of contrast.

In the next section I shall suggest that the term Hellene, as an ethnonym for the Greek people, did not come into common usage until after the Persian Wars, when it is employed regularly in its modern sense by Herodotus. Its use to designate the Greek people in general probably does not antedate the seventh century B.C.

Interestingly the first use of the term in the general sense may be for the name of the judges at the Olympic Games, the *Hellanodikai*. The earliest reference to the *Hellanodikai* (written before Herodotus) is in an inscription dated to c. 600 B.C. [43] Also in the context of the Olympic Games, Herodotus mentions that the Macedonian status of King Alexander I of Macedon in the fifth century B.C. caused his eligibility to be called into question:

saying that the contest should be for Greek, not for foreigners (φάμενοι οὐ βαρβάρων ἀ-γωνιστέων εἶναι τὸν ἀγῶνα ἀλλὰ Ἑλλήνων); but Alexander proving himself to be an Argive, he was judged to be a Greek (Herodotus V.22).

The term Hellene does not have a broad ethnic sense before the seventh century B.C. and it is doubtful whether the concept predates this time.

7. Self-Awareness

The critical test for ethnicity is self-awareness. Some groups of people are very much aware of their self-identity, which for them has an immediate reality. Other ethnographic cases are known where there is no strong collective self-identity, no wish to define tribes or other units so as to assign oneself and one's kinsfolk to one, and strangers to another.

Often, although not in the case of the Greeks, societies which we would describe as "tribal" have an "ethnicity" imposed on them.[44] This was the practice among colonial powers in the last century, who for bureaucratic convenience wished to ascribe all "natives" to one "tribe" or another. It was the practice too among classical historiographers, who sometimes classified barbarian tribes into larger classificatory units, which for the barbarians themselves would have had no clear meaning. The term "Celt" is one such. For although we, following the classical authors and later analyses, would conceive of the inhabitants of south Britain in the first century B.C. as "Celtic," it is clear that to the inhabitants both the name and the concept would have been unfamiliar.[45]

Very often such self-awareness comes about through opposition. Hostility and conflict lead one to define one's own group more closely – and to name it – in the face of the enemy. Moreover, such conflict can bring together allies in a military pact, a *symmacheia*, and thus bring about a unity which never previously existed.

If we take literally the Homeric account of the Trojan War, the situation can be analyzed in very much those terms. Homer has no consistent term for the allies, led by Agamemnon. And he has no such term because, in the Homeric account, there had been no preceding political unity. Nor indeed did one then develop. It was not until the Persian Wars, in the early fifth century B.C., that a military alliance in some ways analogous to the combination against Troy, led to a keen awareness of Greek against Barbarian.

That there was an awareness of Greek identity before that time cannot be doubted, but its reality was exaggerated for political purposes by the Athenians in the later fifth century, when they sought to establish the unity of the Greece which they hoped to lead.

The Panhellenic movement of the fifth century B.C. laid great stress upon the Olympic Games as the early focus of Hellenic unity. Raschke has emphasized the "strangely Athenian symbolism"[46] of the west pediment of the Temple of Zeus at Olympia. Mallwitz[47] has conclusively shown that Olympia's sagas and myths developed from Geometric times, with significant Mycenaean antecedents. And he has concluded that the Games themselves did not begin until about 700 B.C. although the cult itself goes back to Protogeometric times. It was in the seventh and sixth centuries, therefore, that the concept of "Greekness" in relation to the Olympic Games grew up. It may well be that Olympia, like the other great homes of periodic festivals, was originally the center for a local *ethnos* or tribe, and then for a group of tribes, an *amphyctiony*, before becoming a great center for much of Greece. Indeed, so effective a center was it, after the institution of the Olympic Games, that it came to define Hellenism itself, for which the ultimate arbiters were the *Hellanodikai*. But it was the Persian Wars, and the existence of a barbarian enemy against whom all true Greeks felt obliged to unite, that confirmed that Hellenic reality.

Some of the details of this process, and in particular the way in which the increasingly self-conscious definition of "barbarian" refined the concept of "Greek" has recently been explored by Edith Hall[48]

It is, of course, a question worth posing (but difficult to answer) as to whether there was corporate self-awareness amounting to ethnicity in the Mycenaean world. We have seen that the picture which Homer gives of the Trojan War suggests that the Mycenaeans were on the brink of such a concept, although they did not use the terms Hellas and Hellenes in that sense. But perhaps to say this is to take Homer too literally, and too readily to accept the historicity of his Trojan War.

It is instructive, nonetheless, to compare the map prepared by Sir Denys Page from his reading of the Catalogue of Ships in the Iliad[49] with a first attempt at Mycenaean political geography which I outlined some years ago.[50]

Did the Mycenaeans (in our modern archaeological sense) ever think of themselves as one people? Indeed, did the Minoans see themselves as one people? These are difficult questions to answer.[51] My guess would be that they will have done so only when each was united in some common cause against a threatening foe. If there ever was a War of Troy in which many Mycenaean allies participated, those allies are likely to have thought of themselves as a coherent group and perhaps, in opposition to the Trojan forces, as a "people." I would guess that the Minoans, in the face of the mainland invasion of the fourteenth century B.C. likewise saw themselves as a coherent "people" threatened by aliens. We cannot be confident, however, that the concept of the land which we call Hellas, and the people who came to call themselves Hellenes, was formulated until the seventh century B.C., to become an actual political reality in the Persian Wars two centuries later.

Conclusions

Who, then, were the Greeks? We have seen that their name (their ethnonym) and their self-awareness, cannot with confidence be traced back before the seventh century B.C. But that self-awareness was founded upon realities of much longer standing.

It was founded upon a common way of life which sprang from that brand of Mediterranean polyculture coupled with the life of the sea which we can trace back to the third millennium B.C. Beyond it stretch at least three millennia of maritime trading links, reflected in the obsidian trade. And over much of that time, it can be suggested, the Greek language was evolving, within what is now Greece, from that early Indo-European base which may have reached Greece with farming itself before 6000 B.C.

These continuing interactions were the ingredients which promoted the formation first of the Minoan and then of the Mycenaean palace civilizations. Themselves in a sense urban, or at least proto-urban, they laid the basis for the true urbanism of the *polis* a thousand years later. It is no coincidence that a map of Mycenaean settlement and a map of the extent of the *poleis* are approximately coterminous, and that both correlate with the region of true Mediterranean climate and vegetation.

But if developing culture and evolving language were fundamental elements in the process, so too were transformations on the spiritual level. We have seen the radical changes which took place in the successive Aegean religions, each of them apparently a result of local interactions. There was no "Coming of the Greek religion" to the Aegean, just as there was no "Coming of the Greek language." And the product of one of these transformations, the sanctuary at Olympia, with its periodic festival, became the focus for the crystallization of Hellenism, the development of a clear self-awareness, which drew together all these other strands of communality. The Greeks already knew who they were before the Persian Wars. Indeed, no doubt it was this awareness which promoted the resolution which led to victory, just as victory confirmed the bond of communality.

I have tried, then, to show that the Greeks really were, in a sense, autochthonous, "ever in process of becoming." We have no need of intrusions, incursions, immigrations. We need admit of these things only if there is clear evidence for them. Today, through half a century of work, following the death of Evans, and through his own preceding work and that of his contemporaries, we can begin to glimpse more clearly the possibility of describing and explaining, in Aegean terms, how these things came about. There is much to learn. But perhaps we can claim that gradually the outlines are becoming clearer.

"Ever in Process of Becoming"

NOTES

[1] J. L. Myres, *Who Were the Greeks?* (Berkeley: University of California Press, 1930), 538.

[2] Horace, *Epistulae*, 2.1. 156-7.

[3] Myres, *op.cit.*

[4] M. R. Nilsson, *The Minoan-Mycenaean Religion and its Survival in Greek Religion*, 2nd edition (Lund, Skrifter utgivna av Kungl. Humanistiska Vetenskapssamfundet i lund 9, 1950).

[5] A. M. Snodgrass, *Archaic Greece, The Age of Experiment* (London: J. M. Dent, 1980).

[6] V. Ehrenberg, *The Greek State* (Oxford: Blackwell, 1960), xi.

[7] E. Gellner, *Nations and Nationalism* (Oxford: Blackwell, 1983).

[8] Herodotus VIII, 144.

[9] T. Dragadze, "The Place of 'Ethnos' Theory in Soviet Anthropology," in E. Gellner (ed.) *Soviet and Western Anthropology* (London: Duckworth), 162.

[10] "We the Greeks."

[11] J. L. Caskey, "The Early Helladic Period in the Argolid," in *Hesperia* 29, 285-303.

[12] I. Morris, *Burial and Ancient Society* (Cambridge: Cambridge University Press, 1987).

[13] C. Renfrew and M. Wagstaff (eds.) *An Island Polity, the Archaeology of Exploitation on Melos* (Cambridge: Cambridge University Press, 1982) 288 and 5..

[14] E. Kirsten, *Die griechische Polis als historisch-geographisches Problem des Mittelmeerraumes* (Bonn, 1956) 101.

[15] A. M. Snodgrass, *Archaic Greece. The Age of Experiment* (London: J. M. Dent, 1980),45.

[16] Kirsten, *op. cit.* 100.

[17] C. Renfrew, *The Emergence of Civilisation. The Cyclades and the Aegean in the Third Millennium B. C.* (London: Methuen, 1972), 331.

[18] L. L. Cavalli-Sforza, A. Piazza and P. Menozzi, *The History and Geography of Human Genes* (Princeton: Princeton University Press, 1994).

[19] A. C. S. Hill, B. Gentile, J. M. Bonnardot, D. J. Weatherall and J. B. Clegg, "Polynesian Origins and Affinities: Globin Gene Variants in Eastern Polynesia," in *American Journal of Human Genetics* 40, (1987), 454-63.

[20] A. J. Ammerman and L. L. Cavalli-Sforza, 1973. "A Population Model for the Diffusion of Early Farming in Europe," in C. Renfrew (ed.), *The Explanation of Culture Change: Models in Prehistory.* (London: Duckworth, 1973), 343-57.

[21] J. Chadwick, "The Prehistory of the Greek Language," in *Cambridge Ancient History* II, 2 3rd edition (Cambridge: Cambridge University Press, 1975), 816-7.

[22] J. Chadwick, "Who Were the Dorians?" in *Parola del Passato* 31 (1976a), 103-17. "The Mycenaean Dorians," in *Bulletin of the Institute of Classical Studies* 23 (1976b), 115-6.

[23] V. I. Georgiev, "The Arrival of the Greeks, Linguistic Evidence," in R. A. Crossland and A. Birchall (eds.) *Bronze Age Migrations in the Aegean* (London: Duckworth, 1973), 243-54.

24 C. Renfrew, *Archaeology and Language: The Puzzle of Indo-European Origins* (London: Jonathan Cape, 1987).

25 J. B. Haley and C. W. Blegen, "The Coming of the Greeks," in *American Journal of Archaeology* 32 (1928), 141-54.

26 Georgiev, *op.cit.*

27 M. Zvelebil and K. V. Zvelebil, "Agricultural Transition and Indo-European Dispersals," in *Antiquity* 62 (1988), 574-83.

28 C. Renfrew, J. R. Cann and J. E. Dixon, "Obsidian in the Aegean," in *Annual of the British School at Athens* 60 (1965), 225-47.

29 J. M. Renfrew, *Palaeoethnobotany. The Prehistoric Food Plants of the Near East and Europe* (London: Methuen, 1973), 132. C. N. Runnels and J. Hansen, "The Olive in the Prehistoric Aegean: the Evidence for Domestication in the Early Bronze Age," in *Oxford Journal of Archaeology* 5 (1986), 299-308.

30 C. Renfrew 1972, *op.cit.* 397.

31 Ibid, 48.

32 Renfrew and Wagstaff, *op.cit.* 225.

33 Ibid, 226.

34 M. Ventris and J. Chadwick, *Documents in Mycenaean Greek* (Cambridge: Cambridge University Press, 1956).

35 M. R. Nilsson, *op.cit.*

36 A. A. D. Peatfield, "Palace and Peak: The Political and Religious Relationship between Palaces and Peak Sanctuaries," in R. Hägg and N. Marinatos (eds.), *The Function of the Minoan Palaces* (Stockholm: Skrifter utgivna av Svenska institutet i Athen, Paul Aströms Förlag, 1984), 89-93. See also Peatfield, "Minoan Peak Sanctuaries: History and Society" in *Opuscula Atheniensia* 17 (1990), 117-31.

37 Ibid. 418.

38 Ibid. pl. 37a.

39 Desborough *et al.* 1970

40 Renfrew, *op. cit.* Chapter 10. C. Renfrew, *The Archaeology of Cult: The Sanctuary of Phylakopi* (London: Thames and Hudson, 1985), 416.

41 S. Zimmer, "The Investigation of Proto-Indo-European History: Methods, Problems, Limitations." in T. L. Markey and J. A. C. Greppin (eds.), *When Worlds Collide: Indo-Europeans and Pre-Indo-Europeans.* (Michigan: Ann Arbor, 1990). 332.

42 Pauly Wissowa VIII. 1, 155.

43 J. Helm (ed.), *Essays on the Problem of Tribe* (Seattle: American Ethnological Association, 1968).

44 Renfrew, 1987, *op. cit.*, ch. 9.

45 W. J. Raschke, "Images of Victory: Some New Considerations of Athletic

Monuments," in W. J. Raschke (ed.), The *Archaeology of the Olympics* (Madison: University of Wisconsin Press, 1988), 46.

[46] A. Mallwitz, "Cult and Competition Locations at Olympia," (1988) in Raschke, *Archaeology*, 79-109.

[47] E. Hall, *Inventing the Barbarian, Greek Self-Definition through Tragedy* (Oxford: Clarendon Press, 1989).

[48] D. L. Page, *History and the Homeric Iliad* (Berkeley and Los Angeles: University of California Press, 1959), 124-5.

[49] C. Renfrew, "Retrospect and Prospect," in J. Binliff (ed.), *Mycenaean Geography* (Cambridge: British Association for Mycenaean Studies, 1977), fig. 1.

[50] See J. F. Cherry, "Politics and Palaces: Some Problems in Minoan State Formation," in C. Renfrew and J. F. Cherry (eds.), *Peer Polity Interaction and Socio-Political Change* (Cambridge: Cambridge University Press, 1986), 19-45. P. P. Betancourt (ed.), "The Scope and Extent of the Mycenaean Empire," *Temple University Aegean Symposium* 9 (Philadelphia: Temple University, 1984).

2

The School of Greece

John Boardman

The success of the new Athenian democracy would probably have been judged by other Greeks more in terms of Athens' military success and status than in terms of the enhanced quality of life enjoyed by its citizens. Pericles' funeral speech, in which Thucydides probably caught accurately enough the mood of the day, dwells on both aspects. He was speaking to Athenians but the message was for all Greece. The physical expression of this mood was the rebuilding of Athens, and the policy that determined the subjects for the architectural sculpture of the buildings would have reflected that intention. We might imagine a committee of, say, Pericles, Pheidias, the Archon Basileus, the Priestess of Athena, with others, devising the program. The subjects chosen and executed on the temples of Athens and Attica spoke clearly enough to Athenians and other Greeks. Their message should not be altogether indecipherable today, but there were subtleties, innovations and cross-references that can tax our ingenuity.

This paper dwells on just two themes which contributed to the decoration of the Parthenon: the Twelve Gods and Pandora. I believe that in their use of the Olympians the designers were making a panhellenic claim for Athens which embraced but went beyond the patronage and protection of their city goddess, and that in Pandora they had adjusted an old story to make comparable claims for their city at a more human, therefore democratic, level.

The Olympians figure prominently on the eastern aspect of the Parthenon no less than four times. No other cult building in Greece gives them such prominence, indeed no other presents them in any comparable way except once, in the east frieze on the Athena Nike temple on the Acropolis, clearly dependent on the example of the Parthenon. In the pediment they attend the birth of the city goddess, answering the west pediment where the dispute between Athena and Poseidon for possession of Attica was narrated for the first time, so far as we can judge, in any medium. In the metopes they fight the Giants, a subject that answers the west metopes where the Athenians fight Amazons, itself a clear parable for the Athenian defeat of the Persians. The gods secured Olympian rule on earth against the challenge of the sons of Earth, just as the Athenians secured the freedom of Greece against Amazons/Persians. On the frieze the gods await the Panathenaic procession, honoring its participants in a manner that surely expresses the heroic aspect of the citizenry that had led Greece to freedom. Athena sits with them, so this is no simple votive procession to the goddess of the temple, but a demonstration of piety to her in the presence of the whole Olympian family.

Open the temple doors onto a view of the gold and ivory cult statue of Athena Parthenos. The subjects of the east and west metopes are repeated on the inside and outside respectively of the goddess' shield: gigantomachy and amazonomachy, the latter perhaps with explicit reference to the Amazons' attack on Athens if the architectural features in the background are correctly interpreted. And on her base the gods again attend, here for the creation of Pandora and her endowment with mortal finery and skills. We have only Pliny's and Pausanias' word for the identification, but copies of the base do more than hint at a parade of gods in the form in which we see the creation and Olympian blessing of Pandora on fifth-century Athenian vases.

Thanks to Hesiod, Pandora has enjoyed a bad press. We should ignore the misogynist aspect of Hesiod's story, just as antiquity did until mythographers of the Roman period thought to record it again. By this I refer to her release of ills for mankind and holding back of Hope. The story admitted a number of variants and various interpretations, and even Hesiod is none too clear about details except to insist that her behavior was not in man's or mankind's interests and was prompted by jealous Olympians.

The Pandora of fifth-century Athens incorporated various aspects of the primaeval character revealed by her name: a beneficent all-giver to mankind who arose from the earth (so she could also be called Anesidora, who rises to give), but a creation of the Olympians rather than Earth herself (mother of the hostile Giants) and so an agent of their goodwill to mankind in general, and Athens in particular. Lurking behind the story also were various older variants: her role as first woman, a creation of foresight (Prometheus), and her relationship to the story of the creation of mankind involving Deucalion. She could even be inserted into Athens' royal family tree.

Our evidence for these views of her are mainly late and should not influence unduly our understanding of what she meant to fifth-century Athens. Athens makes her more consciously an antithesis to hostile chthonic forces, although with such a name and background it was natural for her to arise from earth (as could goddesses — Persephone and Aphrodite — who are so represented in fifth-century Athens with comparable iconographic conventions). Significantly, where she is named Anesidora, arising to give, she is shown not rising, but as the model figure being equipped by Athena and Hephaestos (on an Athenian vase earlier than the Parthenon, and as she seems to have been on the Parthenos base). When Ge rises from earth in fifth-century Athens it is first to deliver Erichthonios to Athena, and only at the end of the century in supplication for her defeated brood of Giants. There is a strange nexus of old themes here and we must be on our guard against trying to reconcile all of whatever date and source. I have little doubt that Pandora meant more to fifth-century Athenians than most modern scholarship credits, and that her significance had been as soon forgotten in antiquity once the season of its creation and significance had passed. It is not surprising that there could be some confusion between her and Pandrosos on the Acropolis. Both had problems with the unauthorized opening of containers from which evils escaped (*kedea lugra* dire woes: snakes) leaving a blessing behind (Hope: infant Erichthonios, an alternative to being a gift of Earth). This is simply a further thread in the tangled story.

So, on the east pediment of the Parthenon the Olympians present Athens' newborn warrior goddess, sprung from the head of Zeus. On the metopes and frieze they demonstrate Olympian rule on earth and honor Athens and Athenians. And on the goddess' base within the temple, they present Pandora, embodying all their gifts to mankind, hinting at an equation between Pandora and Athena, and more than hinting at Athens' role as their agent in the schooling of Greece.

3

Liberty and the Ancient Greeks

Oswyn Murray

> The end of democracy is liberty.
> Aristotle, *Rhetoric* [†]
>
> Liberty is not a means to a higher political end. It is itself the highest political end.
> Lord Acton, "The History of Freedom in Antiquity" [‡]

I

There is a grave danger in celebrating the birth of anything, except perhaps a baby. Institutions, countries, ideas do have origins, starting points, but they also change over time. They are not like biological organisms determined by their genetic makeup. Indeed, the more successful an institution or idea is, the more it will change and the less the search for origins will therefore tell us. That is because human society is complex, and adaptability is the price we must pay for success. Only unsuccessful societies stick close to their origins; the rest of us change.

So what is the point of thinking about the democratic institutions of the ancient Greeks 2500 years after they were first created? It is, I think, the point of all historical study, to make ourselves aware of the *differences* between societies, differences which lie behind the apparent similarities. The danger in studying ancient democracy as the origin of modern democracy, and emphasizing the continuity between the two, is that it distorts our perception of the past in the

---

[†] 1.8.5.1366a4
[‡] *Essays on Freedom and Power* (Cleveland 1948) p. 74

interests of creating a charter myth for the present: an explanation of the rightness of our own institutions couched in the non-rational mode of ancestor worship. This is to make history harmless. History should be used to change our present perceptions, to make us realize how relative our own society is, how non-necessary and random are its interconnections. Similar words, similar ideas, disguise new ideas, new worlds of thought. Only history can tell us how transitory our own world view is, and how it is bound to change. Only history can give us the humility and the freedom to build a new and, hopefully, a better future. Ideological anniversaries are especially good times to think about this purpose of history, for the comparison of our own political vocabulary and our own political institutions with the distant world from which they came is one of the best ways of understanding both how much change has happened and what are the hidden assumptions behind our most beloved dogmas.

At this point I would have liked to present a video, but the different technologies of video machines and the printed page prevent it. So I shall have to recreate a word picture of a recent television program in England.

Scene: A map of time, flags for the various nations, a satellite picture of the world. To the theme of Beethoven's Eroica Symphony, a voice intones:

"Two thousand five hundred years of democracy. Let us explore what that means to the peoples of the world."

Shot of the Parthenon.

"But first to Ancient Greece where democracy began. Here, Yannis Koros, Professor of Political Science at the School of Windsurfing, Mykonos University, is waiting to speak to us."

Professor Koros is a well known British comic, Rory Bremner. He is dressed in dark glasses, a flowered shirt and shorts, and standing on a beach. In a heavy Greek accent he begins,

"Yess, democracy iss a Greek word, ze Greeks invented it 2500 years ago. It comes from ze Greek, *demos*, meaning people, and *crass* meaning – stoopid."

This is not, of course, a new joke. Rory Bremner's remark recalls the claim of the Athenian democratic politician Alcibiades in the fifth century B.C.: "As for democracy, we men of sense knew what it was . . . but there can be nothing new to say about what is agreed to be absolute insanity" ("*homologoumenes anoias*," Thucydides 6.89.6).

The program continues with a series of clips designed to show the varieties of modern democratic politics. There is the more informal atmosphere of the oldest of all parliaments, the Spanish Cortes (a picture of a little man in moustaches and a funny hat with a sub-machine gun in the Spanish parliament, shooting at the senators as they duck behind their seats), and the grand ceremonial of British democracy (the opening of parliament with all the lords in red robes and eighteenth century wigs, and the queen in a crown), Russian tanks in Prague, U.S. tanks in Kuwait, and so on. The comedy had a serious point: it is as difficult for us to understand the so-called democracies of other countries as it is for them to recognize what particular form of democratic madness it is that we practice.

But to talk about the differences between ancient and modern democracy is an easy target, because everyone recognizes that they are very different things. Modern democracy is representative. Political interest groups with different ideas on how to run the society have been formed by a process of historical development. The people vote between different views and different individuals. The winner becomes a form of more or less powerful elected dictator for a fixed term. He or she can usually only be overthrown during that term from within the party, and the people have only limited power and limited access to the organs of publicity (journals, television) which might influence public opinion for or against the specific proposals in play. The government also relies on an army of unelected professional or political "experts" to help it run society.

Ancient democracy in Athens was, of course, quite different. There were no political parties and no bureaucracy, no judges and no lawyers. Everything was performed directly by the people. Democracy was defined as "ruling and being ruled in turn" (below p. 47). Everyone took a turn. Election was thought by the Greeks to be an oligarchic principle. The only democratic form of selection was the lot. Every man in turn was eligible to be chosen at random to sit on the city council; no man could serve on the council more than twice, or as president of Athens for more than one day in a lifetime. The lot was also used for all offices except military ones. Policy was indeed formulated by a loose group of leaders called "the orators and generals" (*rhetores kai strategoi*)[1]; but it had to be argued for in a mass assembly, which all male members of the city were entitled to attend, to speak, vote and change their opinions from one day to the next.[2]

Democracy in this sense really was "people's power," derived from *demos* and *kratos*. Indeed, I may remark in passing that it is not certain that 1993 is actually the 2,500th anniversary of the word "democracy." *Demokratia* is an aggressive slogan for radicals, formed in opposition to the older *aristokratia* ("power to the best"). It was surely born in an age of conflict, which may also have seen the formation of the dismissive *oligarchia* ("rule of the few"). Neither of this pair of words is found in any text before the late fifth century B.C.; but I believe it likely that both may have been coined around the year 462/1, during the political agitation which created the radical democracy of Ephialtes and Pericles.[3] It might be safer to wait another 46 years before celebrating the arrival of *demokratia*, "people's power."

The earlier word for democracy, the word we are celebrating this year, is not *demokratia* but *isonomia*. It was in the late sixth century B.C. that against *eunomia*, the "good order" promoted by the egalitarian warrior state of Sparta, there emerged the principle of *isonomia*, "equal order" or "equal government," which promised to all male citizens an equal share in the privileges and duties of citizenship. It may well have been Cleisthenes of Athens who coined this new political slogan. Certainly as far as we can tell it was he who, in 508/7 B.C. first worked out in detail the institutions designed to ensure that a previously aristocratic city-state should become a city of "equal order," and so became the author of the idea of democracy.[4] The later reforms of the mid-fifth century and the subsequent reforms of the end of the fifth century followed the same general principles of Cleisthenes, and merely sought to perfect the organization of democracy in the sense of the absolute sovereignty of the people.

So we know that our democracy is very different from Greek democracy, but we also believe, rightly or wrongly, that many of the *principles* that lie behind the institutions are the same in each case. The ideological construct behind any socio-political system consists of a bundle of interlocking ideas and ideals, which are often not fully expressed and sometimes are even in conflict with each other. Their relative importance may change over time or when applied in different countries. To say that a government is democratic is not to say the same thing in every case; it is to claim that it shows enough of a range of political attitudes and possesses enough of a range of institutions to fall within the broad category of democratic systems. In asserting that, I do not wish to be thought to support the view that all countries that call themselves democracies are so. We all know that the word "democracy" is a yes-word that everyone wishes to claim as their own. No country admits to being an oligarchy or a tyranny; all are in their own eyes special sorts of democracy, with or without elections, civil liberties, secret police or freedom of speech. But the fact that politicians misuse and abuse language is no reason for philosophers and historians to stop trying to understand the essential characteristics of the idea of democracy.

II

To our modern notion of democracy nothing is more crucial than the idea of liberty or freedom (English is unique among European languages in having two words, which, however, have always been used in an identical sense by all philosophers, and I shall not try to distinguish them). And my argument today stems from the belief that the differences between ancient and modern democracy are not just differences in institutions or size. They are actually differences of a much more basic nature, to do with the modern insistence on the central importance of a certain type of liberty in democratic thought.

Our conception of liberty is a complex one, involving both a whole series of rights and privileges in the relations of the individual to the state, and a claim for the importance of autonomy between states. It is not easy to separate out the different strands in this general picture, but traditionally philosophers have distinguished two basic clusters of ideas. There exist first the various rights and duties which stem from the principle of what Locke and other writers called "natural liberty." Isaiah Berlin, in a famous essay, "Two Concepts of Liberty" (1958), called this "negative freedom," or "freedom from" – the freedom of the individual to live his life without constraint from government interference or control by his fellow citizens. This liberty is conceived of as the sort of freedom that an individual might have if he lived outside the social community, and it is claimed by liberal thinkers like John Stuart Mill that it has an overriding value, subject only to the needs within society to ensure that one individual's liberty is not another individual's subjection.[5]

Then there is another group of ideas centered around the notion of social or political freedom: the right of the members of an institution to participate in and control the activities of the state, and their right not to be interfered with by others (individuals or societies) in that activity. This second type of liberty, "the liberty of man in society" (Locke) or civil liberty, was called by Berlin "positive liberty," or "freedom to." In some senses that is an accurate description: civil liberty is freedom to participate in the running of the state and to influence the direction which it takes. Again, this consists of a variety of different sorts of freedom; but they all imply that the members of a community take some responsibility for establishing the rules by which society is ordered.

In the relationship between these two types of liberty, one particular issue has been taken by philosophers as central: the status of decisions arrived at by the community of participants. What happens when a democratic society seeks to impose rules on its individual members? Are civil liberty and personal liberty fully compatible?

This problem in modern libertarian thought has been intensified by the fact that, ever since Rousseau, the conception of positive liberty has usually involved ideas of how societies ought to be run and how humanity ought to behave. The democratic liberty to determine the future of society can easily become the liberty to redesign it, to show the uneducated or unaware that a better life exists if only they change their ways. In this direction there is an inevitable collision between the claims of positive freedom, involving the duty of the individual to reach a natural state of perfection or grace and of society to help this process, and those of negative freedom, involving the individual's right to remain unreformed.

Neither of these types of freedom, in fact, is necessarily related to democracy. It is obvious enough that a Platonic or Christian state of positive freedom, in which humanity is able to reach its highest level of attainment, is probably better achieved (as Plato saw) through the rule of philosopher-kings or priests – an enlightened despotism, not a democracy. And equally, the only form of government wholly compatible with negative freedom is anarchy. As Mill saw, popular democracy is just as likely to oppress the personal liberties of its subjects as any other form of government. And there may well have been many enlightened monarchies, colonialist regimes and empires, which offered minority groups among their subjects far more personal liberty than they will ever be able to achieve under so-called democracy – as any former member of the Austro-Hungarian Empire in the Balkans might agree.

If we associate both forms of liberty with democracy, it is, in fact, largely for historical reasons. The theory of positive liberty was developed by Rousseau in relation to his idea of the Social Contract, whose original force is reaffirmed by the continual expression of the general will. By this means he sought to reconcile the constraints necessary to social life with the demands of natural liberty.[6] It is Rousseau's political theory which is democratic, not his ideas about liberty, but the historical climate of the French Revolution subsequently suggested a close connection between the two, as the expression of the general will came to be used to justify infringements of the liberty of the individual.

Similarly, the development of the idea of personal liberty is part of that movement in the Enlightenment which produced the other great modern revolution which still wins our approval, the American Revolution. The ideal of personal liberty was developed at the same time and in the same context as there emerged the theory of representative democracy and the theory of free trade or liberal economics as foundations for the organization of the state. But there may also be practical reasons for our making this connection between democracy and personal liberty, if it is true that the best form of government for the survival of such liberty is a democratic form.

Mill indeed tried to create a necessary connection between personal liberty and democracy, and between both and the growth of economic prosperity. But his arguments are weak, depending on the hypothesis that the investigation of a plurality of paths will lead to the truth, whereas, of course, what is necessary is to find the true path. And even Mill is inclined to believe that democracy itself too often degenerates into the tyranny of the majority:

> In our times, from the highest class of society down to the lowest, everyone lives under the eye of a hostile and dreaded censorship. Not only in what concerns others, but in what concerns only themselves, the individual or the family do not ask themselves – what do I prefer? – or, what would suit my character and disposition? or, what would allow the best and highest in me to have fair play, and enable it to grow and thrive? They ask themselves, what is suitable to my position? what is usually done by persons of my station and pecuniary circumstances? or (worse still) what is usually done by persons of a station and circumstances superior to mine? I do not mean that they choose what is customary in preference to what suits their own inclination. It does not occur to them to have any inclination, except for what is customary. Thus the mind itself is bowed to the yoke; even in what people do for pleasure, conformity is the first thing thought of; they live in crowds; they exercise choice only among things commonly done: peculiarity of taste, eccentricity of conduct, are shunned equally with crimes: until by dint of not following their own nature they have no nature to follow: their human capacities are withered and starved: they become incapable of any strong wishes or native pleasures, and are generally without either opinions or feelings of home growth, or properly their own. Now is this, or is it not, the desirable condition of human nature? (*On Liberty*, p. 119)

In fact, one could argue for a closer logical connection between positive liberty and democracy, for if liberty is to be reconciled with the authority of the social body, then it can only be so reconciled if the social body is a truly democratic embodiment of the general will, in whose service, all might well be brought to agree, is perfect freedom. For the laws in a direct democracy are expressions of the general will, and at least for the majority there should be no conflict between obedience to these laws and the positive freedom to follow that which one has freely chosen to accept. In his rejection of the idea that a minority could continue to have rights to oppose the general will, Rousseau is indeed very close to the ideal of the overriding sovereignty of the people in democratic Athens; but he was, of course, opposed to all forms of representative democracy, for only direct democracy could serve as an adequate expression of the general will.

Very early in this debate about liberty, it was noticed that the issues at stake in the modern world did not seem to be the same as those in the ancient world. In 1819, the French liberal conservative Benjamin Constant published his famous essay, "On the Liberty of the Ancients Compared with that of the Moderns." The ideas in this essay go back at least to 1806 (he himself traces them back to Condorcet), and the immediate aftermath of the French Revolution, which (it seemed to Constant) had been distorted by the ideas of Rousseau on the right of society to impose liberties on others for their own benefit.[7] Constant accepted that Rousseau's ideas were derived from the ancient world – that is, that the positive or civil conception of liberty had its roots in classical Athens; liberty for the ancients was "the active and constant participation in collective power" (p. 501); it established the concept of the social will, which then authorized the state to demand conformity with the decisions arrived at democratically.

But Constant claimed that the modern liberal idea of liberty was completely different, and had been unknown in the ancient world. He contrasted the two ideas of liberty:

First ask yourselves what today an Englishman, a Frenchman, an inhabitant of the United States understand by the word liberty?

It is for each person the right to submit only to the laws, not to be arrested, imprisoned, executed or maltreated in any way, through the arbitrary will of one or more individuals. It is for each person the right of expressing his opinion, of choosing his work and practising it, of being in control of his property, even of misusing it; of coming or going without seeking permission, and without rendering account of his reasons or journeys. It is for each person the right of meeting with other individuals, whether to discuss matters of mutual interest or to worship in the cult which he and his associates choose, or simply to fill their days and their hours in a way most congenial to their inclinations or their fantasies. Finally it is the right of each person to influence the administration of government, by the nomination either of all or of a certain number of officials, or by representations, petitions, requests, which the authorities are more or less required to take into consideration. To this liberty compare now the liberty of the ancients.

That liberty consisted in exercising collectively but directly most aspects of absolute sovereignty, deliberating in the public square about war and peace, concluding with foreigners treaties of alliance, voting on laws, pronouncing legal judgments, examining the accounts and the decrees and decisions of magistrates, making them appear before the assembled people, putting them on trial, condemning or acquitting them. But at the same time that this was what the ancients called liberty, they admitted as compatible with their collective liberty the total subjection of the individual to the authority of the community. (p. 495)

The modern conception of individual freedom was completely unknown to the ancient world. Only in Athens was there some sign that "the subjection of the individual existence to the collective body was not quite as complete as I have just described" (p. 496). The reason for this was the greater presence of trade in Athens; and even there the institution of ostracism[8] demonstrated that "the individual was still fully subordinate to the supremacy of the social body at Athens" (p. 501).

According to Constant (p. 499f), the reasons for this break between ancient and modern liberty were to be found in the differences between their social systems. Antiquity lacked the incentive to invent the conception of individual liberty for four reasons:

First, the size of ancient cities made every citizen a member of the political community. The need for *individual* liberty is closely related to the size of the state and the diminution of individual power within the collective.

Second, slavery provided the ancient world with time for deliberation on public matters. Ancient liberty was dependent on ancient slavery.

The third and fourth reasons were economic. Commerce as practised in the modern world does not give time to the ordinary citizen to partake in collective decision making, whereas the primitive nature of commerce in the ancient world gave people plenty of time for political debate.

Finally, commerce itself actively promotes the conception of individual independence: "It assists their needs and satisfies their desires without the intervention of authority." Indeed, "wherever governments involve themselves in our business affairs, they do it worse and more expensively than ourselves":

It results from what I have said that we cannot any longer enjoy the liberty of the ancients, which consisted in the active and constant participation in collective power. Our liberty for ourselves must consist in the peaceful enjoyment of private independence. (p. 501)

This view of the basic difference between ancient and modern ideas of liberty has been generally accepted by modern writers ever since. Discussion has centered, not on disputing Constant's claim, but on discovering better reasons for the difference that he detected.[9] So Isaiah Berlin in the introduction to the 1969 reprint of his essay could still say:

It is an interesting but perhaps irrelevant historical question at what date and in what circumstances the notion of individual liberty in this [modern] sense first became explicit in the West. I have found no convincing evidence of any clear formulation of it in the ancient world. Some of my critics have doubted this, but apart from pointing to such modern writers as Acton, Jellinek, or Barker, who do profess to find this ideal in ancient Greece, some of them also, more pertinently, cite the proposals of Otanes after the death of pseudo-Smeridis in the account given by Herodotus, the celebrated paean to liberty in the Funeral Oration of Pericles, as well as the speech of Nikias before the final battle with the Syracusans (in Thucydides), as evidence that the Greeks, at any rate, had a clear conception of individual liberty. I must confess that I do not find this conclusive. (p. xi)

Indeed, the contrast between ancient and modern liberty has become strengthened by the triumph of the liberal free-trade capitalist consensus, which sees all forms of state-related liberty as potentially dangerous. As a result, a libertarian like Berlin can even claim that ancient liberty is not liberty at all. The claim to self-government, the assertion of political independence is, according to Berlin, wrongly called liberty. This is rather a search for status or recognition, and has nothing to do with liberty; and of course it is true that many such searches end up with less (individual) liberty (pp. 154ff.).

I do not intend to spend time refuting this extreme view, because it so plainly runs against modern usage. It seems pointless to deny that the freedom fighters of all the oppressed peoples of the world have indeed been fighting for freedom, or that they have envisaged their liberties in ways far closer to the ancient Greek conception of the word than to modern liberal views. Of course, if you believe that political liberty is not liberty at all, then there is only one concept of liberty left, and we have erected an absolute barrier between the ancient and the modern world.

Recently, however, there have been two attempts to reopen the question of the incompatibility of ancient and modern views of liberty. The first is by the greatest living authority on Athenian democracy, the Danish scholar Mogens Herman Hansen. Hansen has combined the claim that the architects of modern democratic theory (the French, the Americans and the various nineteenth century liberal political thinkers) were not influenced by any knowledge of Athenian political institutions, with the somewhat paradoxical claim that in fact the same ideals of liberty, equality, democracy can be found in the ancient world as in the modern, and, moreover, that in Athens, at least, the freedom of the individual to live as he pleased was a conscious ideal of Athenian democracy.[10]

The second attempt to assert the continuity of ideas of freedom is contained in the work of the sociologist Orlando Patterson, in his work *Freedom: Freedom in the Making of Western Culture*.[11] Patterson's attempt to write a continuous history of the idea of freedom is not yet complete; he promises a second volume on the modern idea of freedom from the eighteenth century onwards. Until that promise is redeemed, we cannot know why he has chosen so far to ignore the debate of the last two centuries about the nature of ancient freedom. But the picture he draws already shows the difficulty of attempting to believe that the concept of liberty has a continuous history. Patterson accepts the traditional distinction between personal freedom and civic freedom, but believes that both existed in the ancient world. He adds to these, however, a third type of freedom: "sovereignal or organic freedom," "the power to act as one wishes regardless of the wishes of others, as distinct from personal freedom, which is the capacity to do as one pleases, *insofar as one can*" (p. 3f).

> This conception of [sovereignal] freedom is always relative. At one extreme stands the person who is absolutely free with respect to another, namely the slave-master or absolute ruler or god; at the other extreme is the person who has no freedom with respect to another, namely the slave in relation to his master. Between the two are all other human beings with more or less power or freedom, with respect to others. (p. 4)

I do not want to discuss this theory in detail, partly because it seems to me not, or not yet, to have faced the traditional question of the distinction between personal and civic freedom, but also because I am not convinced that Patterson's "sovereignal freedom" is freedom at all. It seems to me much more like what earlier writers would have called "power." There is, of course, a well recognized relationship between the concepts of freedom and power, but it is not to me convincing to claim that freedom is power, or to deny that between freedom and power there is a form of direct and permanent opposition which is quite different from the occasional incompatibility between personal and civic freedom. But in the course of his argument, Patterson does make a number of points which I believe to be true, and he has at least succeeded in emphasizing the elements of continuity between ancient and modern ideas of freedom.

III

Let us look at the evidence. Like ourselves, the Greeks possessed a group of words relating to the general conception of forms of freedom political and personal, but naturally these words do not wholly correspond to our words or our conception of the spheres of freedom. There is clearly *some* difference between ancient and modern views of freedom.

The basic Greek word usually translated as "freedom" or "liberty" is *eleutheria*. It is, for instance, the slogan *Eleutheria* which in the nineteenth century was used to formulate the claim of the Greek nation to possess the same rights and liberties as other Western nations. But in origin, *eleutheria* is much more restricted; it refers to the distinction between two statuses, slavery and freedom. To be free is to be independent of others, to be a slave is to belong to another. Freedom and slavery relate to each other as opposites, and cannot be understood without awareness of this opposition. In this sense, at least, *eleutheria* implies freedom from control by others, in a world which included the possibility of controlling others absolutely, and Patterson is quite right to claim that the Greek conception of liberty is closely related to the existence of the opposite phenomenon of slavery.

But this liberty, though it relates to the individual, is a liberty of status, not a personal liberty. By being *eleutheros* ("free"), you are first, negatively, not a slave. And since most non-slaves are citizens, the word can be used positively to designate those who are of citizen status, who belong to the civic community. It can also be used metaphorically of someone who behaves in a free, un-slavelike way and so can come to have an almost aristocratic connotation – someone who behaves as the ideal well-bred person should. Another related adjective, *eleutherios*, actually means an aristocratic person.

So freedom for the Greeks, even in the sense of being a free *man* ("free" is seldom used of women, except in the context of the direct opposition free-slave) had long included an element of domination, or of a claim to aristocratic status. In the democratic city-state a free man was also a warrior citizen. And it is in fact Herodotus who first made the claim for a connection between political freedom and military success in Athens, for it was, he says, as a result of Cleisthenes making Athens a democracy that the Athenians were able to defeat their rivals and become a great power.[12] Democratic freedom creates military success. It is indeed one of the main themes of Herodotus' history that the great war between Persia and Greece was a war between slaves and free, in which the victory of the free proved their superiority.

But already this freedom, which began by referring to the legal and social status of individuals, has become a political freedom, related to the right to participate in the government of the city. Later, Aristotle elevated this sense of the superiority of a self-governing Greek community into an ethnic theory, that Greeks are superior to barbarians precisely because they are biologically capable of being free and self-governing, whereas Persians and others are natural slaves in their political systems and in their national characters.

There is no doubt at all that this civic sense of freedom, based on the relationship between free citizens participating in the democracy, is the dominant conception of freedom in ancient Greece. It is indeed comparable to our own sense of political freedom within a democratic system, of which it is the ancestor. And in the Greek world it gave rise to a number of other ideals, which are also included in our own conception of political freedom.

The first of these is inter-state freedom, or political independence. According to Thucydides, the subject allies of the Athenians in the fifth century were not free but slaves of Athens; but the official language of the Athenian empire claimed the opposite, that the allies were "autonomous." *Autonomia* (formed like *eunomia* and *isonomia*) meant "freedom" in the sense of being self-ruling,[13] and corresponds almost exactly to the sense in which freedom-fighters or rebel secessionists claim political freedom from control of foreign domination. Self-determination, though it may lead to lesser personal and economic freedom, is nevertheless a freedom, as the American experience of history has shown.

A second area of comparison with modern concepts of freedom is that of "freedom of speech." But here some differences begin to emerge. Whereas the Romans possessed no separate word for freedom of speech and regarded it as an intrinsic part of *libertas*,[14] the Greeks not only regarded free speech as a basic element characteristic of any democracy, they also possessed two specialist terms to describe the activity of exercising freedom of speech.

The first of these was *isegoria*, the equal right of addressing the Assembly.[15] Every citizen in Athens had this right, at least from the mid-fifth century, and the

Liberty and the Ancient Greeks

records of debates in the Assembly show that most proposals were, in fact, made by citizens who were not famous politicians, even if they were politically active. In any one generation perhaps about a thousand citizens might be found proposing decrees or amendments to decrees, the majority of whom are virtually unknown otherwise.[16] This right is, of course, far greater than that possessed in modern democracies, for it is more than political freedom of speech; it is, rather, freedom to initiate political change, the right of any citizen to address the sovereign assembly and propose laws without holding any official position.

But freedom of speech to us means not only the right to intervene in politics at whatever level, but also the right to express, and even to act upon, personal opinions when they run counter to the will of the community. It includes such freedoms as freedom of religious and political association in a secular state, freedom to express revolutionary ideas about the overthrowing of a constitution approved by the majority, civil disobedience, freedom to refuse to take part in constitutionally decided activities, conscientious objection, agitation against wars like the Vietnam War, opposition to officially declared economic policy through strikes, opposition to the effects of a government-supported, military-industrial complex, or the right to partake in issues such as animal rights or the green movement. We often judge our governments by their tolerance of these threats to the existing system, and especially by their tolerance of minority groups who do not conform to and even seek to overturn the wishes of the majority.

This modern aspect of liberty is ultimately derived from a belief in the importance of freedom of conscience. It has, I think, religious roots in the traditions of Non-Conformism and the history of the persecution of sects such as the Protestants of continental Europe, the Quakers, Catholics and Non-Conformists in England, or the Mormons in nineteenth century America. But though it originally referred to *groups* holding particular beliefs, it has often come to be equated with the right of the *individual* conscience to oppose the majority view in a democratic system.

Every society has its own limits of tolerance in relation to this type of freedom of speech. But, despite the existence of such limits in ancient Athens, their tolerance was remarkably wide, probably as wide as our own, if not wider, in that in ancient Athens there was no protection against libel and very little against false or malicious accusations. Personal abuse and allegations of dishonesty or corruption were part of the normal workings of the Athenian democratic system: negative campaigning is not a modern invention. The Greeks even had a special word for the privilege of rudeness in saying what you really thought with impunity: *parrhesia*.[17] It is the virtue which allows Diogenes the Cynic, when

Alexander the Great says "Ask whatever you want," to reply "Get out of my sunlight." It became a particular privilege of ancient philosophers to practise this sort of rudeness on kings and emperors.[18]

But freedom of opinion in antiquity could also involve moral issues.[19] Whatever interpretation we put on Sophocles' *Antigone*, it is clear that Antigone defies the laws of the city in burying her brother, in favor of a higher law, the unwritten law of the gods. We should note that this is not quite personal freedom of opinion. Antigone's views are not her own; she rests her case on a higher law, that of the gods. But at least we may say that the possibility of a form of freedom of conscience involving an individual asserting an opposition between religion and the state was openly accepted and discussed. Whether Antigone is right or wrong is one of the main focuses of the play, and we are surely meant to see this question as genuinely controversial for Athenians at the time.

It is true that Athens showed on at least one occasion an intolerance which surprises us: Socrates was put on trial and condemned to death for "refusing to recognize the gods recognized by the state and introducing other, new divinities. He is also guilty of corrupting the youth." (Xenophon, *Mem.* 1.1.1.) The second charge may well have been thought to be justified by Athenians at the time. The orator Aeschines says that Socrates the sophist was executed "because it was shown that he had educated Critias" (1.173), the ruthless tyrant who ruled Athens as a Spartan puppet at the end of the Peloponnesian War. And the other accusation of impiety was always dangerous in the Greek world, because it was seen as putting at risk the relationship between the human community and the divine world; impiety (*asebeia*) was an offence in law. But despite the impression that the ancient sources influenced by the example of Socrates give, *asebeia* very seldom led to prosecution. Most of the alleged examples turn out to be inventions, and the one that is best attested (Diagoras of Melos) involves the accusation of revealing the secrets of the Eleusinian Mysteries, a rather special and aggravated type of sacrilege – not just denying the existence of the gods, but positively disrupting divine worship, breaking the rules and committing blasphemy.[20]

Of course, every society imposes limits on free speech. The fact is that the Socratic tradition has tried to create an image of the Athenian democracy as intolerant of the activities of its intellectuals. But in antiquity, Athens was famous for her tolerance of critics. We should remember that Socrates' death was not intended by the state, but brought on himself by his own intransigence in refusing to propose an appropriate penalty, and then refusing to escape.[21] Any society that can put up with the declared anti-democrat Plato has a pretty good record on human rights.

Freedom of speech and the acceptance of a limited right to oppose the state remain in the political sphere. We have still not reached the area of personal liberty, the right to be independent of the state, the right of non-interference from the state. One aspect is the right to live undisturbed as a private individual. In practice that, too, existed in ancient Athens. Some people held it a virtue to live the life (in Laurence Carter's evocative phrase) of "the quiet Athenian."[22] In court you could even claim that you had never done any harm, never taken part in politics, provided (and this is significant) that you could also claim that you had always fulfilled your public duties. Pericles in the Funeral Oration may set up an ideal of a citizenry which takes "equal care for its private and its political activities, and that regards those who pay no attention to public affairs as not unambitious but useless" (2.40.2), but there were some people who believed that you could be a good citizen and not engage in politics. Later, in the Hellenistic age, quietism acquired a whole range of philosophical justifications: Cynic, Stoic, and Epicurean. But many of these, in fact, evade the question. The right to live outside the structures of the city, or the right to "escape notice living" is not quite the right to live as you please within the civic community.

The best evidence for the existence of a true form of personal liberty in relation to democracy is given by Aristotle at the start of Book 6 of the *Politics* (6.2.1317a40-b17). It is part of his report of what defenders of democracy say: According to them liberty (*eleutheria*) is the foundation of the democratic constitution, and only in a democracy does true liberty exist. This liberty has two aspects. The first is "ruling and being ruled in turn," from which spring all the essential characteristics of democracy as a form of government: offices filled by lot, for a short term, rejection of experience and status as criteria for office, popular juries, equality of justice, payment for public duties, decision of all issues by the majority of the poor. This is, of course, the ancient version of democracy as *political liberty*. But there is also a second principle behind "ruling and being ruled in turn":

to live as you like (*to zen hos bouletai tis*), for this they say is the function of freedom, just as that of slavery is to live not as you like. This is the second defining characteristic of democracy, whence is derived not being ruled, preferably by anybody, otherwise by alternation; and this contributes to liberty in accordance with equality.

This second principle of freedom is actually more fundamental than the first, for it implies that the best system of government is anarchy, not to be ruled at all, the second best that everyone should rule in turn. It therefore lies behind the first principle.

Who are these democrats whose views Aristotle is reporting both here and in an earlier passage? I agree with Hansen in thinking they are not a hypothetical possibility, but real people living in "democracies thought to be especially democratic," in which, according to Aristotle, freedom is valued above the law. They are presumably primarily Athenian.[23] Hansen is probably also correct to see this view as a reflection of the standard Athenian defense of democracy. The problem is that Aristotle's interpretation of the views of such democrats is highly tendentious, for they seem rather to hold a doctrine of living indeed as one pleases and without interference from other private individuals, but in accordance with the laws.[24]

According to Aristotle, then, personal liberty is a fundamental principle of ancient democratic thought, just as it is of modern; and M.H. Hansen has made this passage the basis of his assertion that there is no essential difference between ancient Greek and modern ideas of liberty. But if we try to give such theoretical statements concrete meaning, it is not easy to move far beyond the traditional point that Pericles makes in the Funeral Oration, that the Spartans live according to a rigid social discipline, whereas Athenians do not (Thuc. 2.39). Certainly all Athenian citizens were protected by law from arbitrary execution, from torture and from forced entry into private property. But these relate to a minimal limitation of the rights of the city against the individual; they are not the basis for any positive and overriding theory of a right to individual freedom.

The idea of individual freedom was then capable of being formulated as an abstract principle in democratic Athens; but it remained subordinate to a conception of freedom that is essentially political. The difference between ancient and modern conceptions of liberty is not absolute; it rather lies in a major difference of emphasis. And that is actually more significant than the claim that the Athenians could not imagine at all the idea of personal freedom. They could *imagine* it, they could consider it as a principle, but they were not particularly interested in developing it. Personal liberty was less important than the institutions which protected and maintained political liberty. The question we must then ask is, what are the reasons for this difference of emphasis between the ancient and the modern world?

I begin from the arguments of Constant. He is surely right to claim that in a small, face-to-face society, ruling and being ruled in turn, "the active and constant participation in collective power," is a far more effective way of ensuring liberty in general. Our emphasis on personal liberty belongs to a world where we are no longer constantly involved in the decision-making process. The state has become something separate from the general will of the people, and the protection of the individual against the state is therefore a more important issue. Ancient Athens had less need of formal institutions to protect the individual against the state and, if a few dissident intellectuals suffered as a result, at least they suffered less than they would have under any other form of government.

Slavery too has its importance in the history of liberty, though not quite in the sense that Constant suggested. As Orlando Patterson has pointed out, it serves to define liberty by its opposite at all times in the ancient world. Ancient liberty is therefore something rather different from modern liberty in that respect, though not as different as we may like to think. For slavery may be regarded as essentially a form of economic exploitation and it could well be claimed that the institutions of wage labor based on the compulsion of the fear of unemployment and the exploitation of the third world are both forms of economic control not so very different from ancient slavery.

Constant's other arguments are less convincing. It is highly doubtful whether free time for political discussion was a major factor in the development of political life in ancient Athens, or that it depended either on the comparative absence of organized commerce, or the presence of slavery. Equally, there is no necessary connection between the freedom of the individual and free-trade economics. Economic freedom often, in fact, works in ways opposed to the interests of the freedom of the individual.

Rather, I would lay emphasis on what I see as a fundamental difference between ancient and modern society. As Isaiah Berlin pointed out "conceptions of [individual] freedom directly derive from views of what constitutes a self, a person, a man" (p. 134). In my view, the weakness of the Greek conception of liberty relates to weaknesses in their conception of the self. The Greeks saw man as a social animal, in terms of his interaction with society, in terms of his duties and obligations, his skills and his achievements. They saw individual man as an agent in a social context. They classified man into various types. They idealized man. And in this context I have deliberately used the word "man," for it seems to me that there is a significant contrast here between the perception of men and the perception of women. In the case of women, Greek literature was far more concerned with the individual uniqueness of a character, at least in epic and drama. Many of the most convincing portraits in Greek tragedy (and even comedy) are portraits of women, as if men were more able to penetrate the internal conflicts and problems of women than they were to analyze their own problems. If I am right, perhaps this was because women did not appear in public life and therefore could not be seen in the same public context as men – they had to be regarded as individuals who were largely outside the political society and could assert against society the right to a certain degree of personal freedom, even if only through dramatic activities like confrontation with the civil authority, infanticide, suicide or murder.

In contrast, men were bound by social conventions. Their expectations were in accord with the expectations of society for them; they could not doubt or fall into guilt or despair. Oedipus may be misled or uncertain, but he does not fall into self-doubt. This limitation in the conception of the individual may also help to explain other weaknesses in art and literature. There is no true portraiture in Greek sculpture, which is otherwise so prone to naturalistic representation. Greek sculpture idealizes the concept of man even when it purports to portray a particular man. The portrayal of individuals as they really looked had to await the death-mask of the Etruscans and the development of Roman portrait busts.[25] So too with the literary genre of biography; in Greek literature, biography is a late and undeveloped genre, which began, I believe, in an interest in the lives of philosophers and poets. It always dealt in stock characters and stereotyped situations. It portrayed the individual in his external relations, his achievements and his failures, and in terms of a set of standard virtues and vices. Again, it was essentially the Romans - and that much maligned author, Suetonius – who pointed the way to a more vivid depiction, in describing eccentricities and individual characteristics.[26] It is not surprising somehow that the eighteenth century so admired the rather wooden and stylized biographies of Plutarch, or that in the Romantic age they went out of fashion. It has often been said, and I repeat it only because I believe it to be true, that Saint Augustine is the first self-doubting, self-aware individual in Western literature. In his *Confessions* we meet for the first time a truly modern man, whose soul demands the right to personal liberty, in terms of a personal and agonizing choice.

The path that I have been following is not a new one, for it results from reflection on the intellectual pilgrimage of my teacher in ancient history, Arnaldo Momigliano. As a young man he had been brought up in the Italian liberal tradition of his Jewish family, and had come under the influence of the anti-Fascist intelligentsia of the thirties, notably the ancient historian Gaetano De Sanctis and the idealist philosopher, Benedetto Croce.[27] Already in 1931 he was puzzling over the famous essay of Benjamin Constant, which Croce had brought to his attention.[28] Liberty was not, however, a subject that a young and vulnerable Jewish professor could espouse in the Italy of the thirties. Instead, he turned to the less dangerous subject of peace. His inaugural lecture in Turin, only recently published, was devoted to "Peace in the Ancient World."[29] When he was dismissed from his post and found refuge in England, he combined these

Liberty and the Ancient Greeks

two interests and evolved a huge project which was to be a *History of Liberty and Peace in the Ancient World*. Only a month ago the first drafts of his thoughts on this subject were published posthumously in the text of a paper delivered at Oxford in May 1940.[30] A few weeks later, in June, 1940, he was (like all refugees) called for internment as an enemy alien. It is said that when he arrived at Oxford Police Station he was asked to empty his pockets. He pulled out the book he was reading, John Stuart Mill, *On Liberty*. Yet like the great work of Lord Acton on liberty, the book he planned became "The Madonna of the Future;"[31] it was never completed because he felt that he could not answer the question posed by Constant until he had understood the nature of the Greek conception of the individual. For many years he studied Greek biography and evolved an elaborate (and, in my opinion, ultimately mistaken) view of *The Development of Greek Biography*, in order to establish the existence of a concept of the person. In his later years, he recognized explicitly the relationship between modern anthropological theories of the person as a social construct and the Greek conception of the person.[32] But even this brought no easy solution. Before he died in 1987 at age 79, he had also become fascinated with the role of biography in late antiquity, in that crucial time that saw the development of a new sensibility in Saint Augustine.[33] The path I have been following is the Ariadne's thread that he held in his hands.

Let me sum up: We can, I think, learn two lessons from this study of the similarities and differences between ancient and modern ideas of liberty. The first is one that is mightily unpopular with modern liberal philosophers. It is that the historical origins of the modern conception of personal liberty lie in Christianity. Twice Christianity has intervened in our story to set the scene for the liberty of the individual. The first time is symbolized by the intervention of Saint Augustine, and the Christian view of the nature and importance of the individual soul before God. This development of a respect for the self was a necessary precondition for the development of an idea of individual freedom. Moreover, in order for man to be free of the State, the Church had first to proclaim the freedom of God from the State. As Momigliano said in 1940:

Constant saw two extremes of the development, but Lord Acton caught hold of the central point. As the Church, in the name of the religious conscience, was really the first to put an absolute limit to the authority of the State, modern liberty would be unthinkable without the idea of the Commonwealth of God, as Christianity conceived it. Individual rights would not have been recognized without the preliminary opposition of a religious conscience to the authority of the State. (*Nono Contributo* p. 501)

The other time that religion has intervened in our story is with the Reformation and the insistence on the right of the inidividual to defy both Church and State in determining his own relationship to God. The Non-Conformist tradition is the real origin of the modern radical conception of personal freedom, for it imposed on the individual the right, indeed the duty, to make a free choice for the salvation of his soul.

My second point is a word of caution. It is the ancient conception of political liberty which is intrinsic to both the ancient and modern ideas of democracy. The modern conception of personal freedom, on the other hand, is related to democracy only by historical accident. It may happen to be true that most democratic states have a better record on personal liberty than other types of state. But there is no necessary reason, as Constant and Mill saw, why democracies should not tyrannize over the rights of minorities, let alone individuals. And many enlightened despotisms have historically been a safer refuge for individual liberty. Personal liberty indeed, taken to its limits, is ultimately a concept which leads to anarchy rather than democracy.

In our political life we should not therefore over-emphasize personal liberty. We should remember that in all periods and under all conditions no single aspect of the democratic ideology is sufficient. The ancient Greeks saw democracy as closely related to freedom (*eleutheria*), but also to the rule of law (*nomos*), justice (*dikaiosyne*) and equality (*isotes*), and above all to a sense of community (*koinonia*). The French Revolution saw the same - liberty, equality, fraternity. Let no one say that they are incompatible, for unless they can be combined, no just and harmonious society can ever be created. Even those most individualist of political thinkers, the American founding fathers, added life and the pursuit of happiness to liberty. Liberty alone is not enough. Unless, that is, we define liberty in the broad and generous terms that Shelley did, in his great hymn to freedom:

What art thou, Freedom? O! could slaves
Answer from their living graves
This demand – tyrants would flee
Like a dream's dim imagery:

"Thou art not, as impostors say
A shadow soon to pass away,
A superstition and a name
Echoing from the cave of Fame.

"For the labourer thou art bread,
And a comely table spread
From his daily labour come
In a neat and happy home.

"Thou art clothes, and fire, and food
For the trampled multitude –
No – in countries that are free
Such starvation cannot be
As in England now we see."

(*The Mask of Anarchy* LII-LV)

NOTES

[1] M. H. Hansen, "The Athenian 'Politicians,' 403-322 B.C.," *The Athenian Ecclesia II: A Collection of Articles 1983-89* (Copenhagen 1989) 1-23.

[2] K. J. Dover *"Anapsephisis* in Fifth-Century Athens," *Journal of Hellenic Studies* 75 (1955) 17-20 = *The Greeks and Their Legacy. Collected Papers II* (Oxford 1988) 187-93.

[3] Herodotus 6.43.3 (of the Persians in 492 B.C. and 131.1 (of Cleisthenes himself) are the earliest appearances of *demokratia*; but it is generally agreed that Herodotus is using anachronistic language. More significantly, the word seems to lie behind the phrase *"demou kratousa cheir* in Æschylus' *Supplices* 604 (around 460 B.C.); it has also been proposed as a possible restoration in the oath of the Athenian treaty with Kolophon, IG I^3 37.49 (?447/6 B.C.) — but see R. Meiggs, D. M. Lewis, *Greek Historical Inscriptions* (Oxford 1969) no. 47.48. My interpretation of *demokratia* as polemical is controversial: See M. H. Hansen, *The Athenian Democracy in the Age of Demosthenes* (Oxford 1991) 69-71.

[4] For the origin of *isonomia* see M. Ostwald, *Nomos and the Beginnings of the Athenian Democracy* (Oxford 1969).

[5] The editions I cite are Isaiah Berlin, *Four Essays on Liberty* (Oxford 1969); John Stuart Mill, "On Liberty," *Utilitarianism, Liberty and Representative Government* (Everyman 1910).

[6] On the problems of reconciling liberty and the general will in Rousseau, see Patrick Gardiner, "Rousseau on Liberty," in Z. Pelczynski, J. Gray (eds.), *Conceptions of Liberty in Political Philosophy* (London 1984) 83-99.

[7] I cite this work from the selection of Constant's political writings, *De la Liberté chez les Modernes* edited by M. Gauchet (Paris 1980); for earlier drafts of his ideas, see p. 686 n. 2; for the reference to Condorcet, see p. 496 and the note on p. 688 n. 6.

[8] Once a year the Assembly was asked if they wished to hold an ostracism. If there was a majority in favor, a special ballot was held, in which all male citizens were entitled to write the name of that individual whom they would most like exiled. The candidate who received the highest number of votes was required to leave the city and live in exile for ten years, without loss of citizen status or property. At one or more stages a quorum of six thousand votes was required. Over 6000 clay ostraca have been excavated so far, mostly covering the five years of annual ostracisms, 487-3 B.C. During the Persian War, the exiles were recalled and some were even elected generals. In the mid-fifth century, ostracism was used to remove or threaten political opponents (Themistocles, Kimon, Thucydides son of Melesias, Hyperbolos), and was then largely replaced by political prosecutions of various types.

[9] The best scholarly accounts of the differences between ancient and modern ideas of liberty are M. I. Finley, "The Freedom of the Citizen in the Greek World," *Talanta* 7 (1976) 1-23 = *Economy and Society in Ancient Greece* (New York 1982) 77-94; K. Roaflaub, "Freiheit in Athen und Rom: eine Beispiel divergierender politischer Begriffsentwicklung in der Antike," *Historische Zeitschrift* 238 (1984) 529-67; R. Mulgan, "Liberty in Ancient Greece," Pelczynski and Gray o.c. (n.6) 7-26. The most detailed historical account is K. Roaflaub, *Die Entdeckung der Freiheit* (Munich 1985).

[10] "The Tradition of the Athenian Democracy A.D. 1750-1990," *Greece and Rome* 39 (1992) 14-30; *Was Athens a Democracy? Popular Rule, Liberty and Equality in Ancient and Modern Political Thought, Historisk-filosofiske Meddelelser* 59 Det Kongelige Danske Videnskabernes Selskab (Copenhagen 1989).

[11] *Freedom: Freedom in the Making of Western Culture* (London 1991); see my review in the *Times Literary Supplement* October 25, 1991 p. 8.

[12] Herod. 5.78: The word he actually uses for democracy is *isegoria*, again the first attested use of the word; see further below.

[13] M. Ostwald, *Autonomia: its Genesis and Early History* (American Classical Studies 11, 1982); Roaflaub, *Entdeckung der Freiheit* (n. 9) 189-207.

[14] Ch. Wirszubski, *Libertas as a Political Idea at Rome during the Late Republic and Early Principate* (Cambridge 1960); cf. P.A. Brunt, "*Libertas* in the Republic," *The Fall of the Roman Republic and Related Essays* (Oxford 1988) 281-350.

[15] G. T. Griffith, "*Isegoria* in the Assembly at Athens," *Ancient Society and Institutions. Studies Presented to Victor Ehrenberg* (Oxford 1966) 115-38; J. D. Lewis, "*Isegoria* at Athens: when did it begin?", *Historia* 20 (1971) 129-40.

[16] These are the conclusions of M. H. Hansen, "The Number of *Rhetores* in the Athenian *Ecclesia*, 355-322 B.C.," o.c. (n.1) 93-127. The estimate he gives is 700-1400 citizens.

[17] G. Scarpat, *Parrhesia* (Brescia 1964).

[18] Diogenes Laertius 6.38 etc. There are many similar anecdotes of later philosophers and kings.

[19] There is a fascinating collection of evidence on such issues in the delightful and learned book by David Daube, *Civil Disobedience in Antiquity* (Edinburgh 1972).

[20] See esp. K. J. Dover, "The Freedom of the Intellectual in Greek Society," *Talanta* 7 (1976) 24-54 = *The Greeks and Their Legacy*, o.c. (n.2) 135-58.

[21] See I. F. Stone, *The Trial of Socrates* (London 1988).

[22] *The Quiet Athenian* (Oxford 1986).

[23] The earlier passage is *Pols.* 6.9.1310a25-38, which I paraphrase here. For discussion, see Hansen *Was Athens a Democracy?* o.c. (n.10) p.8.

[24] See esp. Herod. 6.82.2-3; Thuc. 2.37.2; 7.69.2 Demosthenes 25.25. Aristotle's interpretation is a standard one among critics of democracy. See Hansen o.c. p.35 n.48.

[25] See R. R. R. Smith, "Greeks, Foreigners and Roman Republican Portraits," *Journal of Roman Studies* 71 (1981) 24-38.

[26] In holding this, I am opposing the views of A. Momigliano, *The Development of Greek Biography* (Harvard 1971), on which see further below.

[27] See Carlo Dionisotti, *Ricordo di Arnaldo Momigliano* (Bologna 1989), Oswyn Murray, "Arnaldo Momigliano in England," in M.P. Steinberg (ed.), *The Presence of the Historian: Essays in Memory of Arnaldo Momigliano* (*History and Theory* Beiheft 30, 1991) 49-64.

[28] *Riv. Fil.* 9 (1931) 262-4 = *Quinto Contributo alla storia degli studi classici e del mondo antico*

(Rome 1975) 906-7; he returned to this preoccupation in the last thing he wrote, the preface to a reprint of his early work, *Filippo il Macedone* (Milan 1987) xv-xvi.

[29] First published in Dionisotti o.c. 97-130; now in *Nono Contributo* (Rome 1992) 409-23.

[30] "Liberty and Peace in the Ancient World," *Nono Contributo* 483-501.

[31] The reference is to Henry James's short story, which Mary Gladstone drew to Acton's attention in 1880.

[32] "Marcel Mauss and the Quest for the Person in Greek Biography and Autobiography," *The Category of the Person* ed. M. Carrithers, S. Collins, S. Lukes (Cambridge 1985) 83-92, later elaborated in "Marcel Mauss e il problema della persona nella biografia greca," *Ottavo Contributo* (Rome 1987) 179-90. I am not convinced by G. W. Bowersock's autobiographical thesis in his interesting essay, "Momigliano's Quest for the Person," in Steinberg o.c. (n.27) 27-36.

[33] "Ancient Biography and the Study of Religion in the Roman Empire," *Ottavo Contributo* 193-210.

4

How Democratic Was Ancient Athens?

Robert Browning

From the late eighth century B.C. onwards, in many Greek states, men began to question the age-old rule of the local big-wigs and to take hesitant steps towards a concept of citizenship which implied certain rights and duties. Sparta was perhaps the first city to establish constitutional government. We know virtually nothing about the Spartan reformer, Lycurgus; his date is quite uncertain and his very existence has been questioned. Sparta, however, never became a democracy. In Corinth too, the ruling family was deposed and a kind of dictatorship set up by Periander, a noble who enjoyed the support of those who had previously been excluded from power. But Corinth, nevertheless, remained a tight oligarchy. In Athens there were stirrings about the same time. A law code was promulgated about 620, which set limits to the arbitrary power of the aristocratic families. A generation later, Solon saw the need for radical change, but the constitution he devised kept public office in the hands of the well-to-do. We know very little of the detailed arrangements which he inaugurated, and in particular how elections worked. Solon succeeded in establishing a legal state, but not a democracy. Yet he set in movement a process that could not be stopped. Increasing trade in the eastern Mediterranean in the sixth century was leading to greater independence of both peasant and artisan from the traditional patterns of control.

It might be appropriate at this point to read a short passage from Professor George Forrest's *The Emergence of Greek Democracy*. "My theme," he writes, "is the gradual development throughout Greece between 750 and 450 B.C. of the idea of individual human autonomy, of the idea that all members of a political society were free and equal, that everyone has the right to an equal say in determining the structure and activities of his society. Athenian democracy was the result of a thoroughgoing application of this idea in practice, the most thorough we know of in the history of Greece and, thanks to the peculiar conditions of life in a Greek city-state, it was possible for the Athenians to apply it in such a way that the individual was given greater direct responsibility, a more immediately obvious and therefore more real political equality than he has ever known elsewhere."[1]

So much for the general concept of Athenian democracy. The world celebrated in 1992 the 2,500th anniversary of the constitution of Cleisthenes, established in 508 B.C. This is as good a date as any to mark the beginning of a democratic system which endured, with two short interruptions – one due to a half-hearted *coup d'état*, the other to foreign occupation – until a Macedonian army of occupation put an end to it in 322 B.C. We must bear in mind that in ancient Greece, as in the world of today, democracy cannot be "installed" like air-conditioning or central heating. It calls for the unlearning of old ways, for the gradual response to new conditions, and for a radical change in the relations between man and man, and between individual and community. There are no short cuts.

Cleisthenes was leader of an aristocratic faction. When he was defeated in the traditional struggle for power, he, in the words of Aristotle, "added the Demos to his faction,"[2] and was elected to a magistracy. He then set about restructuring the political geography of Attica. He abolished the traditional four tribes and their subdivisions, through which the nobility had controlled the life of the city and its territory. Henceforth, the basic political and administrative unit was to be the deme (of which there were 139), a geographical and social unit, either a village in the countryside or a city ward. The demes elected their own officers and managed their own affairs, but they were also the channel linking the ordinary citizen with the central government. In other democratic states, such as Thasos, the people of the countryside were virtually ignored. Athens politicized and democratized the countryside. This factor gave Athenian democracy a durability lacking in other Greek cities. The demes were grouped together in various ways designed to obviate the formation of powerful regional groups. It was through membership of his deme that a man became a citizen of Athens. As a citizen, every male Athenian aged 18 or more was automatically a member of the Assembly, the supreme legislative and executive organ of the city, which met at least forty times a year. Not every citizen attended all meetings, but it appears that an average attendance of some 6,000 could be counted upon.[3] The people – the *demos* – had firmly taken power into its hands.

Was Cleisthenes a principled democrat or an aristocrat disgusted by the endless infighting of his fellows and aiming at efficient and stable government? He is a shadowy figure. We never hear his voice. Yet the sureness of touch with which he transformed forever the political structure of Athens and broke the power of the mighty without touching their prestige or their wealth, suggests that he had long pondered, and no doubt discussed with his fellow-citizens, just where the locus of power must be situated. This does not mean that he was not perhaps something of an opportunist also. What he did was to establish the demes as local centers of power; the Assembly, which ideally comprised the whole citizen body, as the organ of sovereignty, and the Council of 500 as a steering and executive committee of the Assembly, with wide powers both to prepare business for the Assembly and to supervise the carrying out of its decisions. Members of the Council were selected by lot each year from citizens aged thirty or over who volunteered. No one could serve on the Council more than twice in his lifetime, and never in two successive years. The Council had a standing committee of fifty, which changed every 36 days. Service on the Council was a demanding task. A simple calculation suggests that approximately half of the citizen body must have served at least one year on the Council, and so have had direct experience of all the problems of government, from foreign relations to finance. Athens was a participatory democracy in a very literal sense. I will return to this point in dealing with one of the criticisms voiced again and again in antiquity, and provided with a metaphysical backing by Plato.

Most officials were appointed by lot, usually in collegial groups. They had to be over thirty years of age, and no one could hold a particular appointment more than once. An exception to both of these conditions was made for some offices for which expert knowledge was thought necessary. For instance, the *strategoi* – "generals" is the standard but inadequate translation (let us recall that the poet Sophocles was elected to this office) – were directly elected by ballot and could be re-elected. They not only commanded a division of the army but were also in command of naval forces and were sometimes empowered to negotiate with distant foreign states without seeking the approval of the Assembly in Athens. Their powers were great, especially if they were re-elected. Pericles was *strategos* for thirty years. The historian Thucydides observed that in those years Athens was in name a democracy but was in reality ruled by one man. This is rather a one-sided view, as we shall see when we consider the limitations on the power of *strategoi* and on all officials. Another class of officials elected by ballot and not by lot were the members of certain financial boards. Their influence on the conduct of state policy was less than that of the *strategoi*.

It is impossible to calculate how many citizens had a year or more of experience of public office as a result of appointment by lot. It may seem today a strange way of doing things. But as penetrating an analyst as Aristotle (who incidentally did not much like democracy) approved of it and saw in it one of the distinguishing marks of Greek democracy.[4] It had two justifications, one theoretical, the other practical. It gave reality to the idea that power belonged to ordinary people and not to an elite, and it made it difficult for cliques to manipulate appointments to public office, or to bribe or curry favor with future office-holders.

There still remained one important part of the machinery of government which was not under the control of and participated in by the whole citizen body – namely, the law courts. The venerable Council of the Areopagus (its origins probably went back to remote antiquity) whose members were former magistrates, still exercised wide-ranging judicial powers. For a generation after the reforms of Cleisthenes it was necessarily dominated by members of the aristocracy, elected or appointed to office under the old system of rule by the old landowning families, and must for a long time have been a citadel of discontent with popular rule and of more and more nostalgic yearning for the "good old days." At the same time, it was an anomaly in democratic Athens, since its members held office for life. It was, in fact, a kind of Roman Senate in embryo. If circumstances permitted it might, like the Roman Senate, have imposed limits on the effective exercise of power by the people and concentrated more and more authority in its own hands without any corresponding responsibility. Minor cases seem to have been tried by *archons* and other magistrates elected by lot, but there was often a right of appeal to the Council of the Areopagus. There was thus an internal discrepancy in the judicial system.

Around the year 462 (forty years after Cleisthenes), in circumstances the details of which escape us, the judicial system was radically modified. It seems likely that a small group of aristocrats espoused the cause of popular sovereignty. There was tense confrontation. One of the popular leaders, Ephialtes, apparently an Athenian of humble origin, was assassinated – one of the very few political assassinations in the 180 years of democratic rule. What the reformers succeeded in doing was to strip the Council of the Areopagus of all its judicial powers, except for certain cases of homicide and certain religious offenses. At the same time, the magistrates elected by lot were no longer to try cases, but merely to investigate whether there was a *prima facie* case to answer. The actual trial was to take place in a new kind of court. Maybe this was first seen as a minor modification of procedure. But it became a key feature of the developed democracy.

The new court consisted of 6000 Athenian citizens aged thirty or more who volunteered to serve. They sat in groups of several hundred (always an odd number, to avoid a tied verdict) and voted by ballot after hearing both sides. There was a complicated system for allocating members to particular courts, designed to prevent bribery or other illegal influence. In order to enable poorer citizens or those living far from the city to play their part in the court, which sat for perhaps 200 days a year, its members were paid a small salary, roughly the equivalent of the minimum that a free workman might earn.

The powers of the new court were wide-ranging and enabled it sometimes to overthrow a decision of the sovereign Assembly and to punish those who had proposed it, if it could be shown that it was in conflict with the existing laws of the city. It could thus act as a constitutional court and thus find itself involved in political conflicts between different pressure groups (to speak of political parties in ancient Greek cities is a misleading modernization). It also examined the accounts and the activities of all officials, whether appointed by lot or by election, at the end of their period of office.

Some have seen in the occasional conflicts between Assembly and courts a limitation of the sovereignty of the people, especially since many of those who took part in the meetings of the Assembly were excluded from sitting on the courts because they were too young. This view is, I think, to be rejected. Assembly and Court were both organs of the people, of the whole citizen body (which may have numbered 40,000 in the mid-fifth century and nearer 30,000 in the fourth. It was to the people, and not to any single one of its organs, that the ultimate power of decision belonged. The age limit of thirty for service in the court, in the Council or in elected office, which excluded many of those who might attend, speak and vote in the Assembly, is based on the unquestioned belief in antiquity that age brought wisdom, and was never perceived by contemporaries as unjust or unreasonable. The generation gap was not a feature of ancient society. It is worth recalling that according to Aristotle some saw the control of the courts by the people as giving the people ultimate control of their constitution.[5]

One last feature of the Athenian constitution calls for mention, one apparently introduced from the beginning by Cleisthenes. This is ostracism. Each year the Assembly was required to decide whether an ostracism should be held. It usually decided not to hold one. But if it was decided to hold one, then a kind of referendum of the whole citizen body took place, in which each citizen who took the trouble to vote could write on a sherd of broken pottery (an *ostrakon*) the name of one fellow-citizen who, he believed, should be exiled for ten years, without loss of civil rights or confiscation of property. There had to be at least 6000 votes in favor of ostracising any particular individual. Cleisthenes' original intention may have been to forestall a *coup d'état* by a potential dictator among the old aristocracy. In later years it occasionally served to defuse a political conflict which was paralyzing the process of government. After the fifth century ostracism was abandoned. Perhaps it was seen as too cumbersome and too open to political manipulation. (Stocks of ready-made sherds with the name of a public figure have been found.) In any case, the threat to the democratic regime was much diminished in the fourth century, and other ways had been found of dealing with potentially dangerous individuals. Be that as it may, the institution of ostracism – so strange to us – was in intention another aspect of the sovereignty of the people, in which all who wished could take part on a basis of equality.

Lastly, let us remember that all citizens were liable for military service until they reached old age. Those who could afford a horse or an expensive suit of armor served as cavalry or heavy infantry (*hoplites*). The rest served as light-armed troops or as sailors or rowers in the Athenian navy. They were paid for their service.

Now that we have put the Athenian constitution in place in its main outlines, and bearing in mind that there are many details of its workings about which we are in the dark, let us turn to criticisms made of it both by its contemporaries and by modern critics.

First, a modern criticism which, I think, displays a lack of historical understanding. Citizenship, with all its rights and duties, people say, was artificially restricted. Only free male Athenians over eighteen could take part in the processes of political decision. Women, resident foreigners and slaves were excluded. So, incidentally, were children and adolescents. So out of a population of perhaps 140,000, only 30,000 to 40,000 had citizen rights. True, but no ancient state ever gave active citizen rights to women. This may have been short-sighted or unjust, but let us recall that in my country it was not until 1919 that some women obtained the right to vote, and they did not all obtain it until 1928. In the United States they had to wait until the Nineteenth Amendment to the Bill of Rights was passed in 1920, and in France until 1945, and Swiss women only recently achieved the right to vote in federal elections. Yet these countries were and are democracies, whatever their shortcomings. It is unhistorical to project back more than 2000 years our own quite recent attitudes to distinctions of sex or gender. It should be said that Athenian women enjoyed many rights. They were not mere chattels of a father or a husband, as were women in many ancient societies, including the Roman Republic. As for slaves, what ancient socety gave them any rights, except sometimes that of not being arbitrarily killed by their owners? However, when Athens received the news of Philip of Macedon's victory over the armies of the Greek cities at Chaeroneia in 338 B.C., the emergency measures proposed to the Assembly included the arming of resident foreigners and slaves.[6] In the antebellum South, no slave possessed any of the rights of a citizen and the idea of slaves bearing arms was inconceivable. And even in recent times their descendants have sometimes found it difficult to exercise the full citizen rights which the Constitution guaranteed to them. Perhaps we should not be too censorious in criticizing ancient societies.

Now to more serious criticisms of Athenian democracy. Both in antiquity and among modern scholars it was regularly alleged that the common people, because of their ignorance and lack of education, were incapable of making reasoned decisions on important public matters, and so were unfit to rule. For Alcibiades, the archetypal clever and ambitious young aristocrat, democracy was admitted folly – *homologoumene anoia*.[7] A variant of this criticism developed particularly by Plato, who was no friend of Athenian democracy,[8] is that politics is an art or craft, like carpentry or medicine, and is only to be practised by whole-time specialists who have been properly trained. There was no room in Plato's world for amateurism or do-it-yourself. He goes on to argue that in the end only the philosopher is fit to rule. The superficially attractive but illusory concept of the philosopher-king has haunted European thought since Plato's time. It fails to take into account that politics is not a specific craft, like carpentry or cookery, but a general capacity so to conduct the affairs of a community that it does not disintegrate. Aristotle too, though he accepts democracy as a workable way of running a community, thinks that ideally the ruling and the producing classes should be separate, and neither should try to do the work of the other.[9]

It is no doubt true that Athenian craftsmen and farmers and sailors were on the whole less well educated than the rich, who did not work and who had time and money to study under professional teachers. But let us not exaggerate the gulf that separated them. Socrates, after all, was the son of a stone-mason and a midwife. More important, the whole structure of Athenian democracy ensured that a large proportion of the citizen body had some experience of the problems of government. A man might be active in the affairs of his deme, serve on its council or become one of its officers. Another, or indeed the same man, might serve on the Council or the court, or hold one of the many executive posts. It has been calculated that about half of the citizen population served for one or perhaps two years on the Council of the city, drafting resolutions for the Assembly, supervising the work of magistrates, putting into effect the decisions of the Assembly, administering dockyards and temples, receiving foreign ambassadors, and carrying out a hundred other duties. For a tenth of his period of office, each councillor was a member of the *prytany*, or standing committee of the Council, which remained in permanent session, lodged and fed in a public building in the heart of Athens. A citizen was quite likely, unless he was a principled loner, to hold one of the many magistracies elected by lot (we do not know of all of them). He will certainly have taken part in many meetings of the Assembly, the ultimate organ of the sovereignty of the people. If he was over thirty he is likely to have served on one of the courts for a year or more. In short, the common Athenian citizen was not an ignorant bumpkin, but was tolerably well informed on and experienced in public affairs. Let me quote three witnesses, one an ancient Athenian, the others modern Englishmen acquainted with the workings of public life. First, Pericles, as reported by Thucydides (2.40.2):

> You will find united in the same persons an interest at once in private and public affairs, and in those of us who give attention chiefly to our private business, you will find no lack of insight into political matters. For we alone regard the man who takes no part in public affairs, not as one who minds his own business, but as good for nothing. We Athenians decide public questions for ourselves, or at least try to arrive at a sound understanding of them, convinced that it is not discussion that is a hindrance to action, but rather not to have learnt from discussion before the time comes for action.

Next, John Stuart Mill in *On Representative Government* (pp. 196-198 in World's Classics edition):

> The active participation of Athenian citizens in Assembly, courts etc. provided a unique education in weighing interests other than a man's own, in examining objectively conflicting claims, etc. Thus the ordinary citizen attained an intellectual level unequalled before or after.

Last, Sir Alfred Zimmern, Professor of International Relations at Oxford before the Second World War and an adviser to the League of Nations:

> The Athenian community during the Periclean time must be regarded as the most successful example of social organisation known to history. Its society was so arranged as to make the most and the best of the human material at its disposal...We are apt to forget that we owe the Parthenon sculptures not merely to the genius of Phidias, but also to the genius of the social system which knew how to make use of him. (*The Greek Commonwealth* 365-66)

Mill and Zimmern were no doubt affected by the idealization of ancient Greece so common in the nineteenth century, but they were men of experience and judgement. I quote with some hesitation another witness, Edward Augustus Freeman, a wide-ranging if somewhat opinionated historian who held the Regius Chair of Modern History at Oxford towards the end of the last century, that "the average Athenian citizen was, in political intelligence, above the average English Member of Parliament" (*Historical Essays*, 2nd Series, 1880, 165). The argument that the common man is too ignorant to rule is not a valid criticism of democracy, ancient or modern.

A related argument can be dealt with more briefly. It is that the Assembly, a crowd of 6000 or more citizens, is impetuous, excitable, easily swayed by persuasive speakers, and irresponsible in its political judgements. Plato actually compares the people to a huge animal, whose passions and prejudices a political figure must carefully study, and always give it what it wants when it wants it. No doubt, from time to time decisions were made hastily under the pressure of strong emotions. One example often quoted is the decision to punish the people of Mytilene for revolting in time of war, by killing the men and selling the women and children. But the citizens themselves had second thoughts and, on the next day, an extraordinary meeting of the Assembly reversed the barbarous decision which it had made on the previous day. We must also bear in mind that though the Assembly exercised sovereign power, it did so within a framework of law. It could not pass a resolution without a previous draft prepared by the Council. It could not pass resolutions which were in conflict with the laws which it had already approved. There were procedures to bring to trial those who proposed resolutions which were not in accordance with the laws, or which manifestly conflicted with the interests of the Athenian people. Not only the proposers of such resolutions, but even the chairmen of the Assembly who put them to the vote were liable to prosecution. These procedures were developed and refined – and used – throughout the 180 years of democratic government in Athens. But the ultimate sovereignty of the people was not challenged, and government by the people never became government by officials, as it did in the Roman Republic and in some Greek cities. Lastly, the criterion of democracy is not that its decisions are invariably right and that it never makes mistakes. This is more than can be asked of any government.

Another criticism levelled against Athenian democracy by modern students of politics is that in the absence of political parties there was no possibility of "change of government." This criticism, it seems to me, is invalid on two grounds. First, political parties with a continuing identity and a consistent policy are an invention of the nineteenth century. Second, and more important, there was no "government" in Athens other than the citizen body. There was no permanent bureaucracy. There were regular speakers at the Assembly, but they had no special authority. Every time they rose to speak they put their credibility, and sometimes even their liberty, at risk. However often they had won the favor of the Assembly on previous occasions, there was never any assurance that they would win it next time. A speaker might have friends, supporters and canvassers, but in Moses Finley's words, "he walked alone."[10] A man was leader solely as a function of his personal, unofficial status within the Assembly itself. The test of whether or not he held that status was simply whether the Assembly did or did not vote as he wished, and therefore the test was repeated each time he rose to speak. Conversely, each member of the Assembly voted as he pleased. There was no party discipline to direct his voting.

If there was no government, there was no opposition. The old landed aristocracy in the course of the fifth century dwindled into a group of disgruntled internal émigrés, squabbling among themselves, and by the middle of the fourth century had ceased to exist as a coherent group. There was still a conflict of interest between rich and poor, but that is another matter.

Perhaps the most serious criticism made of Athenian democracy both in the past and in modern times is that it was rendered possible only by the exploitation and oppression of the city-states throughout the Aegean which formed the so-called Athenian Empire. The term was first used in the nineteenth century and has overtones not entirely appropriate to the situation of ancient Athens. First, let me briefly remind those who may have forgotten of the history of the "empire."

After the defeat of the Persian invaders at Salamis, Plataea and Mykale in 480-478, Sparta, the second most powerful city in the alliance against Persia, withdrew into isolation and showed no enthusiasm for pursuing the war and expelling all remaining Persian garrisons from the Aegean area. The cities of the islands and the Thracian and Asia Minor coasts, therefore, sought the protection of Athens in a voluntary confederation in 478/7. What was needed was a powerful fleet, sound finances and the will to continue the struggle. These Athens alone possessed.

At first, representatives of all the member cities, of which most were very small, met regularly to decide policy. Athens, which provided most of the ships and all the commanders for expeditions, was able to control the votes of most of the smaller and poorer cities and so, in effect, to dominate the confederation. She soon began, for strategic reasons, to coerce a few cities which had remained aloof from the confederation or which sought to leave it. Cities so coerced remained under close Athenian control. Thus there gradually developed a kind of three-tier membership of the confederation: a few large cities contributed their own ships, many smaller cities contributed money instead, leaving the Athenians to furnish ships for them, and a growing number of cities were under more or less tight Athenian control. There also developed a pattern of Athenian jurisdiction in member cities, arising out of contracts between Athenians and foreign citizens, the details of which varied from city to city. It was aimed at preventing civil disorder, protecting democratic regimes and forestalling revolts. No doubt it was sometimes exercised with a heavy hand. Another cause of resentment was the establishment of Athenian settlements near or in the territory of certain member cities, particularly on the Thracian coast. By the time the great conflict between

Sparta and Athens began in 431, which was to last almost thirty years, Athens was beginning to treat many members of the confederation as if they were her subjects. It could scarcely have been otherwise, as war drew nearer. Yet the great majority of the subject cities remained loyal to Athens until the victory of Sparta and the final dissolution of the confederation, which had become an empire. The Athenian empire was unique among empires in that the ruling city relied on the support of the common people in the subject cities.[11]

The argument linking democracy with empire was put in a sentence twenty years ago by Claude Mossé in her excellent study of the origin, development and eventual collapse of the democratic constitution of Athens. Athenian democracy, she wrote, depended on the existence of the empire. Any threat to the empire was a threat against the regime.[12] There is much truth in this at first sight. But the democratic constitution lasted 180 years, while the confederation or empire lasted only 75, so the formulation needs modification. In fact, I think it is true only of the thirty years of the Peloponnesian War and a few preceding years, when the Greek cities were divided into two hostile groups, when much of the soil of Attica was occupied by a Spartan army, and which ended with the imposition of a brief but brutal tyranny in Athens.

War corrupts and brutalises all who engage in it, and democratic Athens was no exception to this rule. She unilaterally increased the contributions demanded from subject cities, interfered more and more in their internal affairs, and punished with often pitiless severity any which defected. But if we look at the 47 years of relative peace which preceded the outbreak of the great war, a different picture emerges. The cities of the confederation, whose original aim was to prevent any future Persian invasion of the Aegean area, had the choice between contributing ships and men to the common defense force, or paying money and leaving the defense of the region to the Athenians. Most of the cities were quite small and naturally preferred to pay money rather than maintain a navy of their own. Then, when we look at the actual cash contributions required from each city and measure them against the probable population, we realise that they were quite modest – in modern terms only a small proportion of the GNP. In return for their payments, the cities gained nearly fifty years of peace and freedom from foreign invasion or control, not to mention Spartan aggression. They gained a place in a rapidly developing network of trade centered on Athens. If they were themselves democracies – and many were – they gained protection from antidemocratic coups and civil war. It was not a bad bargain. It is interesting how many fathers in subject cities named their sons Demokrates, Philodemos or the like. Later empires, beginning with that of Rome, relied on the support of the aristocracy or the rich in their subject territories. The Athenians relied in general on the loyalty of the common people.

It is true that the accumulated tribute of the subject cities may have helped Athens to make democracy work by paying citizens for carrying out some of their civic responsibilities. But these payments continued and even increased after the empire had been dissolved and Athens itself had become impoverished. So this argument does not clinch the matter. What Athens did use some of the tribute money for was to rebuild the great temples on the Acropolis and elsewhere in Athens. But these were restorations of temples destroyed by the Persians while Athens was bearing the the brunt of the war with Persia. Athens kept her part of the bargain. It was Athenian citizens who fought in the skirmishes and minor wars. It was Athenian citizens who manned the warships which year in, year out patrolled the Aegean Sea. It was Athenian citizens who kept the peace. This complex question calls for more detailed discussion. But I feel that the existence of the empire is not a sufficient explanation of the success of the democratic constitution of Athens.

To sum up, Athenian democracy was not a perfect society. It made mistakes. It was capable of harshness and cruelty. It needed political leaders, but it kept them under tight control. Military leaders, especially in the fourth century, might enjoy great influence and authority so long as they were victorious. But they paid a heavy price for failure – fines, exile or death. Civilian leaders, men who made speeches and proposed resolutions in the Assembly, were often prosecuted if their policies turned out to be unsuccessful. The principle of the responsibility of a public figure was always maintained. Yet for two centuries, Athens trod the narrow path between civic unity and civil war. The history of most Greek states, in particular in the difficult economic climate of the fourth century, was punctuated by savage internal strife and mutual massacre. Democratic Athens swung between power and prosperity and impoverishment and impotence without lasting civil strife. It needed leaders, but never developed a ruling elite which excluded the people from power. When in the end the democratic constitution was overthrown in 322, it was the result of an overwhelming military defeat and the occupation of the city by the Macedonian army. Most of its citizens became mere inhabitants, with few civil rights. Its loss of independence was a fate which it shared with the other cities of Greece, and perhaps it marked the end of the viability of the city-state as an autonomous political unit.

During its 180 years of democratic government, Athens saw an unparalleled flourishing of art, literature, philosophy and science, which has become part of the common heritage of mankind. An important part of that heritage has been the idea of democracy, of the full participation of equal and autonomous human beings in the decision-making processes of their community.

I have quoted some positive verdicts on Athenian democracy by nineteenth-century thinkers. Americans doubtless know more than I the place of that democracy in the thinking of the founding fathers of the United States, so I will not recapitulate it here. But, as the devil can quote Scripture, so the opponents of the American Revolution sometimes turned to Greece for cautionary examples. In 1778 – mark the date – my fellow-Scotsman John Gillies wrote that if any people ignored the unhappy history of Greece, and, "disdaining to continue happy subjects of the country under whose protection they have so long flourished, would set on foot a republican confederacy, let them tremble at the prospect of those calamities which, should their designs be carried into execution, they must both inflict and suffer."[13] Was John Gillies right? It is for you, the people, to decide.

NOTES

[1] G. Forrest, *The Emergence of Greek Democracy* (London 1966) 44.

[2] Aristotle, *Constitution of Athens* 20.1.

[3] M. H. Hansen, "How Many Athenians Attended the Ecclesia?", *Greek, Roman and Byzantine Studies* 17 (1976) 115-134, reprinted in M.H. Hansen, *The Athenian Ecclesia* (Copenhagen 1983) 1-23.

[4] Aristotle, *Politics* 4.9.4.

[5] Aristotle, *op.cit.* 2.12.3.

[6] Lycurgus, *Against Leocrates* 41; Hypereides, *frg.* 27, 29; Plutarch, *Lives of the Ten Orators* 849a. Cf. the discussion in K.-W. Welwei, *Unfreie im antiken Kriegsdienst, I,* (Wiesbaden 1974) 54-56. Pausanias (1.32.3, 7.15.7) states that in 490 the Athenians by a *bouleuma* gave freedom to their slaves who fought at Marathon, but his evidence is questionable, since Herodotus mentions no such measure in his account of the battle. The slave orderlies who accompanied hoplite soldiers occasionally took part in the fighting (Cf. Welwei, *op. cit.* 54, n.1).

[7] Thucydides 6.89.

[8] Plato, *Republic* 8 553b ff. and elsewhere.

[9] Aristotle, *Politics* 7.2.1.

[10] M. I. Finley, "Athenian Demagogues," *Past and Present* 26 (1962) 15. This whole article is full of insights into the working of Athenian democracy.

[11] G. E. M. de Ste. Croix, *The Class Struggle in the Ancient Greek World*, (London 1981) 290-291. For a further discussion of this feature of Athenian rule cf. Notes 26 and 27 on pp. 603-605 of the same work.

[12] Claude Mossé, *Histoire d'une démocratie. Athènes* (Paris 1971) 58.

[13] F. M. Turner, *The Greek Heritage in Victorian Britain* (New Haven, London, 1981) 192.

5

Cleisthenes and His Reforms

Robin Lane Fox

The anniversary celebrations of democracy began with a heartening prelude. Like the Athenians in 510 B.C., we too watched a "fall of the tyrants" prior to democracy's year. From South America to Cambodia, the democratic alternative has asserted itself and, world-wide, tyrants have been driven out, put on trial or replaced by parties with democratic names. In 508/7, when the Athenians first voted for a democratic system, democracy was only the most recent of the various alternatives to tyranny. We, however, live for the first time in a world without alternative systems, except for the uneasy combination of secular leadership and religious community in Muslim societies.

Historians do not expect history to repeat itself and are rightly wary of finding nothing but the present (or an ideal future) in the past. Their own times, however, suggest new questions which are worth putting to old evidence: contemporary change is the life-blood of significant interpretations of the ancient world. Other contributors to this series have pointed to differences between the Athenians and ourselves, to a different emphasis in political theory, democratic practice, democratic ideals. In the light of our recent experience world-wide, I wish to reflect on an area on which my fellow contributors have had less to say: the texture of events which surround Cleisthenes' great reform, first proposed at some point between late summer, 508 and late spring, 507, in my view in July/August 508. We should not expect exact parallels between his times and ours nor should we look only for analogies. Comparative studies have always attracted historians and indeed have their own degrees in modern universities. Yet no two eras are alike: contrasts, not similarities, are what comparisons help to bring out.

One contrast is obvious. Nowadays, when tyrants fall in Argentina or East Germany or the Philippines, people want democracy because democracy is a system which is well known, widely invoked and entrenched in prosperous societies elsewhere. My first question, then, is: what were Cleisthenes' precedents in 508/7? With hindsight we can see several, but hindsight has its dangers. When early Greek societies introduced appointments by use of the lot or when they allowed the reference of particular legal trials or items of policy to the people as a whole, we might nowadays describe these elements as "democratic." They were not seen as democratic steps at the time; the participants had no ideas or examples of *demokratia*, or the ultimate power of the people as a goal before them. Only to us, not to them, were some of their moves a move in this direction.

Some modern historians emphasize citizenship as the central issue in Cleisthenes' reforms and his support. We are not sure exactly how he changed the procedures for being accepted as an Athenian citizen and although some residents had recently been disenfranchised, they cannot have been his main support, as his reforms were voted into existence. A widening of citizens' rights was more important. I define the novelty of his reforms as the recognition that the people, in pre-arranged assemblies, were the supreme political authority in Attica. Proposals were put to them by a Council, but without the people's amendment or acceptance, proposals could not be enacted. Membership of this Council of 500 changed yearly, and any Athenian (in my view) could serve twice in his adult lifetime. To our eye, the surprising fact about this democracy is that it was so direct, a participatory system, not a representative one; since the later 18th century, and especially since the writings of de Tocqueville, we have come to equate democracy with a parliament of people whom we choose to represent us. For Cleisthenes, *l'état, c'est nous*: no civil service, no bureaucrats, no political parties. Remarkably, "*nous*" included peasants as well as aristocrats, and after his reforms, each counted for one, and only one. The inclusion of the peasantry and the absence of a property qualification for voters are exceptional features in the political history of the world.

Some people think first of use of the lot when they think of Greek democracies. In fact, political use of the lot was not originally democratic. According to one view, Solon had already introduced it for appointments to the chief magistracies, or archonships, in Attica in 594: its effects were controlled because it was used to choose between candidates already selected on a short list. Use of the lot was also familiar to many Greeks in their own families. In ancient Greece, inheritances were divided, often in equal shares, between sons and traditionally, the lot had been used to assign the shares. Those who arranged the shares did not know which share the lot would give them and so they would be more likely to put equal shares into the draw. Actually, Cleisthenes, the first democrat, is not known to have extended the use of the lot in any important way. If the lot had been used to choose *archons* in 594, it had almost certainly ceased by 508, returning only in 487/6. His main political changes concerned the Council and the power of the Assembly. What precedents can we see here, using our hindsight, not his?

"The people" certainly confront us as an entity in Greek political life before 508. "Public" property is attested in various forms in Greek city states and was described by an adjective which meant "the people's." It ranged from military equipment to mining resources or public slaves. The word "people" here did not refer to the commoners, but the people as a whole. In this sense, too, "the people" had sometimes been summoned in order to share in important decisions. From the 730s onwards, colonies had been sent abroad from Greece and, in most cases, the ruling aristocrats had presumably decided and enforced obedience. In a time of collective crisis, however, a drought perhaps or a war, decisions might be more general. In the 630s we know of a famous pact, agreed to by the islanders of Thera (modern Santorini) before sending a colony to Libya (it ended up at Cyrene). We know the pact through a later version, reinscribed on stone at Cyrene in the mid-fourth century. It begins with the formal words, "It seemed good to the Assembly," and although the wording is unlikely to have been so formal in the 630s, some such pact had existed. We can follow knowledge of it back to Herodotus who visited Cyrene at some point in the 440s or early 430s. His language for it is formal, more so than historians often realize, and clearly he had been told of a "general resolution" taken on Thera. In the face of a crisis (probably a drought), some such popular decision in the 630s is credible. In the 540s, the Ionians of Phocæa probably would have held a public meeting when they resolved to abandon their city in the face of Persian conquest. According to Herodotus, they took with them the "statues from the temples and the other dedications, except what was bronze or stone or a painting," a tantalizing hint of early art treasures in Ionia now lost to us.

Before Cleisthenes, a crisis which brought the people together could be internal as well as external. Solon tells us how he "summoned together the people" as the *archon* for 594, when he wanted approval for his remedies for Attica's social and political crisis. A few years before, on Mytilene, Pittacus had been appointed "mediator," or "umpire" (*aisymnetes*), by a similar meeting, by all the "people gathered together," according to the poet Alcæus, who disapproved of the event. However, the point about an emergency meeting is that it is not a constitutional meeting, rooted in a system in which the people have political authority. It may show that they are capable of such authority, but unless there is another emergency there is no particular reason why anyone in the ruling class should allow the capability to be exercised. Cleisthenes allowed that very thing, but before 508 we know of only a very few examples of regular, defined "popular power." Outside the Greek world, examples have been sought in the urban assemblies of Babylonia or Phoenicia, but any idea of a defined citizenry with political rights is missing and there is no anticipation, here, of the Greek experiment. Within the Greek world, the most famous forerunner is Sparta. At an uncertain date, before 670 B.C. (in my view, c. 710-700), the Spartans adopted a constitution which gave political rights to a citizen-body for the first time in history. We know about it through the ancient wording of their oracular enactment, or *rhetra*, which is preserved for us in much later sources. It fixed the due times for popular assemblies and prescribed the introduction and discussion of items of business. Unfortunately, our only text of it is notoriously corrupt and we cannot be sure what rights were specified for the *damos*, or people. In my view, they concerned the power of deciding "yes" or "no" for proposals put to the Assembly. There was no right to move amendments or to turn to a subject which was not brought forward by the Council. It may well be that the people (*damos*) were assured of authority (*kratos*), for these words are the likeliest restoration of the sense of the most corrupt part of the text. Does this "*kratos*" for the Spartan "*damos*" amount to *demo-kratia*, two centuries before Athenian Cleisthenes?

The meetings of the male citizenry at Sparta could involve several thousand people and their recognized "*kratos*" is significant. It is not enough to object that the citizenry were all soldiers, trained to obey superiors. In form, if not in spirit, their meeting might still be democratic. Nonetheless, I think this notion is mistaken. The Spartan political system did recognize citizen-rights, but it worked by checks and balances, not by full democracy. In my view, the people had only been given this limited *kratos* as a check-and-balance because of recurrent crises between the two kings, the peculiarity of Sparta's constitution. This double kingship survived the reform and remained a major force in the system. It was accompanied by an unrepresentative council of men over sixty years old, appointed for life. Neither the kingship nor this Council belongs in a democracy, nor, I suspect, does the "Little Assembly" (known through one reference to events in the 390s). The role of the Spartan people to declare "yes" or "no" is a precedent for one aspect of Cleisthenes' reforms, one power of a citizen Assembly. The other aspects are all missing at Sparta, down to the method of voting. The powers of the Spartan citizenry were merely greater, but not much greater, than the role of popular citizen-assemblies in Roman politics, active outside the Greek sphere. A few historians would wish to describe the Roman republic, too, as democratic on the

Cleisthenes and His Reforms

strength of this one element. Much more points the other way: the Roman analogy puts a further distance between Sparta and Cleisthenes' reforms.

The precedent of Chios is more tantalizing. In 1909, scholars published the upper part of an inscribed stone which had been found near Tholopotami in the south of the island, at a distance from the main harbor-town. Its lettering is unlikely to be older than c. 560, but it certainly precedes Cleisthenes. It refers to enactments of the people, or *rhetrai* (significantly the same word as in Sparta). The *rhetrai* concern sacred property. It mentions a magistrate of the people, or *demarch*. It also mentions a "people's council." This council is empowered to impose fines and hear appeals from magistrates' decisions; it is also to "transact the other affairs of the people."

In 508/7, Cleisthenes' reforms provided a new people's council and are said to have instituted *demarchs* for the 140 demes, or villages, of Attica. Do we see his model here on Chios? The most recent historian to study it has posed the options clearly. "The Chiotes had formalized the exercise of popular sovereignty, limited as in other Greek states of this period by...traditional privileges and probably...by property qualifications. The system could be described as a moderate oligarchy or an incipient democracy, depending through which end of the telescope it is viewed."

On Chios there is no doubt which end of the telescope is correct. Chios did not graduate into democracy and if this system was a beginning it had still begun nothing as late as 412 B.C. when Thucydides' language strongly implies that the island was still ruled by an oligarchy. The inscription looks democratic to us with hindsight, but Cleisthenes' reforms had to intervene to give us that perspective. At the time, the Chiotes would have seen it differently. Who exactly are "the people" in this context? All the Chiotes, including peasants, or a narrower group with rights, perhaps only those citizens who could arm themselves for war?

In Ionian Greek cities especially, we find other mentions of *demarchs*, mostly in inscriptions and always after Cleisthenes. Nonetheless, they probably point back to an earlier institution. Elsewhere, especially in Doric states, we find *demiurgoi*, people active in public business. Are these magistrates an early echo of popular rule? Much depends on their setting, of which we know nothing. Are they elected by the people, from the people or merely for the people? And again, who are the people? All the people or just the non-noble commoners, the *demos* in a sectional sense? If so, how big a section? In Attica, in 594, Solon's own poems do refer to "leaders of the people" and to "restraining the people," in both cases leading and restraining them against or apart from the aristocracy. They are nowhere near a "pro-democracy party," but who are these non-nobles? Are they the commoners, peasants and all, or just those citizens who are able to provide arms? Again, we do not know, whereas Cleisthenes, we do know, took the broad definition of *demos*.

In Sparta, the *demos* had *kratos*; on Chios, the *demos* had "other business" besides the imposition of fines. On Chios, a people's council was chosen from the tribes. So was a council in Attica after Solon's reforms in 594. Elsewhere, councils and assemblies had long been paired as political institutions: we hear of them on Lesbos c. 600, even before Solon. We can see, then, why Cleisthenes looked to both institutions in order to bypass aristocratic rule and change the old system. But we still have no close model for the leap he took: the giving of sole and final authority to the people on a majority vote, whose voting was to include landless petty craftsmen, the hewers of wood and part-time humpers of baggage, and to count them for as much (just one) as the grandest aristocrat whose family provided priests or priestesses for Attica's most venerable cults. Nearer to 508, can we find this option being aired (if not enacted) elsewhere?

For guidance we can only look to Herodotus, but his Histories were composed almost a century later and risk being anachronistic. He is certainly anachronistic when he makes a Persian nobleman propose democracy as an option for Persia before Darius' accession in 522 B.C. Here, later Greek theorizing has probably misled him. Many would say that he is also anachronistic when he makes Histiæus, tyrant of Miletus, warn other tyrants from Ionia of the dangers of the urge for democracy in their home cities in c. 510 B.C. The warning is set on a bridge on the Danube River. Many would doubt its historicity and at best, Herodotus could only have had a second-hand oral tradition of what Histiæus had said so far away. Probably he has put words into his mouth, although *"demokratia"* is the word which he chooses. More tantalizing are events on Samos when the tyrant Polycrates fell in 519 B.C. According to Herodotus, his secretary Mæandrius offered to "put rule of the city in the midst of them" (what we might call "in the public sphere") and to offer *"isonomia,"* equality before the law. His own fee for this advice was a personal sum from the tyrant's treasure and a priesthood in perpetuity of Zeus the Liberator for himself and his family. The men of Samos turned him down.

Herodotus had lived on Samos and had good informants about Samian history. I am prepared to trust the substance of what he ascribes to Mæandrius. Nine years later, the tyranny ended in Athens and then, after a two-year interval, Cleisthenes also proposed "rule in the midst" and, according to one modern view, the ideal of *"isonomia."* In Attica, people accepted him. Modern scholars have been keen to suggest benefits and crooked corners in the system which

Cleisthenes and His Reforms 77

might have favored Cleisthenes' family, but nobody has ever suggested that he claimed a pay-off and a personal priesthood. Should we see him as Athens' Mæandrius, but cheaper?

The sixth century B.C. was already an age of compound political words. Spartan *eunomia* was a virtue of obedient citizens, not a constitutional ideal. In Attica, however, Solon had rebuked wicked people who wanted "equal sharing" (*iso-moiria*) of Attica's rich land; in Herodotus, we hear of "*isokratia*," a word for "equal" oligarchic rule. In the face of Persian power, I suspect, Ionian Greeks had already invented another major idea in world history: "self-government" (*auto-nomia*), our "autonomy." The idea presupposed an external power strong enough to infringe it. *Iso-moiria, iso-kratia, auto-nomia*: why not play further with words and propose *iso-nomia*? On Samos, Mæandrius is said to have offered it. In Attica, two young aristocrats were praised in an aristocratic drinking-song soon after 508, for bringing *isonomia* by killing one of Pisistratus' sons. Was not this idea in the air, in Ionia and elsewhere? Is the originality of Cleisthenes that he first brought the idea down to earth?

Cleisthenes, we know, had spent years as an exile: with so many examples before us, from Lenin to Uganda's Museveni to the recent, short-lived democrats in Burundi, we should allow for the impact of exile as a means of picking up new ideas and seeing with greater detachment the flaws of the political system at home. At Delphi, perhaps, did Cleisthenes discuss *isonomia* with visiting Ionians? Maybe, but it is far from certain that they would have taken it to mean popular rule by all citizens, rather than equality for them before the rule of law. We should certainly not think that Ionian reformers were all tending in the same democratic way. In the 540s, the Phocæan exiles who left Asia eventually settled at Massilia where they established an extremely secure oligarchy, based on a life-long council of 600 and an inner group of 15. The system lasted for several centuries. In the 520s (probably) the progressive city of Miletus was torn by political strife. Arbitrators arrived from Paros and gave control of the city not to the people but to those citizens who were found to have tidy farms.

We would trivialize this era of Greek history if we reduced the options after a tyranny to one and the same sort of oligarchy. I think that we trivialize Cleisthenes if we reduce his reform to other people's notions of *isonomia*. The word did not necessarily mean the "people's power" which he introduced. The surviving Attic decree which is most likely to be our nearest in date to Cleisthenes begins bluntly: "It seemed good to the *demos*." Might he not have promised *demokratia* already in 508/7, a new (but intelligible) compound? In our surviving literary texts, we do not happen to meet this word, or its constituents, until a work of the 460s, Æschylus' *Suppliants*. Yet Herodotus ascribed it to Cleisthenes' reform in one of his allusions to it and the plain fact is that we have next to nothing written between 510 and 480 anyway. Was *"demokratia"* an impossible slogan in 508? We simply do not know.

On our evidence, what we can reasonably guess is that Cleisthenes had no real predecessor and no off-the-peg model. *Isonomia* was a word of the time, but what exactly did it mean? If he wanted to end the old aristocratic days of faction, the way to do it was through a popular Council, a popular Assembly and a new infrastructure for both. For that much, there were precedents, but for their purpose and scope, I guess that the inspiration was the one we can observe for political reformers in our own times: the wish to reform existing politicians' most recent bad examples. Like philosophers, politicians go forwards by negative arguments with their immediate predecessors. Perhaps Cleisthenes had a new word for his aim: *demokratia*, with all its promise. However, I suspect that the main elements and the drift of it spoke for themselves, that people accepted them in 508 without a slogan and that like "inflation," "paranoia," or the "High Renaissance," the label "democracy" arose later, when people reflected on experience.

II

In 510 B.C. the tyranny fell in Athens and the last of the tyrants fled east to the Persian Empire. Spartan troops had played a major part in the liberation but they withdrew from Attica, leaving Athenians to construct their own alternative. We would dearly like to know more of the next two years. In spring, 508 the aristocratic Cleisthenes was "defeated" (Herodotus implies) by the aristocratic Isagoras, presumably in the contest to choose Athens' supreme magistrate for the following year. Isagoras took up office, but Cleisthenes turned to the people who were "formerly rejected" (Herodotus again) and proposed his reforms. Isagoras called for Spartan intervention; Cleisthenes withdrew. The intervention failed and by spring, 507 the way was clear for Cleisthenes' reforms to sweep the political field.

The exact chronology is unclear and our only source for a sequence of events is Herodotus. His image of the conflict has been widely trusted, in the absence of any other, but he may well be basing himself, as elsewhere, on the distorted oral tradition of later Attic aristocrats who were not natural democrats. Surely there were more contenders than Isagoras and Cleisthenes? Cleisthenes had already been the chief *archon* and could not legally take the job again: was he campaigning for an associate? Herodotus is, however, clear that nobody had tried to give power to the *"demos"* ("formerly rejected") until 508, two years after the tyranny's ending. When Cleisthenes was losing, he played this new card.

Cleisthenes and His Reforms

Why did the people accept it and carry out his reform? Unlike the peoples of Eastern Europe, they could not point to an existing democratic model where things already seemed to go better. Interpretations are needed at several levels. We need to infer responses to the proposed reforms "on the day," and then to propose reasons why those responses were so widespread. "On the day," we can point to Cleisthenes' offer of the power of decision and an equal right to speak in debates on it, offers connected with the value of freedom. People might doubt its practicality, but who would refuse the possibility? His proposals for a division of the citizenry into ten new tribes were more complex and, in themselves, not particularly appealing. At the local level, however, two attractions have been suggested by modern scholars: the *demarchs*, who were to be appointed in each deme or village, and the role of the deme, not the *phratry*, or "brotherhood," in admitting each year's young men to the citizen registers. Demes, or villages, had existed in Attica long before 508, but the affairs of these local communities would presumably have been managed by the local great families. Now, an official would rule instead, giving the deme a role of its own. Presumably, meetings of deme-assemblies would come in too, just as we find them in our later evidence. Any Athenian in Cleisthenes' audience could quickly see the significance of this new by-pass of the old aristocratic system: Aristotle's *Constitution of Athens* credits him with the innovation of the *demarch*. The deme's new role in citizenship had the same implications. Previously, aristocratic families dominated many *phratries*, or brotherhoods, membership of which (I assume) was a necessary precondition of Attic citizenship. *Phratries* continued to matter, but membership of a deme now mattered beside them; aristocrats no longer had the sole power of interfering with membership of the Attic citizenry.

In my view, the new Council of 500 was at least as great an attraction as the new local network. Perhaps the finer points emerged only in later discussion, but there is no evidence anywhere for the widespread modern view (which I reject) that at first, membership was denied to the lowest social class. In its mature form the Council, we know, was chosen yearly and was open to any male citizen over the age of 30, provided that he never served more than twice in a lifetime. In a male citizenry of not more than 30,000, these rules meant that a high proportion of Athenians would be councillors for a year at the center of political business. Nobody is credited with introducing the rules for Council membership after 508, and I accept that they were Cleisthenes' from the start. Other jobs and magistracies eventually totalled at least 600, many of which were appointed by lot. In 508, their numbers would probably have been far fewer and the use of the lot less prevalent. In 508, the chances of holding such a job were more remote, and less of an inducement for accepting the proposals.

In my view, the new Council and the new role for an Assembly were the decisive political attractions. The *demarchs* and the demes' role in citizenship (possibly) would have been attractive at an every-day local level. At all levels, however, these attractions only existed because of a readiness to break with the *ancien régime*. My view also assumes a widespread concern for political decisions which were "national," not merely local. This readiness and this concern are extremely rare in all subsequent political history: why did enough Athenians share them in 508?

In Eastern Europe, we have seen the power of the idea of democracy as a "return to normality." In the ancient world, we have plenty of evidence for changes and revolutions which are presented as a return to the past. Since Solon's reforms in 594, Athenians had lived by a written law code with a Council of 400 and an Assembly of uncertain powers and composition. Solon's reforms and poems had expressed a strong opposition to excess, insatiability, monopoly of power, faction, and above all, violence. These political values, like Solon's laws, had not disappeared since 594 just because people infringed them sometimes. Nonetheless, we do not hear of Cleisthenes promising a return to Solon. Nor, significantly, were Athenians being asked to return to normal. In 508 Cleisthenes' proposals were not normal anywhere else.

A "return," then, was not the mood, although Solon's framework remained a necessary pre-condition. Recent events have acquainted us with two other models, which I will characterize as the "Spanish" and the "reactive." In Spain, the last years of a long tyranny helped to pave the way for democracy by liberalization, economic growth and delegation (some of it unofficial, like the "workers' commissions" within the trade union structure). When Franco died, the transition, on the whole, was strong and smooth. Elsewhere, democracy has been adopted by reaction against a preceding tyranny: against Galtieri, Marcos, or the awful frauds of the Eastern bloc. Here, people know what they do not want, more than they then know how to proceed.

Many historians have emphasized a "Spanish model" for Attica in the later sixth century. For nearly forty years, almost as long as Franco's regime, the tyrant Pisistratus and his sons had ruled conspicuously. In the time of Solon, the divisions in Attica are said to have been "the plain, the shore and the hills." In 508, we find that they are the "inland, coast and city." Under the tyranny, therefore, the city-districts had become significant. The city of Athens was dignified by a wide range of public buildings, ranging from its water-springs (the Fountain House) to shrines for the gods (including the great predecessor of the Parthenon on the Acropolis). Attica was patterned by a road-system which may have met, symbolically, at a new Altar of the Twelve Gods in the central Agora. Judges travelled into the outlying demes to dispense justice. Under Pisistratus' sons, the first Athenian state coinage was struck. It is tempting to present these changes as a centralization. It is tempting to modernize further and consider the newly prominent city, the state coinage and the new buildings as a sign of economic growth for the Athenians. "All roads now ran to Athens." Would not a new city, newly prosperous, naturally turn to its own central Assembly when the tyrants' family was forced out?

These further temptations, at least, should be resisted. Much of the building work would have been done by slaves. Studies in progress on the accounts for the later Parthenon on the Acropolis imply that even in the 430s the numbers involved were still quite small. Some Athenians may have had slaves to hire out, but the tyrants could always import their own. As for the fine sculpture, it was often assigned to non-Athenian masters, the Ionian leaven in the variable dough of Attic art. How do we distinguish between economic growth for all Athenians, for a few citizens or merely for the tyrants' own revenues? From our present archæological knowledge, we cannot compare a pattern of (probable) growth between Solon and Pisistratus (594-546) with a pattern under Pisistratus' sons (528-510). Studies of Attic pottery and its increased export to the Etruscan west in the tyrants' lifetimes tell us only about one little industry, whose goods happen to survive. Of the others, we can only guess. The tyrants' buildings are the most visible evidence; the tyrants owed much to the competitive spirit of their epoch, which they shared with their fellow nobles. "Anything you can do, I can do better..." Better than a Polycrates, building on Samos, or better even, than the Athenian tyrants, if you were an Alcmaeonid in exile, rebuilding at Delphi in marble while the Pisistratids inside Athens built only in limestone. The resulting buildings say more about the tyrants' ambitions and powers of taxation than about a panAthenian boom.

Nowadays our representative form of democracy is powerfully associated with a free-market economy and growth. The tyrants had owned land, like other aristocrats; they had hired their own foreign guards and they may have considered all or part of Attica's silver mines to be their own possessions. These assets were their own, not "the state's." During their rule, therefore, there was scope for a tension between owners (tyrants, against the rest) rather than between two forms of ownership (public or private). By 510 a new capitalism was not challenging the tyrants' "command economy." When the tyrants fell, the Athenians apparently regarded the tyrants' personal assets as "theirs" to be confiscated and used as public revenue or property of the *demos* as a whole. Some of it was promptly put up for sale to help with the state's public expenditure. There was reluctance, we are told, to bid for Pisistratus' property. Other assets of the tyranny were retained: the silver mines, evidently; the public slaves; possibly the road system which confronts us later as "public." It had been dignified with monuments by one of Pisistratus' sons in a manner which implies that it was regarded as the family's possession.

We do not know when these confiscations and sales were carried out, but we would assume that they followed immediately after the flight of the tyrants' family. If so, those who voted for Cleisthenes two years later were not voting for confiscations or public sales. The sales had already occurred. Nor were they voting because his reform bill was good for business or would best safeguard newly won growth. One of democracy's modern supports, concern for the free market, was irrelevant: after the tyranny, more, not less, passed into the public ownership.

What about centralization, paving the way for a sovereign assembly? Centralization is a comfortably modern notion. What exactly could it mean in a world without cars, radios or telephones? People had always been able to walk to Athens or ride on a donkey, long before the Pisistratids put a smooth surface on the roads. Their road system was more relevant for the overland transport of bulky goods, including building supplies. Recently, the complex grouping of demes by Cleisthenes has been related to the course of Attica's roads, and the aim of his local reforms has been interpreted as the wish to move soldiers quickly and assist military mobilization. This "Autobahn" theory of his system's infrastructure infers too much from coincidence; it sits oddly with spatial inconsistencies at the level of the demes in *trittyes* and presupposes too much about the purpose of road-surfaces, and the frequency of army exercises or mobilization by grouped units in Attica. As for the city's new prominence, we can calculate from the deme-names of known Athenians (given in 508 and never altered, so far as we know) that less than a fifth of the citizenry lived in city-districts in 508. The tyrants had not created some vast new city, a teeming Bangkok or a modern Athens, attracting a migrating country population who needed the vote. The divisions between city and country were not our sharp divisions between urban cement and green fields. The countryside ran into a town whose male citizenry in 508 probably totalled no more than 5000.

Above all, Attica had none of the problems of ethnic or religious minorities which bedevil modern states and encourage centralized claims to majority rule. Athenians lived by the myth that they were the original inhabitants of the old Ionian land. Citizens belonged to tribes and *phratries* (brotherhoods), which reinforced the notion of common kinship. Solon had already spoken of the goddess

Cleisthenes and His Reforms 83

Athena's protection of the city, "holding her hand above it," an image which remained famous but which was not a "national orthodoxy:" the Athenians were polytheists for whom a minority religion was inconceivable. Some people might prefer one god, but everyone honored many, and Attica teemed with the cults of hundreds of different local heroes. Polytheism on this scale could not be centralized. The tyrants did develop some of the existing festivals of the gods and on the usual view, which I accept, they added a new festival, the Dionysia, the future setting for Attic drama and theatre. In this case, however, we should probably not think of a program of drama and competitions attached to the new festival from the start. The important point is that the tyrants did not originate this type of celebration. The most significant pan-Athenian festival preceded their rule, the Panathenaia of the 560s.

Even when festivals were expanded with more games and more competitions, the motive was not necessarily to bring more Athenians into Athens city or to centralize a cult. Like the Emperor Augustus, the tyrants must have realized the wisdom of giving fellow-aristocrats the scope to compete in politically harmless displays. Festivals allowed people to win honors and prizes, usually at the tyrant's bidding, and to compete without political challenge. We should also wonder about the financing and accounting of the city's new temples. No accounts survive, in significant contrast to the later projects of the democracy. At least one project, the huge Temple of Olympian Zeus, was too grandiose for any classical Greek successor to complete it. Was it really an uncontroversial exploit at the time? I suspect that unfinished exploits of this nature had intensified public interest in the conduct of public works, which becomes such a feature of the mature democracy.

In short, the tyrants were no Franco, paving the way for a democratic successor: for two years after their fall, nobody proposed democracy at all. Instead, we should explore the negative model, democracy by reaction. By 508, Athenians were ready to react twice over, once against tyranny but once, too, against any return of tyranny's predecessor: the faction and strife of aristocratic leadership. Here, Athenians' memories and family traditions were of years of instability and even bloodshed, before Pisistratus established himself. They did not want tyranny back, but thanks to tyranny they did not feel tied to aristocracy, either. In order to survive, the tyrants had exiled some of the leading families from Attica. In their absence, ever more Athenians had found that they could manage without the old local overlords. Tyranny thus weakened the old customary regime, not so drastically as the Russian seizure of Hungary or Poland affected rule by the large landowner, but nonetheless to a point from which the clock (as in 1989) could not simply be turned back.

Tyranny had also compromised important people who remained in Attica. The highest organ of state was the Areopagus, or Supreme Council, whose only members were ex-magistrates, enjoying tenure for life. We can infer from surviving fragments of the list of Attica's highest magistrates that during the tyranny, the tyrants helped suitable candidates to be chosen for the job. Like the political clique of an ex-president, members of the Areopagus in 508 were mostly tyrants' men, discredited by their patrons' fall. Significantly, there is no tradition of opposition by the Areopagus to Cleisthenes' proposals. Its members were too compromised to be credible opponents.

Both by their patronage and by sentences of exile, the tyrants had weakened Attica's upper class. In 508, therefore, a reaction against its renewed dominance was a practical option. There were also grievances which a shrewd reformer could reverse. The moral and political abuses of the tyranny's later years had turned enough people against experiments with another tyrant in the seat of power. There was also the matter of finance. In Greek history, direct taxation is associated with tyrants: a true tyrant, Pisistratus is said to have collected a tithe from his subjects, while his sons are said to have taxed at the rate of five percent. If both traditions are accurate, the sons may already have begun to lessen an unpopular burden. After their fall, however, direct taxation of all the citizenry is never attested again in Attica. Was it Cleisthenes who offered to abolish it, a further sweetener to win supporters?

There were also two real fears for a secure future. When the tyranny fell, the citizen-body was promptly reviewed and a number of residents in Attica were denied citizenship. Presumably, the first to lose out were supporters imported by the tyrants, not least their personal guards. However, the process could easily be carried further in a society where citizenship was based on the groups of *phratries*, traditionally dominated by an aristocratic family. The first batch of excluded citizens were not in themselves a serious constituency on which to push through political reform; they no longer had any say in Cleisthenes' audience, the Assembly. But they mattered as a warning, a foretaste of what might follow for others if groups of aristocrats tried to purge their rivals' supporters.

There was also the spectre of foreign intervention. The tyranny had been put down with Spartan help. If one great family fell out with another, might not either party summon Sparta to its aid, and promise alliance in return? In 508/7, opponents of Cleisthenes, Isagoras and 300 supporters, did exactly that, and lost ground because of it.

On the longer view, we can point to the tyrants' state coinage, the roads, the travelling deme-judges as significant steps to a more unified Attica. But when the Alcmaeonids failed to win the archonship in spring 508, these steps were

Cleisthenes and His Reforms

not the reasons why Cleisthenes, an Alcmaeonid, turned to the people and offered them powers instead. Nor were they the immediate reasons why the people voted for them, in the face of their archon Isagoras and the Areopagus. In an unstable situation, where past memories were bad and Sparta would soon be called back into Attica, the new democratic option was a way to break the cycle and to stop faction or a narrow pro-Spartan oligarchy from taking over instead.

III

There remain the perennial questions about Cleisthenes' motives and the detailed scope of his reforms. Notoriously, Attic tradition made little of him. He is not known for any reward or any presidency, not even for a statue. It seems that we should exclude the importance of personal charisma in his success, which might have drawn people to vote for Cleisthenes the man as a good man, while only half understanding what he was offering. We are uncertain exactly how much he proposed, but the uncertainty is evidently ours, not a majority of his voters'. We may suspect that it was Cleisthenes who introduced Athenians to voting by an individual show of hands, a practice they adopted for all controversial matters. In Sparta, by contrast, elections were "by shout, not vote" and magistrates decided for whom the crowd had shouted louder. The show of hands made an individual's vote visible and responsible in a way that a shout in a crowd did not. We can also suspect that Cleisthenes introduced a system of *prytaneis* for his new Council, whereby each tribe's fifty councillors were to be on special alert for a tenth of the year. This system existed before 462, as we can infer from the opening prescript of the Phaselis decree (itself dated before 462 by a modern restoration which is almost certain). We can wonder, too, about the practice of "scrutiny" before holding office and of "accountability" afterwards, two major institutions in the later democracy, which applied them to any elected official. Here, Cleisthenes probably left both in the hands of the Areopagus, but did he propose their extension to more offices than before? We can wonder about the arrangements for liturgies, public duties allotted to the rich who had to finance them. We might even wonder about the institution of public burial in a public tomb, for Athenians killed in battle. Were liturgies extended in the aftermath of 508? Did the honor of public burial begin with the victories of 506, which saved the democracy from invaders? Was Cleisthenes active in either sphere or both?

What we can infer from the situation in 508 and the democratic sequel is that Cleisthenes shared a major preoccupation with the new democrats in Poland or Czechoslovakia in 1989: he wanted to fragment power and break up blocs of it in his system. His concern was not representation, but the avoidance of undue concentration. I accept that the limiting of service on the Council to twice in a lifetime was Cleisthenes' original scheme. It helped to fragment power and to prevent cliques of pre-arranged "companionable associates." I also accept the tradition that he introduced ostracism by the people, the process whereby Athenians voted on potsherds against any one of a wide range of contemporary persons of importance. So long as at least 6000 votes were cast, the candidate with the most votes against him left Attica for a period of ten years. Aristotle implies that the aim of ostracism was to prevent another tyrant, but the view needs modification: an aspiring tyrant would have enough popular support to ensure that he was not the person ostracized. A better interpretation is that the law was aimed against leaders of a minority opinion or faction, rejected by the majority but nonetheless able to disrupt the political process, to polarize opinion repeatedly and prevent a coherent decision from going forwards and moving on. Isagoras had already signalled such a possibility, by summoning Sparta on behalf of a minority against Cleisthenes' proposals. If power was to lie with an assembly, majority decisions must be allowed to prevail. In recent British terms, a Wedgwood Benn (in the 1970s), a Heseltine (in 1986) and a Thatcher (in 1990) would have been ostracized and left to cool off abroad for ten years, buried in different ways in the graveyard of European issues. Our own experience of yesterday's men (and women) reminds us how shrewd Cleisthenes was. Politically, a ten-year absence breaks old warhorses and when they hobble back, they seem wonderfully out of date: ostracism is a prime reason for Athens' political stability until 411.

The most discussed aspect of the entire reform is its infrastructure, an aspect which was essential to its success but probably less immediate in its appeal. It too is best understood by the same notion: "fragmentation, not representation." Since the fundamental study by D. M. Lewis in 1963, thirty years of scholarly work has mostly tended in this direction. For historians, not everyday Athenians, the key element in Cleisthenes' infrastructure has turned out to be the "third," or *trittys*. Each tribe had three: according to the Aristotelian *Constitution of Athens*, which I still accept, they were one city "third," one inland, one coast. Each third was made up of a deme or demes, and scholarly interest has focused on the yoking of particular demes into a third. Sometimes, the natural groupings of neighboring demes were ignored and the substance of Lewis's case still stands, that an explanation for these unnatural combinations may be sought in the desire to break up known groupings which had a common cult, controlled by an aristocratic family, and a strong identity as a community. There is also the question of the connection, or separation, of adjacent thirds into one and the same tribe. Here, too, there are interesting combinations. They are made more interesting by the further observation that demes in the thirds along Attica's south coast are

Cleisthenes and His Reforms 87

not distorted out of their natural groupings, that here, the coastal, inland and city thirds are sometimes contiguous and that contiguous ones can be linked with areas in which Cleisthenes' own family, the Alcmaeonids, is known or inferred to have had local roots. The tradition is that the thirds were allotted to the tribes by lot, but the lot can be manipulated and we would also like to know by whom, and where, the allotment was carried out. If the final pattern was intentional, it did not favour Cleisthenes personally. At most, it gave members of his family group, the Alcmaeonids, greater influence in a tribe, increasing their chances of serving on the Council or being elected as generals. We must always remember that (as events showed) in the context of the new political system, these advantages were not great.

Cleisthenes' infrastructure endured in Attica for centuries. With it came meetings in the demes themselves, presided over by annually elected demarchs, who were accountable to their fellow-demesmen. Localities' procedures thus mirrored the central system's, although the exact stages of their development are uncertain and questions of the demes' influence on the center itself are still open. They are crucial questions, because in the new democracies of the 1980s, we are witnessing the importance of the local political cultures on which the central systems attempt to operate. In Attica, Cleisthenes inherited localities which were willing to submit to an alternative to traditional rule by local great families. One of the strengths of his reform, and a key to its success, is its basis in this alternative local network. By 508, people wanted a change from the aristocratic past. Aristocrats still presided over local cults, still owned the same family estates and dominated most of the "brotherhoods," or *phratry*-groupings, to which adult Athenian males belonged. But the deme, *demarch*, deme-assembly and the new tribal council now existed beside them. Within two years, the Athenians mustered to fight their neighbors on two fronts in order to preserve their new freedom. Their double victory in 506 must have enhanced their self-confidence as a political group. In 490 and in 480, victories over Persian troops, first at Marathon, then at Salamis, entrenched it yet more deeply.

In our new democracies, the source of self-confidence and the acid tests of strength are economic, not military: if the economy fails, a government can turn against its minorities in a final bid for majority favor. In 508, neither the economy nor a minority nor an elected government in power for a fixed term were part of the political scene. The question, rather, is how and why such a complex infrastructure as Cleisthenes' new system was put into place.

In 1977, in an important study, the late Professor Andrewes reasoned convincingly that Cleisthenes' main reforms must have been brought to the Assembly in a single bill. People were asked to return to a deme of their choosing and register there; a new infrastructure was promised, but the details of its final shape, so Andrewes inferred, would be presented as matters for a committee that would report back to the Assembly with a detailed scheme. Andrewes left open the question of the timing of Cleisthenes' local reforms. He was inclined to think of six months at least, between the first proposals to the Assembly, registration of each Athenian in a deme and the complex connections of demes into thirds, and thirds into tribes. Others have suggested an even longer period: as much as six years, because Aristotle dates the introduction of an oath for members of Cleisthenes' Council to the year 501/0. Would not this oath mark the first meeting of the new Council? However, this inference is quite unconvincing. The oath needs merely to have been introduced to formalize what the Council had been doing already in the hectic years after 508/7. It may have been proposed off the cuff by a constitutionalist, in the calm wake of events.

We are left, not with a wait of six years, but with the nub of Andrewes's problem. At the first Assembly, Cleisthenes need only have referred to institutions which sounded familiar to his audience: demes, *trittyes*, tribes, a Council, an Assembly. Numbers and structures, merely, were to be different: ten tribes, not four; thirty *trittyes*, not twelve; 500 in the Council, not 400. I doubt if he had to invent any new demes or even any new names for them: the change lay in their role, not their identity, for the 140 communities in Attica had already had a long village life. If he also mentioned ostracism, people may have known that practice too. Before 508, some such system of blackballing might have been practised in one or other of Attica's Councils, in the Areopagus or (more probably) in Solon's old Council of 400. If a People's Council on Chios could impose fines, could not a Council ostracize a member in Athens? From now on, Cleisthenes perhaps proposed, ostracism would be a process in which all Athenians could share, not just the members of one Council. A prehistory for this process would help to explain why it could have occurred to him and above all, why he would have expected his voters (and the victims) to go along with its complex operation.

After the first Assembly, what next? Everyone returned to register in a deme, not so that each deme's boundaries could be mapped out, but so that lists of people and their distributions could be returned. Possibly this listing was assigned to the new *demarchs*, pre-selected (perhaps by the committee) for this wearisome task. It then fell to the committee to draw up the new local map of Attica and report its interconnections to a second, enabling meeting of the people.

Recently, the likelihood has been presented that "the whole conception took as its basis a political 'map' of Athens and Attica which was drawn, in a real and important sense, not by one Athenian Kleisthenes, but by them all." True, the people went to a deme to register, but I would like to revert to a different answer relevant to Andrewes's question of timing. Admittedly, the evidence for it is conjecture, or intuition.

Changes in the number or names of tribes were not new in the Greek world in 508 but they had no necessary connection with democracy. Our evidence from Corinth, either under a tyranny or an oligarchy, shows hints of a system of territorial units, linked to tribes, in a pattern which recalls the *trittyes* (thirds) used by Cleisthenes. Tribesmen could also be regrouped by locality, not by kinship. Again, this type of change did not presuppose democracy. Before 508, might somebody in Attica have thought of these changes before Cleisthenes applied them?

Between the tyranny's fall in 510 and the year 508, some such system might have been aired, even sketched, in one or other political camp which was keen to scupper their opponents. However, I would like to go back further. In 1939, publication began of fragments of an inscribed list of Athenian archons which gave us a sensational insight: Cleisthenes (the restoration of his name is unavoidable) had served as archon under the tyrant's sons in the year 525/4. Like St. Paul, the founder of the new system had known the old one from the inside. I would like to end with a conjecture.

Might not the elderly Pisistratus have recognized in this young Alcmaeonid a nobleman with a bright political future? Night after night, in the tyrant's house, Cleisthenes could have enjoyed a privileged audience and the usual treats of the insider: the anecdotes, the maxims, the veiled remarks about other noblemen. Then, as the evening ended, the old man would rise and depart next door and hunch himself, with satisfaction, over what appeared to be a document spread on his desk. For Pisistratus, too, aristocratic rivalry was a besetting worry. He had built the new roads; he had travelled into the countryside; he had sent judges out into the demes to dispense justice, bypassing one of the nobles' age-old functions. As a noble Eupatrid himself, though slightly less noble than those in the plain around the city, he knew how a noble's power was visible in local cults, in local groupings and in patterns of landholding which could already be rather diffuse. Not every great family lived in one area only, in coast, inland or city: intermarriages split families and sales had greatly complicated the older picture. The deme-judges, perhaps, had reported on local power-blocs which had otherwise been less evident. As a result, the tyrants were placed, like nobody before them, to know the political map of Attica and all its noble networks.

Tyrants elsewhere had changed tribe names and tribal structures; Herodotus remarks on Cleisthenes' kinsman, Cleisthenes, tyrant of Sicyon, as a forerunner of his tribal reform. If we follow an elegant interpretation of the late L. H. Jeffery, Cleisthenes of Sicyon had given his tribes new names, not the abusive names which hostile tradition pretended, but names which linked tribes to localities. In Corinth, a similar structure existed in the state's eight-tribe system. Why could not a tyrant plan to do the same in Attica? Proclaim a new mixing up of the citizenry, link it to locality and thereby bypass the old aristocratic network? The newly mixed citizens would not be given new Councils or new powers of decision. They would merely be grouped differently, away from their previous noble "bosses." As for the new tribe-names, why not play the classic game of a dynasty and name four: one after each child in the tyrant's own family? The Emperor Augustus, Rome's Pisistratus, would have approved.

By the late 530s, map-drawing was intellectually fashionable in Greek thought. I have come to picture the tyrant with a map and a scatter of variously colored pins. Each pin, stuck into the map, could mark the center of influence of a rival family. By regrouping the pins into four colors, one for each of his new dynastic tribes, the tyrant could plot a new structure for his grandest memorial, to be superimposed on Attica's citizenry. The pins of each rival family were wonderfully disconnected on his map, except for the pins of the Pisistratids themselves, located at Brauron, at Marathon, up in the Attic north-east.

Pisistratus died and the sons (I suggest) lacked the will or the confidence to carry out the old man's blueprint. Cleisthenes joined the other Alcmaeonids in exile, but he knew what he most wanted when he returned to Athens from Delphi after the tyrants' fall. Herodotus notes that a store of Pisistratid documents, their all-important oracles, had survived on the Acropolis. Among their heaps of other old papers, I suggest that Cleisthenes made for the old Pisistratid map and kept it, pins and all, on one side.

In summer 508, he was worsted by Isagoras, but he played a new card and offered power to the *demos*, ruining the old games of aristocratic faction which he himself knew inside out. The people acclaimed his reform bill and returned to the demes to register. As the lists came in, Cleisthenes summoned the committee which he had proposed and chosen to link the deme-members to thirds and thus to the ten new tribes. It was not a matter of six years, nor even of six months. Before them, on the table, Cleisthenes spread their blueprint: Pisistratus' own intended map.

It was amazing what the old man had planned for his noble rivals: a bypass of the Boutadai, a fragmentation of the Philaids. In these areas, the blueprint could stay untouched. It was awful, too, what he had dreamed up for the Alcmaeonids, but Cleisthenes and his largely Alcmaeonid committee knew (I suspect) the

Alcmaeonids' network; it was a matter of a few minutes to re-route the pins in south-east Attica and leave their blocs unbroken. As for the Pisistratid bloc, the old man had had the nerve to leave the main bits of it in place. His family, however, had fled and so there was no need to tamper with the map to remove its advantage. On the known Cleisthenic scheme, there is indeed an element of contiguity which would have suited a Pisistratid's influence.

Behind Cleisthenes' map, I am suggesting, there lay a tyrannical forerunner. The general idea is not new: the great historian, K. J. Beloch entertained the possibility in 1913. The pins, the paper, the role of Pisistratus are only my suggestions, but they do remind us that the local reforming of tribes was not in itself democratic and that Cleisthenes need not have been the first Athenian to consider such changes. If a blueprint existed, bequeathed from the tyrant or one of his sons and surviving during the years between 510 and 508, Andrewes's question of timing is eased. Alcmaeonid "details" had to be "corrected:" the blueprint had to be adapted to fit ten tribes, not four, thirty *trittyes*, not twelve. But the basic splitting up had already been done.

I am not thereby transferring the credit for democracy to a tyrant or proposing yet another alternative for our anniversary: 530 B.C plus 2000, perhaps, to join alternatives like 462 or 506 or 501. I wish simply to end with two serious points. When we watch new constitutions being modelled in new democracies, we look nowadays at the center, at how the government will be constituted. The success of Cleisthenes' experiment should warn us to look at the infrastructure too and at "fragmentation, not representation." As for Cleisthenes himself, I see him as the supreme insider, who was given time to think and see flaws while in exile; on his return, he began to lose out and so he deliberately destroyed the old system which he knew so thoroughly. I do not see him as a democrat by accident, but I do see him (and his success) as impelled by reaction against his predecessors. In my view, politicians thrive on previous politicians' bad examples, not on brand new visions. Cleisthenes gave both the deme and the *demos* a new role to stop the old confusions, but his reaction did also include one borrowing: I believe that he gave them their new role with the help of an inherited, Pisistratid map.

BIBLIOGRAPHY

I am most grateful to Ball State University for inviting me to address them in their Anniversary of Democracy series and to its organizer, Professor J. A. Koumoulides, for his great kindness and hospitality.

My approach to Cleisthenes and his reforms owes a profound debt to the scholarship of Oxford's older generation, A. Andrewes, D. M. Lewis and W. G. Forrest and behind them, to the essays of H. T. Wade-Gery. Among general books, W. G. Forrest's *The Emergence of Greek Democracy* (London, 1966) chapter 8 is still outstanding. Full bibliographies and more detailed discussion can be found in another offshoot of this generation, M. Ostwald's *From Popular Sovereignty to the Rule of Law* (USA, 1986) 3-28 and his chapter V of the revised *Cambridge Ancient History IV* (1988).

On particular points in my text, use of the lot is studied by J. W. Headlam, *Election by Lot at Athens* (Cambridge, 1933): its use in inheritance is already in Homer, *Odyssey* 14.209. On "public" and "people's" property, D. M. Lewis, "Public Property in The City" in O. Murray, S. R. F. Price edd., *The Greek City* (Oxford, 1990) 245-264. On Cyrene, R. Meiggs-D. M. Lewis, *A Selection of Greek Historical Inscriptions* (Oxford, 1969), number 5, with Herodotus 4.153 where "*heade*" is a Doric word, later attested in the prescript of Cyrenaean decrees instead of "*edoxe*." On Phocaea, Hdt. 1.164.3; for emergency meetings, Solon F36 (West) and Alcaeus F163 (Page).

On Babylonian "primitive democracy," G. Evans, "Ancient Mesopotamian Assemblies" *JAOS* 78 (1958) 1-11; in Punic texts, M. Sznycer, Semitica 25 (1975), who does not distinguish between "the people" as a political body and "the people" merely as a periphrasis for "Kition," "Carthage," etc. On Sparta, H. T. Wade-Gery, *Essays in Greek History* (Oxford, 1958) 135-155 is still basic for textual problems, though not for dating. On Sparta's system, D. M. Lewis, *Sparta and Persia* (Leiden, 1977) 27-49 and G. E. M. de Sainte Croix, *Origins of the Peloponnesian War* (London, 1972) 124-51; I disagree with S. Hornblower, in J. Dunn. ed. *Democracy* (Cambridge, 1993) chapter 1, who claims Sparta as the inventor of democracy! In contrast, a general sketch is given by W. G. Forrest, *Echos du Monde Classique* 27 (1983) 285. Rome's "democracy" has also found recent champions, but the case is reviewed by J. North, "Democratic Politics in Republican Rome," *Past and Present* 126 (1990) 3-21 and I would withhold the term from Rome altogether. On the Chios council, Meiggs and Lewis, *op. cit.* (1968) number 8 with C. Roebuck, whom I quote, in J. Boardman *et al*, edd. *Chios* (Oxford, 1986) 81: Hipponax F89 (Loeb) refers to the casting of a "*psephos*," or pebble, by a "people's council," probably as a court of law, and probably not on Chios. On Ionian *demarchs* and Doric *demiourgoi*, L. H. Jeffery *ABSA* 51 (1956) 164-5. On "*demos*" as a group, Solon F36 and FF4-5 (West).

Council and Assembly on Lesbos: Alcaeus F128 (Page); Herodotus on *demokratia*, 3.80 and 4.137; on Maeandrius, 3.142. On "*eunomia*," A. Andrewes, *CQ* 32 (1938) 89-91 is still important; *isomoiria* in Solon F34 (West); Hdts. 5.92 refers to *isokratia*, arguably the word for aristocratic "oligarchy" and Sparta's own system in the eyes of her allies in the sixth century. On autonomy, M. Ostwald, *Autonomia: Its Genesis and Early History* (Chicago, 1982) correctly traces the word's sparsely surviving history to the fifth century, but I still agree with E. J. Bickerman, *RIDA* (1958) 339-41, who posited a sixth century origin in Asia

Cleisthenes and His Reforms 93

Minor. The personal name, Isodemos, in seventh century Sicyon also deserves notice: Nicolaos of Damascus F61 (Jacoby). The Attic drinking-song is reconsidered by R. Thomas, *Oral Tradition and Written Record In Classical Athens* (Cambridge, 1989) 257-61, but I still favour the drift of F. Jacoby, *Atthis* (Oxford, 1949) 162. On Phocaea's government, Strabo 4.1.4-5 (her colony); on Miletus, Hdts. 5.29. On the *"demos"* after 508, Meiggs-Lewis, *op. cit.* (1969) number 14 and M. H. Hansen, *Liverpool Classical Monthly* 11 (1986) 35-6.

On *demarchs*, D. Whitehead, *The Demes of Attica* (Princeton, 1986) 121-48: on *phratries*, S. Lambert, *The Phratries of Attica* (Michigan, 1993) is important, differing from the view that the deme simply replaced the *phratry* as the arbiter of citizenship in 508/7 (pp. 261-3). On Pisistratid projects, D. M. Lewis, chapter 4 in the revised *Cambridge Ancient History* IV (1988): on ideas of "centralization," B. M. Levick, *Claudius* (London, 1990) 187. The "Autobahn" theory is P. Siewert's *Die Trittyen Attikas und die Heeresreform des Kleisthenes* (Munich, 1982), justly doubted by A. Andrewes, *CR* 97 (1983) 346-7 and D. M. Lewis, *Gnomon* 55 (1983) 431-6. On Athenian mythology, R. C. T. Parker in J. Bremmer, ed. *Interpretation of Greek Mythology* (London, 1987) 187. On festivals, H. W. Parke, *Festivals of the Athenians* (London, 1979): on the Dionysia, against a later dating, C. Sourvinou-Inwood, in S. Hornblower, R. G. Osborne edd., *Ritual, Finance, Politics...* (Oxford, 1994) 269-290. On the Areopagus, H. T. Wade-Gery, *Essays in Greek History* (Oxford, 1958) 105. On voting, G. E. M. de Sainte Croix, *Origins of the Peloponnesian War* (London, 1972) 348-9 and P. J. Rhodes *GRBS* 22 (1981) 125-32; on *prytaneis*, I disagree with P. J. Rhodes, *The Athenian Boule* (Oxford, 1972) 17 n. 2, as Meiggs-Lewis, *op. cit.* number 31 is dated by *prytany* and since Wilhelm, is restored in a way which dates it before 462. On public burial, A. E. Raubitschek, *AJA* 46 (1940) 53, especially 59 is suggestive. On ostracism, most recently L. G. H. Hall, *Tyche* 4 (1989) 91-100, suggesting precedents, although the religious one, from *phyllophoria*, is not convincing. On the *trittyes*, D. M. Lewis, "Cleisthenes and Athens," *Historia* 12 (1963) 22. On the Alcmaeonid "advantage," W. G. Forrest, *Emergence of Greek Democracy* (1963) chap. 8. On cults, E. Kearns, in P. A. Cartledge, F. D. Harvey edd., *Crux* (Exeter, 1985) 189, not, however, weakening Lewis's case. On the procedure, A. Andrewes, "Kleisthenes' Reform Bill," *CQ* 27 (1977) 241.

My Pisistratid "map" is conjectural, I must emphasize, without ancient evidence. Corinthian tribal reforms, discussed by J. Salmon, *Wealthy Corinth* (Oxford, 1984) 413-19; the Athenian archon-list is Meiggs-Lewis, *op. cit.* number 6. On the scattered estates of great Athenian families by 508, R. Sealey, *A History of the Greek City States, c. 700-338 B.C.* (Berkeley, 1976) 140-1 and 159 n. 2 who rightly rejects Lewis's previous view of the Philiads' landholding. On the tribes at Sicyon, L. H. Jeffrey, *Archaic States of Greece* (London, 1976) 174 n. 2. The best modern map of Cleisthenes' infrastructure is in P. Siewert, *Die Trittyen Attikas und die Heeresreform des Kleisthenes* (Munich, 1982). For the possibility of a Pisistratid antecedent, K. J. Beloch, *Griechische Geschichte* 1.2 (2nd ed. Berlin, 1926) 328-331, brilliantly wild and imaginative pages on "das erste Beispiel von Wahlkreisgeometrie, das die Geschichte kennt:" I share the intuition, not its every argument, but imagine Cleisthenes with a new number of tribes, new detail and a different purpose. Beloch denied *Ath. Pol.* 21.4, on the use of the lot for placing *trittyes* in tribes. M. H. Hansen, *Ancient World* 15 (1987) 43-4, for further discussion: I accept a possible use of the lot, knowing that it could be manipulated by the committee, before reporting the infrastructure to the Assembly. I have knowingly avoided discussion of the complex and unresolved questions of deme-location and *trittyes*-identity and possible connections (which I doubt) with our later evidence for service on the *boule*. I do not, however, share the view that the demotics of 508 were re-assigned in the democratic era after Cleisthenes, although demes' "quotas" of councillors surely were. A major problem is our uncertainty over many demes' exact location, emphasized (with other problems) in D. M. Lewis's important review, *Gnomon* 55 (1983) 431-6, addressing, among much else, the alternative view of *trittyes*' identity developed most notably by J. S. Traill, *Hesperia*, Supplement 19 (1982) esp. 162-171, which I could accommodate, but do not share.

6

Aristotle's Ideals of Life

Anthony Kenny

To discuss Aristotle in the context of a celebration of democracy is an ambiguous venture. Aristotle was not, it must be admitted, a wholehearted democrat. If one were lucky enough to live in a good society, it would be better to have a monarch, who could do much more good than a *demos*; it was only if one lived in a bad society that democracy was the best constitutional arrangement, since it minimized the harm that could be done by rulers. To make Aristotle a democrat, therefore, one has to add the premise – not in itself at all improbable – that most of the people, most of the time, are going to live in bad societies.

But Aristotle's political theories, interesting though they are, have not had anything like the influence on subsequent thought that his ethical theories have, and it is those - or certain aspects of them - we shall examine here, specifically Aristotle's ideals of life. I use "ideals" in the plural advisedly, because in the Aristotelian ethical *corpus* we find not a single ideal, but three ideals presented.

The best known of Aristotle's ethical works is the *Nicomachean Ethics (NE)*, and I will begin with it. The ideal life - *eudaimonia* or happiness - is treated there in the first and last books. There is an ongoing controversy among scholars, to which I have contributed, about the teaching of these two books. The first, in the opinion of most scholars, presents a view of the ideal life as involving the exercise of all the virtues, both moral and intellectual. The last book, on the other hand, seems to present a view of the ideal life as consisting entirely in the exercise of philosophical contemplation. This is disconcerting to most contemporary commentators.

Aristotle began his consideration of happiness in the *NE* by asking which of the traditional careers - that of pleasure, politics, or contemplation - really amounted to happiness. Whatever may be the case with the initial book of the *NE*, the final book, instead of offering, like the *Eudemian Ethics (EE)*, a single life containing all the value sought by the promoters of the three traditional lives, offers us a first-class, perfect happiness consisting in the exercise of understanding. As an alternative, the *NE* goes on to offer a second-class career consisting in the exercise of wisdom and the moral virtues; that too is a form of happiness, but it is not perfect happiness (1178a9-1178b8).

In my view, this intellectualist view is clear in both the first and the last books of the *NE*. Most commentators reject the intellectualist view of book one, and some hardy ones reject it also in book ten. The main reason why interpreters are motivated to reject this intellectualist position is that they do not find the position credible as a piece of philosophy; as admirers of Aristotle they are unwilling to saddle his mature ethical work with such a strange doctrine. In particular, they find the contemplative who is the hero of *NE* 10 a strange and repellent human being. A forceful statement of this view is made by Nussbaum:

> Throughout books 1-10 Aristotle has indicated that the human good is an inclusive plurality of actions according to excellence, in which intellectual activity will be one component, side by side with other constituents of intrinsic worth, such as activity according to excellences of character and activity benefiting friends. Most of book 10 develops this view. But 10.7 abruptly shifts to the defense of a life single-mindedly devoted to theoretical contemplation, seeking to maximize this as the single intrinsic good. Interpreters have tried in various ways to minimize this problem but it remains. According to the view expressed in 10.7 friendship and excellence of character could not have intrinsic value; if we chose to pursue them, it would only be because, and insofar as, they seek to maximize contemplation. But their intrinsic worth is clearly defended in the other books... Perhaps the best that one can say is that Aristotle, like anyone who has been seriously devoted to the scholarly or contemplative life, understood that, thoroughly and properly followed, its demands are such as to eclipse all other pursuits. Although he tried to articulate a conception of a life complexly devoted to politics, love, and reflection, he also felt (whether at different times or in different moods at the same time) that really fine reflection could not stand side by side with anything else. He would, then, be...revising his conception in accordance with a new perception of a conflict between the full demands of one cherished value and all other values.[1]

The specific objection to the position of *NE* 10 may be phrased thus: If Aristotle made contemplation alone a constituent of perfect happiness, then in cases where there is a conflict between the demands of moral virtue and the demands of contemplation, Aristotle must say that the agent should engage in contemplation, even if the alternative is saving his neighbor from a burning house. If the contemplative lacks moral virtue, there is nothing to prevent him from being quite ruthless in pursuing his goal.

However, I think that it is rash to take for granted that the contemplative of *NE* 10 will lack the moral virtues. Does Aristotle in fact believe that he will possess them? Some commentators have answered "yes" and some have answered "no;" all have been repelled by the idea of the ruthless, treacherous theorizer, whether or not they regard him as Aristotle's own ideal. But what demands, according to Aristotle, does morality really make of the person of contemplative excellence?

Before answering this question, let us note that there is a distinction, in Aristotle, between failing to possess the moral virtues and falling into moral turpitude. Somebody, without actually being morally virtuous or admirable, may none the less fulfil mimimum moral demands such as refraining from murder, theft and adultery. The moral virtues are concerned with observing the mean among acts which are basically morally acceptable. (NE 1107a8-17) An Aristotelian moral candidate may, as it were, obtain a pass degree in morality without obtaining the honors degree awarded for the excellence of moral virtue.

The position of *NE* 10 is surely that the contemplative will *possess* the moral virtues, but that their exercise will not constitute part of his happiness. That will be constituted by contemplation alone. None the less, being a human being, and a good human being, he will practice the moral virtues also. (1178b5-7) But the activity of moral virtue is given its definition by the mean, and the mean differs from person to person. The right number of brave actions, for instance, will be greater for the politician than it will be for the theorizer. Wisdom, which determines the mean, will prescribe differently in the two cases, because of the different overarching end which constitutes the chief happiness of each of the two types of virtuous person. It will diminish the demands of the other fine and noble activities, in order to preserve the maximum room for contemplative happiness.

The objection to the theorizer, in this interpretation, is not that he will let his neighbor's house burn down, or that he will steal in order to get an adequate research fund. It is rather that he will not do such things as volunteering to fight in the course of a just war. He is likely to take a course of action such as that taken by W.H. Auden at the beginning of the Second World War, crossing the Atlantic to nurture his talent in less dangerous surroundings.

Even when the harsh lineaments of the contemplative have been softened in ways such as this, his aspect is still repellent to many commentators, and they seek various ways of absolving Aristotle from excessive intellectualism.

The argument between the intellectualist interpretation of *eudaimonia* in the *NE* and the inclusive interpretation will no doubt continue. It is noticeable how in the course of the last two decades the positions of the intellectualist interpreters and the inclusive interpreters of the *NE* have come closer and closer together.

But no explanation succeeds in the three goals which most commentators have set themselves: (a) to give an interpretation of book one and book ten which does justice to the texts severally, (b) to make the two books consistent with each other and (c) to make the resulting interpretation one which can be found morally acceptable by contemporary philosophers. And even if *NE* 1 and *NE* 10 are reconcilable, the *NE* as a whole seems to have two different heroes: the contemplative of 1 and 10, and the great-souled man of 2-4. Both characters are difficult to make palatable for twentieth century readers.

But must we judge Aristotle's ethics solely by the Nicomachean position? Those who are prepared to take seriously the *EE* as an expression of Aristotle's mature theory are able to preserve their admiration intact without doing violence to any of the relevant texts of the *NE*.

For most of the present century there has been a consensus among Aristotelian scholars that the *Eudemian Ethics* is earlier than, and inferior to, the *Nicomachean Ethics*, which alone can claim to be Aristotle's definitive ethical system. In my book *The Aristotelian Ethics* (1978), I tried to show that this consensus is ill-based. In particular, I argued, it is an error to try to settle the chronological relationship between the two treatises before solving the problem of the three books which make a double appearance in the manuscript tradition, as books 5, 6 and 7 of the *Nicomachean Ethics* and as books IV, V and VI of the *Eudemian Ethics*. Only if we can settle, independently of chronological hypotheses, the primitive context of those books are we in a position to make non-tendentious comparisons between the treatises.

I went on to argue, on historical, stylistic and philosophical grounds that the disputed books, as they stand, belong with the Eudemian and not with the Nicomachean context. Having, as I believed, established this beyond reasonable doubt, I went on to claim that the *Eudemian Ethics*, considered as a whole and including the disputed books, had as serious a claim as the *NE* to be considered Aristotle's final and considered system of ethics.

I argued that *EE* is a late work, dating from Aristotle's final period in Athens, between 335/4 and 322. If the *EE* contains the *AE*, it must undoubtedly (on the basis both of content and historical allusion) be assigned to Aristotle's later years; we must therefore reject the view that it is early superseded work.

It is a surprising fact that in the early centuries after Aristotle's death most writers gave to the *EE* the primacy which it has long been traditional to give to the *NE*. Unlike the *EE*, the *NE* was not included in the canon of Aristotle's works established by the edition of Andronicus. In *The Aristotelian Ethics* I reviewed the evidence from pseudo-Aristotelian works, from Theophrastus, Cicero, Xenarchus,

Arius Didymus, Nicolaus of Damascus, Philo of Alexandria, Favorinus of Arles, and Diogenes Laertius. I found that every writer, from Aristotle himself until the second century A.D., who shows a first-hand knowledge of the Aristotelian ethical writings also shows a preference for the *EE* over the *NE*; either in the sense that he refers to it as *The Ethics*, sans modifier, or that he quotes it exclusively, or that he prefers its doctrine, or its terminology, or its systematic structure. No author (except the author of the *Magna Moralia*) quotes the *NE* as "the Ethics;" and the only two authors (Cicero and Diogenes) who show awareness of an ethics with that title both regard it as the work of Aristotle's son, Nicomachus.

Gauthier and Jolif believe that the posthumous editor who was responsible for inserting the Eudemian treatise on pleasure into the *NE* was none other than Aristotle's son, Nicomachus. There is, indeed, much to be said for the idea that the *Nicomachean Ethics* was edited by Nicomachus after his father's death. As Gauthier and Jolif convincingly show, it is the most natural explanation of the traditional title of the work.[2] But if Nicomachus was responsible for an edition, may it not be that it was he, and not his father, who removed the common books from their original home in order to tranfer them into the *NE*? This is a hypothesis which is more economical than the theory of two separate transfers, one by the father and one by the son; it fits the internal evidence for the homogeneity of the third of the common books, and it explains a number of the puzzling features of the external evidence set out in *The Aristotelian Ethics*.

If the *Nicomachean Ethics* was so called because it was edited by Nicomachus, then the *Eudemian Ethics* was presumably so called because it was edited by Eudemus.[3] The preference shown to the *EE* in the centuries after Aristotle's death may be one instance of the general tendency of scholars to give greater credence to philosophers' posthumous works when they are edited by their colleagues than when they are edited by their widows and orphans. Similar reasons may have accounted for the fact that the Eudemian, but not the Nicomachean, version of the *Ethics* was included in the edition of Andronicus. If the *NE* was edited by Nicomachus, that would explain why Cicero and Diogenes Laertius were inclined to regard the treatise as his work rather than his father's.

If we accept the hypothesis that Nicomachus was the first person to add the disputed books to Aristotle's *NE*, the question remains: to what exactly did he add these books? There is a tradition of scholarship according to which Nicomachus' contribution may have been to collect together a number of selfstanding works into a single series. Many years ago, Thomas Case, in his celebrated *Encyclopaedia Britannica* article on Aristotle, suggested that "the probability is that the *Nicomachean Ethics* is a collection of separate discourses worked up into a tolerably systematic treatise." That would explain a puzzling fact for which no very convincing explanation has ever been offered. We know from Elias (*CAG* 18, 32) that in antiquity the *Magna Moralia* was known as "The Great Nicomachean Ethics" and that the *Nicomachean Ethics* was known as "The Lesser Nicomachean Ethics." Since the *Nicomachean Ethics* is much longer than the *Magna Moralia* this has puzzled commentators. They have suggested that since the individual books of the *Magna Moralia* are larger, they were preserved on rolls which were physically larger than the more numerous but smaller rolls of the *Nicomachean Ethics*. No douht this is true; but it is a solution which pushes the question further back. The traditional title of the *Parva Naturalia* suggests that the ultimate solution may be along the lines suggested by Case. The *Parva Naturalia* is not a short treatise, but a collection of only slightly connected treatises. May not the *Nicomachean Ethics* have been originally, then, the *Parva Moralia* in exactly the same sense? If we add the Case conjecture to the Gauthier-Jolif conjecture, we reach a quite plausible explanation for the various pieces of puzzling evidence studied in this appendix and in *The Aristotelian Ethics*. Our *Nicomachean Ethics* consists of an anthology of genuine but separate Aristotelian treatises, of uncertain date, which were collected together into an anthology of ethical writings after Aristotle's death by his son Nicomachus, an anthology in which Nicomachus included three books which belonged to an existing and more lengthy treatise, the *Eudemian Ethics*.

The stylostatistician Richard Bailey drew interesting conclusions from his study of the statistics from the ethical treatises and the *Metaphysics*. Concerning the *NE* books he wrote: "The stylistic evidence seems to force a conclusion that they are somehow spurious, drawn from a quite different population of articles and connectives."[4] Time and again we find that when the *NE* stands apart from the *EE* and *AE*, it stands apart also from the *Metaphysics*, *Politics*, and other works. The explanation of differences between the *NE* and the political and metaphysical writings may no doubt be partly explained by the subject matter; but it cannot wholly be explained by that, otherwise why should not the *EE* stand apart in the same way and to the same extent?

I do not regard these stylistic differences between the *NE* and the central parts of the Aristotelian *corpus* as showing that the *NE* is inauthentic, or even as providing evidence in that direction. Nor do I regard them as giving any indication of its chronological location; there is not, so far as I have been able to discover, any particular work or set of works which resemble the *NE*'s idiosyncracies, and which therefore would provide an anchor to which to attach a hypothesis of dating: the *Topics*, say, for an early date, the *De Anima*, perhaps, for a later one. Rather, these idiosyncracies of style suggest that it is wise to keep open the question whether the explanation of the differences between the *NE* and *EE* may not be something quite other than chronological.

If the differences go back to Aristotle himself, in each case, then they may be due to a difference of intended audiences. The *NE* is more fluent, less austerely philosophical, less telegrammatic in its arguments than the *EE*; it may be designed for a less professional audience than the *EE*, just as, throughout history, it has appealed to a wide readership, whereas the *EE* has never appealed to more than a handful of Aristotelian fanatics. But of course the doublets, *lacunae*, and inconsistencies in both treatises forbid us to think that either of them was brought to anything like publishable form by Aristotle himself.

If the differences between the styles of the two are due, on one side or the other, or both, to the activities of editors, then it seems that we must say that the *NE* has reached us from the hand of an editor different from the one responsible for the edition of Aristotle's other major works. This is, of course, consistent with the fact that the *NE* is the only Aristotelian treatise which we have any reason to believe was edited by Nicomachus. But it would be rash to assume that the peculiarities of the *NE* are personal characteristics of Nicomachus, imposed on a text which, without his editing, would have resembled, in the features that have been studied, the rest of the *corpus*. On the contrary, it could even be that in the peculiarites of the *NE* we have preserved, alone among the *corpus*, some of the stylistic habits of Aristotle himself. Indeed, if it was Nicomachus who transferred the common books from their Eudemian context to keep company with the *NE*, the fact that they retain so many Eudemian features suggests that he was an editor with a very light hand. The *NE* may differ from the other extant works not because it has had more attention from an editor, but because it has had less.

These and other hypotheses seem to me open at the present time. A convincing explanation of those stylistic features that are amenable to statistical study must await a fuller study of the *corpus* as a whole, and a detailed investigation of the separate parts of the *NE* itself.

In the *EE*, happiness is clearly a combination of the activities of various kinds of excellence. According to the *EE*, happiness is the exercise of perfect life in accord with perfect virtue, which in the context must mean the virtue which is a whole of parts.

This theme is taken up later in the same book II at 1220a34. Just as the general good condition of the body is compounded of the partial virtues, so also is the virtue of the soul, *qua* end. But of virtue there are two kinds: moral and intellectual.

After the treatment of individual virtues and quasi-virtues is complete, in the final book, we return to the theme:

About each virtue by itself we have already spoken; now since we have distinguished their natures one by one we must give a more accurate description of the excellence which arises out of their combination, which we now name *kalokagathian.*

To possess this virtue you have to possess all "the partial virtues" (*tas kata meros aretas*). This must mean the virtues of the parts of the soul, just as the partial virtues of the body are the virtues of the various parts of the body. So it must include the virtues of the intellectual part of the soul, including the supreme or theoretical part.

This is in accord with what was said in the common book B, which is Book V of the *EE*, in answer to the objection that understanding (*sophia*) and wisdom are superfluous because unproductive. "They are indeed productive: not like medical skill in relation to health, but like health itself; it is thus that *sophia* is productive of happiness: for being a part of virtue entire by being possessed and being operative it is productive of happiness." (1144a3-6). The possession of *sophia* is part of perfect virtue (which is the same as "virtue entire"). Correspondingly, the exercise of *sophia* is part of perfect happiness. It would be pointless of Aristotle to remind us that this virtue is only part of perfect virtue if he wanted to say that it was the whole of perfect happiness.

Understanding is one of the virtues which causally produce activities which in their totality are happiness, in the way that health (which is a combination of the healthiness of the various parts of the body) produces the activities of a healthy body.

> Most noble is that which is justest, and best is health;
> But pleasantest is it to win what we love.

The Delian epigram is made the introductory text for the *Eudemian Ethics*, and the task of the book is stated as: to show that happiness is at once the noblest and best of all things and also the pleasantest. (1214a1-8)

Among goods, Aristotle says, those are ends which are chosen for their own sake. And of these, those are noble which are praiseworthy, such as justice and just actions, and temperance and temperate actions. Health and strength, on the other hand, riches and honor, power and fortune, though goods, are not objects of praise and therefore not noble. Indeed, though they are naturally good, they may in an individual case be harmful, materially or morally. Aristotle sees these goods as good only provisionally. He calls them "goods *simpliciter*" (*haplws agatha*). This does not mean that they are absolute goods, things that are good come what may; it means just the opposite, that they are only *prima facie* goods which may, in the concrete, not be goods at all. Their goodness depends on the goodness of their possessor. It derives from their being used by a good person. They are not goods when used by a bad man, since for him they are not instruments of virtuous action (1248b27-34). These provisional goods are indeed the ones most competed for and are thought of by many as the greatest goods, but they can be harmful to those of bad character. If you are foolish or unjust or intemperate you will not benefit from them, any more than a sick man will benefit from a robust diet, or a weak man will be able to make use of the armor of the strong.

If the natural goods are to be good for you, you have to already be good. But, for the first and only time in the ethical treatises, Aristotle, in this last chapter of the *EE*, makes a distinction between two types of good people: those who are just plain good (*agathos*), and those who are both good and noble (*kalos kagathos*).

The distinction between these two kinds of people depends on the distinction made above between the two kinds of intrinsic goods. Those goods that are praiseworthy are not merely good but noble. Nobody can be good without performing the virtuous actions which deserve praise. But it is possible to perform these actions for more than one motive. The actions may be done for their own sake, or they may be done with a view to gaining and retaining the non-praiseworthy goods. The character of the person who ranks praiseworthy acts below non-praiseworthy goods is described by Aristotle as follows:

> There is also the civic disposition, such as the Laconians have, and others like them might have. This is a state of the following kind: There are people who think that one should possess virtue, but only for the sake of the natural goods. Such men are therefore good (for the natural goods are good for them), but they do not possess nobility as well as goodness (*kalokagathian*). For the things that are noble do not belong to them for their own sake. (1248a38-1249a3)

This important passage is not altogether clear. Do these people actually possess virtue, in Aristotle's eyes? On the one hand, they are good people, and good people are people who have virtues; it is difficult not to read the passage as implying that they are genuinely virtuous, but virtuous for the wrong reason. But if they do the appropriate actions, but do not do them for their own sake, or because they are noble, are they really virtuous? It is wrong to assume that the Laconian, when he chooses to do a particular just action, does so for the sake of wealth or power or other natural goods. But that is not what Aristotle means in *EE* VIII. The Laconian, like any virtuous man, does virtuous actions for their own sake, because they are the acts that virtue requires; where he differs from the noble person is in the answer he gives to the second-order question: "What is the point of being virtuous?" The *kaloskagathos* gives the answer: "Because virtue is splendid, fine and noble;" the Laconian gives the answer "Because virtue pays." The matter is very well put by Sarah Waterlow Broadie:

> The point concerns different *reflective* attitudes to virtue and virtuous actions *in general*. The

noble person prizes these because they are noble in themselves. The merely good man certainly cares about virtue: he seeks to inculcate it in his children; he deplores its absence in others; in each situation he wants to know what is right to do so as to act upon it; and he may put even his life on the line in doing what he sees himself called upon to do. He behaves as if good conduct matters most, and his behavior itself is a judgment to this effect. But when asked why virtue matters, the answer he gives, if he makes anything at all of the question, is that it is for the sake of the natural goods. We should note that for a person to count as good and as living a life of virtue, it is not necessary that he have any general view about why virtue is important. Nor is it necessary that he think about his own virtues or about his actions as exercises of virtue. He may simply make and stand by good decisions, each as it comes along.[5]

The Laconian, then, has the virtues and does virtuous actions virtuously, that is, for their own sake; his character and his actions are alike good. But are his virtues noble, and does he act nobly? A few lines later Aristotle gives an answer to the second question. At 1249a15 we are told that the person who thinks the virtues are for the sake of exterior goods does noble things only *per accidens*. (It is not suggested that he does *good* things only *per accidens*). But what of the actual virtues themselves? They are noble in themselves (1248b21-5), but are they noble in the Laconian? Perhaps Aristotle's final answer would be that they are noble by nature, but not noble in the case of the Laconian, just as wealth is good by nature but not good in the case of the vicious.

Aristotle goes on to give us a contrast between the Laconian and the truly noble person. The *kaloikagathoi* choose noble things for their own sake; and not only these, but also the things which are not noble by nature, but merely good by nature, are noble for them. For things are noble when the reason for which people do them and choose them is noble, and that is why, to the noble person, the natural goods are noble.(1249a3-7)

The noble person possesses the things that are noble in themselves, namely the virtues; and he does the things that are noble (namely virtuous actions); and he does them for the sake of their own nobility, not for the sake of the non-noble goods which are the highest value of the Laconian. (1248b34-37) But in the case of the noble person it is not only virtuous acts and dispositions which are noble: The natural goods, which for the vicious person are evil and for the Laconian person are merely good, are for him noble too. These natural goods are ennobled by the noble purposes for which the noble person uses them. It is just and fitting that the noble person should have such things as wealth, high birth, and power, since when they are his they are noble. (1249a4-14) The nobility of these objects, of course, is not intrinsic nobility, but derivative nobility, a nobility deriving from the noble purposes of the noble person.

Aristotle says:

> To the *kaloskagathos* what is useful is also noble; but for the many there is not this harmony between the useful and the noble, for things *prima facie* good are not good for them, as they are for the good man; to the *kaloskagathos* they are also noble, for he does many noble deeds by means of them. (1249a10-15)

We may paraphrase as follows: For the noble person, the noble and the useful are in harmony. However, this harmony is highly exceptional. Most people are not good, let alone noble, and so for most people what is useful (i.e. what is *prima facie* good) is not even good: it is useful only to their own bad purposes. In the case of the good but not noble person, the useful and the good overlap, and whatever is useful is good. But instead of what is useful being ennobled by noble purposes, as it is in the case of the noble person, in the merely good person what is noble - namely virtue - is downgraded by being treated, in the utilitarian manner, as useful for non-noble ends.

In various places in Aristotle's ethical treatises we are told that the virtuous man does virtuous actions "for their own sake" or "because they are noble." One of the things we learn from the final chapter of the *EE* is that these two expressions are not equivalent. The Laconian does virtuous actions for their own sake (otherwise he would not be good); but he does not do them because virtue is noble (otherwise he would be a *kaloskagathos*).

The new character who is introduced in the final book is not the *kalos-kagathos* but the mere *agathos*, the "Laconian" character who does virtuous actions for their own sake but not because they are noble. He - like the continent and incontinent persons discussed in *NE* and from time to time in the *EE* - occupies a position intermediate between the virtuous and vicious characters who are presented in an exaggeratedly well-defined trichotomy by the doctrine of the mean.[6]

The introduction of the Laconian, however, does mark two significant elements in which the Eudemian ethical system differs from the Nicomachean.

First, the attitude to natural goods, such as health and wealth, is very different. In the *Nicomachean Ethics* wealth is quickly dismissed as a candidate for the supreme good. "The life of money-making is one undertaken under compulsion, and wealth is evidently not the good we are seeking; for it is merely useful and for the sake of something else." (1096a6-8). Whereas the discussion of the Laconians shows that the *Eudemian Ethics* recognises that there are people who systematically value wealth, health, and power above virtue. The *EE* is even prepared to call such people good, provided their pursuit of wealth is within the bounds of virtuous behavior.

Second, the Laconian passage is the most explicit statement of an important theorem about Aristotelian value-systems, which is elsewhere left tacit. The theorem is this. Every item in a person's hierarchy of choices takes its value from the highest point in the hierarchy. Thus, if in one person's system virtue is for the sake of wealth, virtue is only a useful good, not a noble one, because wealth is something merely useful. If, in another person's value-system, wealth is for the sake of virtue, then wealth too acquires the nobility which virtue has. Aristotle insists that in ordered choices the higher you go up the series of *hou heneka*, the greater the good must be (otherwise you fall into the category of Laconian).

But what of the supreme point in the Aristotelian hierarchy, namely *eudaimonia*? In the *EE*, as in the *NE*, happiness is an end; and we know from the book's first paragraph that happiness is the noblest thing there is (1214a8). But the way in which happiness functions as an end seems to be not that the happy man does things in order to be happy, but rather that he does, for the sake of their own nobility, the noble things which in fact constitute the happiness which makes life worthwhile. (Cf.1215b30, 1216a11-13)

For the ideally virtuous man, according to the EE, the concepts *good*, *pleasant* and *noble* coincide in their application. We can bring this into relief by examining the cases where the two do not coincide.

First, if what is pleasant for a man differs from what is good for him, then he is not yet perfectly good but incontinent. The road to virtue, Aristotle says, is through pleasure:

What is noble must be pleasant; but when these two do not coincide a man cannot yet be perfectly good, for incontinence may arise; for incontinence is precisely the discrepancy between the good and the pleasant in the passions.(1237a8-9)

Second, if what is good for him does not coincide with what is noble for him, then he is not yet *kaloskagathos* but merely good; for, as we have seen, for the noble person the natural goods of health and wealth and power are not only beneficial but noble, since they subserve his virtuous activity. So for this ideal person, goodness, and nobility coincide. What of pleasantness?

Pleasure has already been discussed: what kind of thing it is, and in what sense it is a good; how things which are pleasant *simpliciter* are noble, and things which are good *simpliciter* are also pleasant. But there cannot be pleasure except in action, and so the truly happy man will also have the most pleasant life. (1249a18-21)

Whereas something can be noble or good whether it is a state or an activity, only an activity can be pleasant. States are not pleasant, but only the exercising of states. So it is in the noble activities of the noble and good man that the highest pleasure is to be found, and it is there that pleasure, goodness and nobility meet. But the noble activities of the good man are the exercises of perfect virtue with which happiness was identified in book one. So the promise of book one has been fulfilled, to show how, *pace* the Delian inscription, goodness, nobility and pleasure coincide in *eudaimonia*.

Among the noble activities of perfect virtue are the activities of the philosophic life. If *kalokagathia* is a synthesis of the virtues of the parts of the soul in the way that health is a synthesis of the health of various parts of the body, then it must include the virtues of the intellectual parts of the soul as well as of the passional part. But not only is it part of happiness, it also sets the standard to which the activities of the other virtues must conform if they are to remain within the realm of virtue and happiness. (1249a21-b14)

Virtuous action consists in executing choices about the right amount of things - of the passions and external goods - which are the field of operation of the moral virtues. What particular behavior in concrete circumstances counts as virtuous living cannot be settled, Aristotle tells us at the end of the *EE*, without consideration of the contemplation and service of God. (1249b15-22)

In the *EE*, Aristotle makes a distinction between constituent and necessary or *sine qua non* conditions of happiness (1214b24-7). Using this terminology one can bring out clearly the distinction between the two treatises. Whereas in both *Ethics* external goods are only necessary conditions, in the *EE* wisdom plus moral virtue is a constituent of the primary happiness, while in the *NE* it is at best a necessary condition of it. In the *EE* the best of what can be achieved by action is a state in which all the parts of the soul, *qua* human, are operating well.

That wisdom plus moral virtue is part of happiness, because of being the right functioning of one part of the soul, is stated most clearly not in an exclusively Eudemian book, but in the disputed book on the intellectual virtues, where we are told that wisdom and understanding are both productive of happiness "not like medical skill in relation to health, but like health itself; it is thus that understanding is productive of happiness: for being a part of virtue entire by being possessed and by being operative it is productive of happiness." This passage spells out the contribution of understanding to happiness; the final book of the *EE* spells out in parallel terms the contribution of the life of virtue. The activity of wisdom plus moral virtues is itself part of the exercise of virtue which constitutes happiness; it has an efficient causal relationship to the contemplative happiness, but it is also itself a form of happiness, by being a form of service to God. It contributes to happiness by being part of it, in the way that good breathing contributes to good singing; not in the way that (say) eating certain foods rather than others may contribute to good singing.

Completeness of virtue was introduced as a defining feature of *kalokagathia*; the ultimacy of virtuous activity as an end is the feature which emerges from the contrast with utilitarianism. So, among virtues, *kalokagathia* is the most final. But it is not the most final human good, because virtues are for the sake of their exercising, not the other way round, (1219a32) and so it is the exercise of *kalokagathia* that is the supreme human good which constitutes happiness. This must include both contemplation and morally virtuous activity.

The final chapter of the *EE* spells out the relationship between these elements within happiness.

> Here, as elsewhere, one should conduct one's life with reference to one's superior, and more specifically with reference to the active state of one's superior. A slave, for instance, should look to his master and everyone to the superior to whom he is subject. Now a human being is by nature a compound of superior and inferior, and everyone accordingly should conduct their lives with reference to the superior part of themselves. However, there are two kinds of superior. There is the way in which medical science is superior, and the way in which health is superior; the latter is the *raison d'être* of the former. It is thus that matters stand in the case of our intellectual faculty. For God is not a superior who issues commands, but is the *raison d'être* of the commands that wisdom issues. But *"raison d'être"* is ambiguous, as has been explained elsewhere; this needs saying since, of course, God is not in need of anything. To conclude, whatever choice or possession of natural goods - bodily goods, wealth, friends and the like - will most conduce to the contemplation of God is best: This is the finest criterion. But any standard of living which either through excess or defect hinders the service and contemplation of God is bad. (1249b6-21)

This text incorporates several ambiguities. But what is clear is that Aristotle believes that the intellect is twofold, like the superior, and the theoretical intellect is related to the practical intellect as a *raison d'être*. The way in which medicine rules over the patient corresponds to the way in which the rational part of the soul rules over the irrational part.

The most difficult part of the chapter to interpret is the final section setting out the relationship between the soul and God. In accordance with the general rule that everyone should live in accordance with their superior part or ruling principle *(arche)* a human being should govern his life in accordance with what is required by his rational soul. But while the rational soul is such an *arche* or principle, we need to know what kind of principle it is. In matters concerning our body we need to take account of the requirements (i.e. prescriptions) of medical science; we also must take account of the requirements (i.e. needs) of our health. Both medical science and health are *archai* in different ways; and the latter is the *raison d'être* of the former. We must apply this to the rational part of the soul. There too there is a principle like medicine and a principle like health. The principle corresponding to medicine is wisdom, which, like medicine, issues commands. So in following the requirements of our *arche*, we must: (1) obey the com-

Aristotle's Ideals of Life

mands of wisdom, and (2) take account of the needs of that which is related to wisdom as health is related to medical science. Well, what is this?

From the discussion in the common book B (1145a6-11) we might expect the answer to be: understanding. But here Aristotle, instead of giving an immediate answer, goes on "For God is not a superior who issues commands." This sentence, and especially the "for," is puzzling.

But the sentence becomes clear if we look back to the previous chapter. The cosmic God was the supreme *arche* in the soul, superior to *logos*, *episteme* and *nous*. So, it seems, if everyone should live according to the requirements of his superior as a slave lives according to the requirements of his master, we must conclude that in matters of the soul, we must live in obedience to the commands of God. But this would be an erroneous conclusion, according to Aristotle, for God is not a ruler who issues commands. To avoid this conclusion, we have to distinguish between senses of *arche*: God is indeed the supreme *arche* of the soul, but not in the sense in which the analogy of slave and master would suggest.

The overall sense of the passage is this: In the same manner, there is a twofold *arche* in relation to our intellect. God is one *arche*, but not, like medicine, an epitactic one which gives commands. Wisdom is an *arche* which is epitactic and gives its commands for the sake of God.

In the second common book, at 1145a6-11 we are told:

Wisdom is not in authority over understanding or the better part, any more than the science of medicine is in authority over health; it does not make use of it, but provides for its coming into being; the orders it issues are not issued to it but issued for its sake.

Are we, then, to interpret this final passage of the *EE* in the sense that God is like health, which is the *hou heneka* or *raison d'être* of medicine? Surely wisdom does not "provide for God's coming into being"? Indeed not. There are two kinds of *raison d'être*, and God is not the kind which needs to be brought into existence (like health) or provided with benefits - for God has no needs.

Aristotle is here saying that God is not a *raison d'être* whose good is being aimed at, but a good whose attainment is the *raison d'être* of wisdom's commands. Well then, what is the other *raison d'être* whose good is being aimed at, and what is it for it to attain God? Aristotle gives no explicit reply, but the answer is clear enough from the concluding passage: That which benefits from the commands of wisdom is that which serves and contemplates God, and this service and contemplation is itself the only kind of attainment of God which is possible. And what is it that serves and contemplates God? Either the soul as a whole, or its speculative part. Which of the two is intended must depend on what is meant by "service" here.

Let us look more closely at this final passage of the *EE*.

To conclude: whatever choice or possession of natural goods - bodily goods, wealth, friends and the like - will most conduce to the contemplation of God is best: this is the noblest criterion. But any standard of living which either through excess or defect hinders the service and contemplation of God is bad. This is how it is with the soul, and this is the best criterion, to be conscious as little as possible of the irrational part of the soul[7] in so far as it is irrational. (1249b6-23).

It is not said here that the contemplation of God determines everything in the good person's life; it is the criterion for the choice of natural goods like health, wealth and strength. The noble actions of the moral virtues are chosen for their own sake and have their own internal criterion, namely the mean. A good man exercising the virtue of temperance will indeed be conscious of the irrational part of the soul. He will enjoy food, drink and sex in the appropriate measure, and if he did not he would be guilty of the vice of *anaesthesia*, insensitivity (1221a2,1231a26). But he will not be conscious of the irrational part *qua* irrational, precisely because it will be obeying the commands of reason.(1220b28, 1249b15)

None the less, the final chapter of the *EE* does offer a general standard for the exercise of virtue. The final summary of its content, at lines 23-25, says "So much, then, for the criterion of *kalokagathia* and the point of the *prima facie* goods." We have been offered, then, the standard of perfect virtue. The *prima facie* goods, the natural goods that are not in themselves praiseworthy, are such things as health, strength, honor, birth, wealth, and power (1248b24, 28-30; 1249a10-ll); they are the subject matter of the virtues of magnanimity, magnificence and liberality (*EE* III, 1231b28ff). The subject matter of the virtues of courage, temperance and meekness are the passions of the irrational soul mentioned in lines 1249b22-5. Thus, this last passage in the *EE* does give a standard for the exercise of the six virtues which are discussed in *EE* III and which are included in *kalokagathia*. Each virtue does indeed have its own internal criterion, the mean, but what the mean is in each case is to be determined by wisdom, and wisdom gives its commands for the sake of God.

How are the intellectual and practical virtues related to the supreme principle, God? God is related to the intellectual virtue of *sophia* as being the principal object of its activity of contemplation. But how is God related to the practical virtues? Can he be in any way the object of them? The answer to the question cannot be given until we make the inquiry, postponed earlier, into the meaning of "the service of God" in 1249b20.

Clearly when Aristotle uses this expression he is not thinking of the liturgies he describes in book VIII of the *Politics*. A close Platonic parallel to the present passage occurs in Plato's *Euthyphro*. Socrates argues that the notion of service of the gods is unintelligible; we cannot benefit the gods. *Therapeia* is what slaves give to their masters to help them with their tasks, but what is the task *(ergon)* of the gods? "Many noble things," says Euthyphro. By the service of the gods Euthyphro has in mind acts of justice, like the attempt to punish a murderer (on which he is currently engaged).

If Aristotle does have the *Euthyphro* in mind here, then the service of God could well include acts of moral virtue. These are the *kalai praxeis* of the *kalos kagathos* which are the subject of the early part of the chapter; they could well be regarded as the many noble things which we, under the *arche* of God, find our fulfilment in performing and by which we make our contribution to the splendor of the universe.

In both the *EE* and the *NE* the question is raised: which is the best of the three traditional patterns of life: the life of pleasure, the political life, or the contemplative life?

In the *NE* the answer is that the contemplative life is the most perfect life, and the political life is the next best thing; happiness can be found in either life. In the *EE* the answer is that if the three lives are exclusive alternatives, the best is none of the three. The best life is both political and theoretical. As Broadie puts it: "It is a life of practical wisdom enlightened by nobility and looking towards *theoria*."

The nature of *theoria* seems ambiguous in the *NE* itself, so that it is not strange if later ages wondered whether contemplation is a normal activity, like the research of a mathematician, or a paranormal experience like the rapture of a mystic. In *NE* 10,7, Aristotle seems to be torn between two views. At one time he will say that perfect happiness consists in contemplation because that is the best activity of the most human thing in us (1178a6). At another time he will say that the life of contemplation is something superhuman (1177a26). He will contrast the moral virtues, which belong to the human being, compound of body and soul, with the virtue of the understanding which is, he says tantalizingly, "a thing apart." (1178a22) Having claimed, when discussing friendship, that it was incoherent, when deliberating about the good, to think of the good of some other sort of being, such as a god, he now says that we ought to "immortalize as much as possible," identifying ourselves not with our complex human nature, but only with its intellectual element.[8] And he will offer this as his clinching argument for identifying perfect happiness with contemplation: "The activity of God, which surpasses all others in blessedness, must be contemplative; and of human activities, therefore, that which is most akin to this must be most of the nature of happiness." (1178b21-3)

Is there an inconsistency between saying that *nous* is what is most human in us, and also that it is superhuman and divine? Not necessarily. From passages such as these, Christian theologians built up the doctrine of the human need for the supernatural. A thorough inquiry into human nature, they claimed, would show that humans' deepest needs and aspirations could not be satisfied in the human activities that were natural for a rational animal; humans could only be perfectly happy if they could share the superhuman activities of the divine, and for that they needed the supernatural assistance of divine grace. Aristotle might have been surprised at some of the uses to which *NE* 10 was put by theologians, but he could hardly complain that they were completely distorting its meaning. The tension between nature and supernature is clearly there for all to read.

When we look at Aristotle's account of contemplation from a modern secular viewpoint, the questions which it poses are rather different. Modern commentators, when they strive to understand Aristotle's text, have in mind not a meditating monk but a philosophical, or more generally, a scientific researcher. It is for this reason that so much recent attention has been focussed on the relationship, especially in the *NE*, between contemplative and political happiness. For it is related to the decision to be made in the actual lives of Aristotle's twentieth century readers: how much energy and effort to devote to philosophical and scientific research and how much to social and political activity?

The modern equivalent of the question to which Aristotle addressed himself is the problem of the role of science in society. Whatever contemplation exactly meant for Aristotle, one contemporary equivalent of it is the pursuit of basic science. And the Aristotelian issue of the supremacy of contemplation is parallel to the twentieth century debate about the autonomy of science. The Aristotelian question, "What is the correct attitude for the contemplative *vis à vis* the other moral virtues?", has as its modern equivalent: "What are the limits of the autonomy of science?"

Let us set out briefly an answer to the modern question, and then return to relate it to the Aristotelian discussion. Science, I believe, is autonomous with respect to its goal, but not with respect to its means, its conditions or its consequences. That is to say, the pursuit of scientific truth is an activity which needs no further external good to make it worthwhile, so that science is an independent value in its own right. But in pursuit of this end, the scientist must be answerable to other norms and values in his choice of means for research, in his appropriation of funds for research, and in his concern for the consequences of research. Scientific discovery is an independent goal, and in a sense an absolute goal, but it is not a unique or supreme goal.

Let us consider, first, science as an end. Scientific discovery is an independent goal and, in a sense, an absolute goal. The sense in which it is an absolute goal is the sense in which "absolute" is contrasted with "relative". The quest for scientific truth has been carried out with greater energy in some societies than in others, but that does not mean that it is a value which is relative only to a particular social structure (such as, say, chivalric honor). There is no conceivable human society for which scientific truth would not be a good.

But if scientific discovery is an absolute goal in this sense, it is not absolute in a different sense with which we have become familiar in our discussion of Aristotle. It is sometimes said that making one single value absolute (be it pleasure, wealth, power, family, fatherland, friendship, beauty, truth, love, religion) would amount to admitting that in pursuing this value anything is permissible. Scientific truth is not a value which is absolute in this sense, but there are no values which are absolute in this sense. There is no value in whose pursuit anything whatever is permissible.

The objection may be made that, surely, there must be at least one absolute value, morality itself. (This parallels the idea that *eudaimonia* is the motive of everything we do). If not, if morality is not absolute, are we not all morally adrift in a sea of relativism? No; morality is not a value at all, though it has an intimate connection with value.

Three elements are necessary for morality: a moral community, a set of moral values and a moral code. First, it is as impossible to have a purely private morality as it is to have a purely private language, and for very similar reasons. Second, the moral life of the community consists in the shared pursuit of non-material values, such as fairness, truth, comradeship, freedom. It is this which distinguishes between morality and economics, and between the *kaloskagathos* and the Laconian. Third, this pursuit is carried out within a framework which excludes certain types of behavior. It is this which marks the distinction between morality and aesthetics.

A common morality, therefore, consists of values and norms. No value is absolute in the sense that its pursuit justifies the violation of every norm. Some norms are absolute in the sense that no value will ever justify their violation. This is simply to say that there are no ends which justify every means, and that there are some means which no end will justify. So if we are asked whether morality is absolute we must answer with a *distinguo*: moral values, no; moral norms, yes.

Scientific truth, then, is a value which is independent, in the sense that its pursuit needs no ulterior justification. It is a value which is absolute in the sense that it is not relative to particular societies, but it is not absolute in the sense that it trumps all other moral values or overrides all moral norms.

The discovery of scientific truth is not just a permissible goal to pursue, it is an admirable goal. In Aristotle's terms, it is something noble. It is a pursuit to which it is allowable, and indeed laudable, to devote one's life to. We admire the dedicated scientist more than we admire the dedicated golfer, chef, or banker; and we are right to do so. Why is this? The answer is that the goal which the scientist seeks is a goal which is a good not just for himself, not just for his customers or shareholders, but for the human race as a whole.

Unlike Aristotle's external goods, or goods of fortune, scientific truth is a non-competitive good. It is a good which is indefinitely shareable; it is not a good which is lessened as more people participate in it. When I know a scientific truth, I can share my knowledge with any person qualified to understand it, without in any way diminishing the good I have acquired for myself by my discovery. I cannot, in the same way, share with other people, without diminishing it, the money I have made. I cannot share my political power with others without diluting it. I cannot distribute throughout the human race the pleasure produced by my culinary skill.

It is not easy to specify precisely what makes a truth a scientific truth; many distinguished philosophers of science have failed in the task. But, again taking our cue from Aristotle, we can say that it is clear that it is connected intimately with the notions of necessity and universality, however these notions are to be explained in detail. It is this which makes scientific truth a value which transcends the contingencies of particular historical societies.

The independence of science as an end does not mean that scientific purposes will justify means which would be otherwise immoral. But in addition to the constraints which extra-scientific morality puts upon means of scientific research, the nature of the scientific goal itself rules out certain modes of research behavior as unworthy of science. When we condemn certain means of research as manipulative, or wasteful, or cruel, we are using criteria which could be used equally well to condemn business practices or military operations. But in the pursuit of scientific truth we may condemn researchers for being secretive, or competitive, in a way which would be quite inappropriate if applied to soldiers or businessmen.

It is because the good sought by science is a good superior to that sought by many other human activities that there are some means which would be justified in the case of science which would not be justified in the case of other areas of human endeavour. Thus, for example, the infliction of harm on animals, or damage on inanimate nature, is much easier to justify if necessary in the pursuit of scientific truth than in the cause of sport, or fashion, or art.

We must make a distinction between the means of scientific research and the conditions for scientific research. While some forms of scientific research - such as pure mathematics - are not in competition with other human activities for the consumption of scarce resources, most forms of natural science are expensive and become increasingly so as science becomes more developed and sophisticated.

When we are considering the allocation of funds for applied science, the decisions to be made resemble the generality of investment decisions. In deciding whether to fund medical research or to use the funds for providing more hospital beds, we are making the comparison between immediate and remote goods, but the goods are of the same kind, namely the health of the community. But when we are deciding how much money should be put into the health service, and how much into pure science such as cosmology, we are faced with a choice between incommensurables. Here no principle, whether of welfare economics or of normative morality, offers a clear decision procedure, at least in a society where the basic necessities of life are made available to the citizens.

It is in the evaluation of these incommensurables that we rejoin the issue which was our concern in the interpretation of the Aristotelian treatises. For the political problem of the allocation of funds is the social replica of the individual problem of the choice of the ideal life which has been the topic of this book. And if our reading of the texts has been correct, a different answer is given by the two different Aristotelian ethical treatises. The *NE* places a higher value on the autonomy of science in the life of the individual. The highest form of happiness involves locating it entirely in scientific contemplation, even though the scientist will not lose his humanity, and will perform the practical tasks which arise from his living as a human being in the society of others (1178b6). In the *EE*, scientific endeavor is not a totally autonomous goal, but is one element, even though a specially significant element, in a life which is a harmony of several elements. In every action and sentiment, the Eudemian happy person bears in mind not only the contemplation of God, but also the service of God.

Aristotle's ethical treatises, as the intense attention paid to them in the last decades show, provide a magnificent conceptual framework for the discussion of ethical questions. They seem especially attractive to those who have become discontented with Kantian deontologism or positivist emasculation of ethics. They are found attractive both by religious and non-religious people; by non-religious people because so much of the argument seems to proceed on totally secular assumptions; by religious people because many of the finest moralists in the Jewish, Christian and Islamic traditions were themselves Aristotelians.

But does Aristotle provide any moral guidance? Does he provide anything more than a framework into which different and incompatible sets of norms and values can be fitted? Can one accept his ethical system? Would anyone be able genuinely to adopt the supreme values of Aristotle or endeavor to practice the moral virtues described in the *EE* or *NE*?

One purpose of comparing closely the two treatises is to exhibit that there are such great differences between them that it is misleading to talk simply of Aristotle's ethical system, even though the conceptual frameworks of the two works are similar. But Aristotelian scholarship is not a merely antiquarian pursuit. Reflection on Aristotle can throw light on first-order moral concerns, though Aristotle himself would have been the first to deny that any genuine moral question can be settled by looking up a book. But the close study of these ancient texts can assist us to clarify our own moral concepts, to make explicit our own moral assumptions and to examine our own concept of human perfection. For "everyone that has the power to live according to his own choice should set up for himself some object for the good life... since not to have one's life organized in view of some end is a mark of much folly." (*EE*, 1214b6-10)

Aristotle's Ideals of Life

NOTES

[1] Nussbaum, M. C. "Aristotle" in T. J. Luce (ed.), *Ancient Writers* 1 (New York, 1982).

[2] Gauthier and Jolif believe that when Aristotle died in 322 the *NE* was merely a notebook. Nicomachus, his son, who was very young when Aristotle died, and died young himself, edited the text, perhaps with the help of Theophrastus, who, according to Aristocles in Eusebius, had a hand in his education. The title does not refer to a dedication; one does not dedicate a notebook, and Nicomachus may not even have been born at the time of Aristotle's course. Gauthier and Jolif date the edition shortly before 300. They think it must have preceded the publication of the *EE* (on the grounds that the latter did not contain the disputed books!).

[3] We know from correspondence preserved by Simplicius (in *Phys.* 923,7) that Eudemus concerned himself with the editing of Aristotle's *Physics*, but because there was no other version of Aristotle's physical teaching current, there was never any need to call the *Physics* the Eudemian Physics.

[4] Bailey R. W. "Determining Authorship in Ancient Greek" in *Proceedings of the International Conference in Literary and Linguistic Computing* (Tel Aviv, Israel, 1979).

[5] *Ethics with Aristotle*, 379.

[6] In my book *The Aristotelian Ethics* p. 206, I claimed that the Laconian performed virtuous actions as a means to an end, in a utilitarian manner. Having read Broadie, I now believe that if the Laconian is to be compared to a utilitarian, it is to a rule-utilitarian rather than an act-utilitarian.

[7] Reading Fritzsche's emendation ἀλόγου for ἄλλου (MSS.) Verdenius, "Human Reason and God" in *Untersuchungen zur Eudemischen Ethik*, Symposium Aristotelicum, 1971, p. 294, argues that there is no need to change; the other part obviously is the irrational part. But the end of the sentence is easier to read with the emendation: it is equivalent to; with the other you have to take it, in a very contorted way, as meaning "*qua* hindering from the contemplation of God."

[8] Nussbaum, p. 376.

7

Democracy After 2,500 Years

David Hunt

"Fourscore and seven years ago" is a fine phrase with which to begin a speech and it is one which is liable to come to mind when the theme is democracy. It is also an interval that is comfortably comprehensible. "Two thousand five hundred years ago" sounds less attractive. The figure is too vast and formless to be easily grasped. It transports the mind into remote regions and past civilizations constructed by peoples whose way of life and culture it is difficult to imagine. Moreover, even those who would not claim to be well informed on history are aware that there has been a great discontinuity in the practice of democracy. Can there possibly be any sense in spending time on studying those first steps in a system of government which was abandoned after less than two hundred years in the state that gave it birth? How can there be any lessons derived from such a study, even though that system has been for some time the standard by which others are judged and still, in spite of set-backs and contentions, is reputed the least imperfect of all political systems? My aim is to give as good an answer as I can to such questions and to vindicate the claims of Athens as the native city of democracy.

I do not feel much need to provide a detailed and reasoned argument for the value of history. The fact that it is such an enjoyable pursuit is sufficient reason in itself. Certainly it would have been for Aristotle, who argued that what is pleasant is desirable. History fosters the sense of continuity between people living now and their ancestors who lived many years ago. It gives a feeling of empathy for human nature as a whole, not just for the small sample of it represented by the age in which we are now living. In the past, many people maintained that it also had the advantage of enabling us to make forecasts for the future. In our more austere times this has been denied. Hegel went so far as to say that the lesson of history is that no one learned anything from history. (He expressed the thought less epigrammatically and at greater length.) In taking so forthright a line he deliberately set himself at odds with Thucydides, with St. John the Divine, the author of the Apocalypse, and with Karl Marx, not to mention the modern compilers of books of racing form.

Whatever the truth of this may be, it is a fact of human nature that people always have enjoyed celebrating the anniversaries of notable events. Recently, we in Britain organized ceremonies to mark the fiftieth anniversary of the Battle of Alamein. The Spaniards, at least, have been celebrating the five-hundredth anniversary of Columbus's western journey, although I believe that in some quarters in America doubts were expressed about the real value of his achievement. Taking a longer perspective, as is natural with people who are specially interested in ancient history, many universities and learned societies in Europe and America held ceremonies to honor the memory of Cleisthenes the Alcmaeonid, the Athenian statesman who, in the course of the year 508-507 B.C., introduced the reforms in the Athenian constitution which are accepted as marking the birth of democracy. The official year in ancient Athens ran from mid-summer to mid-summer and so in Britain the ceremonies began in June and culminated the following year in July. The finale was provided by a reconstructed Greek warship of the fifth century B.C. rowing up the Thames to deliver to the Houses of Parliament a memorial stone carved with the basic Attic constitutional laws. It was a reminder of the interesting fact that both in Britain and in Greece and now in the United States, democracy and preponderant naval power have been closely linked.

It is right that in celebrating the birth of democracy we should go back to its Greek roots. This small country gave birth also to so many of the arts and sciences which are practised to this day, in forms that still betray their origin, that the great men of that time – and women in the case of poetry – seem almost to be our contemporaries. Their art is admired, their literature read. As for their sciences, though they may have been superseded, their principles are still recognized. As Heath, the great historian of Greek mathematics wrote, we should regard the works of Euclid, Eudoxus and Diophantus not as voices from the past but as contributions by Fellows of another college. This attitude is most notably instanced in the study of politics. There was no such study before the Greeks, because it was they who invented the *polis*. They are responsible not only for the title of that science but all the technical terms with which it operates. Monarchy, aristocracy, tyranny - they borrowed that word from Lydian - oligarchy, dynasty,

Democracy After 2,500 Years

hegemony are all names of forms of government that were first used by Greeks. The one which has lasted best is democracy.

Like all Greek coinages the word is readily understandable and means exactly what it says: power to the people. The doctrine it asserts is that control over the lives of the members of a state is to be exercised not by monarchs or aristocrats or specially selected and appointed rulers, but by ordinary men and women. Over the last two centuries or so, this form of government has come to be increasingly favored as the most desirable and also the most effective. It is easy to see why it should be popular, because it more or less gives everyone an equal chance, but its effectiveness has been recognized only more recently. In the course of my lifetime I have been most impressed and, I confess, a little surprised, by the way in which democracy passed what was always considered the severest test for any form of government, the test of war. So many people used to say that democracy did no great harm when a nation was bumbling along in peacetime, looking after its affairs as best it could without much sense of strain, but that in war what was essential was stern, central direction, leadership unquestioned and all-powerful. This doctrine was noisily asserted by those eminent corporals, Mussolini and Hitler. Their sycophantic court philosophers constructed a systematic ideology to buttress it. But when the crunch came it was the tolerant old democracies, not the new-fangled, athletic dictatorships, which showed themselves the more efficient.

I should like to expand a little on that theme. The last time I had the honor of delivering a lecture at Ball State University it was on the subject of military intelligence, more particularly on strategic deception. One would have expected that the one thing a dictatorship would be good at would be the creation of a powerful, all-pervading intelligence service. On the contrary, the German service was dreadfully inefficient, corrupt and so gullible that it was easy to deceive it. I ascribed the difference not to any supposition that the British were cleverer than the Germans but to the fact that they benefited from living in a democracy.

What I am going to claim now is that this highly efficient system, which has stood the test of war and has seen its rivals crumble and collapse, derives directly from events that took place in the small country of Attica two and a half millennia ago. I shall also argue that those events were mainly due to one man, the Cleisthenes I have already mentioned. The reforms that he introduced into the constitution of Athens were the work of one eventful year. It might have seemed at the time that they were merely one more turn, probably a temporary one, of the wheel of politics, which had been going through some highly dramatic revolutions over the past forty-odd years. It was later that their full significance became apparent.

Before Cleisthenes, the state of Attica was organized on traditional lines. That was natural both for historical and economic reasons. Attica had been spared most of the migrations and upheavals that affected the rest of Greece at the end of the Mycenaean period, and at least three-quarters of the population were farmers. Nearly all were subsistence farmers who, throughout history, have been a conservative lot. It is true that there was in the city and in its port of Piraeus a population of artisans and artists, some of whose production was for export; there were also merchants, many of whom traded overseas exporting agricultural and manufactured goods. The bulk of the population, however, lived outside the city. There, in the countryside, life was organized on the traditional basis of the extended family. The method by which a man became a citizen was by having his name, and his patronymic, entered on the list of family members which was kept by the "brotherhoods" or *phratries*. This is a form of patriarchal society which will suggest the clans of highland Scotland, a society in which a man's social rights depended on his family lineage. As in Scotland, the heads of families had paramount importance. They could command the services, in politics or in civil war, which often ran into one another, of the members of their extended families. Apart from their patriarchal prestige and power they were large landowners. They controlled local affairs, both economic and civil, in and around their estates. As the course of war or alliances between these landed aristocratic families went, so went the history of Attica.

Cleisthenes was a member of a prominent aristocratic family, the Alcmaeonidae, who owned a great deal of property. They had been engaged for some time before in a vigorous rivalry with the family of Peisistratus, which had established in Athens a personal ascendancy of the type then called tyranny. The word at that time did not necessarily carry the implication of oppression; it merely meant the rule of a single man who was not a traditional king, but had seized power by some abnormal route. Cleisthenes himself had become reconciled to the tyranny, which was not particularly oppressive, and held office as *archon*, one of the nine senior magistrates, under Peisistratus' sons, who succeeded to his position on his death. This gave Cleisthenes life-membership of the court of Areopagus, which besides being then supreme in all juridical matters exercised a strong informal influence on politics. He was, therefore, a member of the establishment, to borrow a contemporary phrase. However, in the last years of the domination of the tyrant's sons, when there was growing opposition to their rule matched with increasingly severe repression, Cleisthenes' family had gone into exile. In the year 511/10, popular unrest assisted by a Spartan army, whose motives are variously assessed, resulted in the expulsion of the Pisistratids. Although the Alcmaeonids, from their exile, had contributed largely to this (notably by persuading the Spartans to take action), their influence at home came second to another clan which had stayed in Attica throughout the tyranny. This clan was headed by a man called Isagoras, and the measure of his popularity was shown in the electoral contest in the late spring of 508 in which he defeated Cleisthenes, who was running against him for the office of senior *archon*. This was the leader of the college, the man who gave his name to the year; it was the office which Peisistratus, the late tyrant, had held during his period of rule.

So far as Cleisthenes was concerned, therefore, the first year of the forty-second Olympiad (which we call 508/7 BC) was the year of Isagoras; that was its official name in the public records. Cleisthenes took his defeat hard; all the Alcmaeonids were notable for arrogance and for resentment of slights. It seems from such historical comments as are available that the election had been fought on the same basis as were previous elections, that is by rallying the support of family retainers and tenants. Beaten on this basis, Cleisthenes decided that Isagoras should have no pleasure of his year. Adopting new tactics, he decided to "take the common people into partnership," in the phrase of Herodotus, and to change the constitution to entrench the power of the common people for the future. His political slogan was "equality before the law" (*isonomia*). Frightened by the popular clamor, Isagoras plotted to overthrow the constitution in favor of an oligarchy of his friends. He called on Sparta for help again, but when that proved inadequate he went into exile. The other magistrates were compromised by the failure of the conspiracy, which had been frustrated by a genuine popular uprising, and the leadership of the citizens' Assembly was gained by Cleisthenes, who had been prominent in the resistance to the Spartan-backed reactionaries. It was he and his supporters who proposed legislation in the Assembly which laid the foundations for the first pure democracy in history.

At first sight it may seem as though what Cleisthenes introduced was a sweeping reform of local government. The institutions at the top levels of the state appeared unchanged. There were the magistrates, in the shape of a board of *archons*, the august Council of the Areopagus, consisting of all living ex-*archons*, and the popular Assembly of five hundred. These were left untouched by him – others were to introduce more sweeping changes later – whereas the lower level underwent a fundamental reconstruction. The word is appropriate: It was when the foundations were changed that the system began to work and, increasingly, to triumph.

One thing Cleisthenes saw clearly: If Attica were to be a powerful state playing its proper part in Greece it must become a unity instead of being at the mercy of warring clans and territorial magnates. The device he selected was to take a new political unit as the building block of the new polity, one based on locality rather than lineage. In future, a man's political status would depend on where he lived. If I may translate into English terms, he got the vote because his name was on the electoral register at the town hall, not in the family Bible at the manor house. This by itself greatly increased the electorate by extending citizenship to new elements; many established foreigners were also enfranchised. These localities were called *demes* and there were one hundred and thirty nine of them. By a complicated system they were grouped into ten electoral colleges, each containing *demes* from all areas of Attica; each electoral college elected fifty members to a council of five hundred. Thus every local interest in the country, and every class among the free citizens, was equally represented in the supreme body, which was solely responsible for making the laws.

The paramount importance of the basic units of democracy, the individual constituencies or voting districts, has never been better demonstrated. I have not gone into the detailed provisions which were designed to ensure that these basic units all had roughly the same value and could not be dominated by factions; they were extremely elaborate. Indeed, the map in the Cambridge Ancient History which attempts to illustrate the electoral geography of Cleisthenes' reforms must remind many people in the United States of the map of the electoral districts of Massachusetts in the days of Governor Eldridge Gerry. Which carries a lesson: If you want to arrange elections with either good or evil intentions you must pay special attention to voting districts. It is also significant that such arrangements come early in the life-history of a democracy. Gerry was a signatory of the Declaration of Independence or, to give it its original title, "The Unanimous Declaration of the Thirteen United States of America." The man who suggested the other half of the word gerrymander was the famous early American painter Gilbert Stuart. Cleisthenes' *demes*, which his enemies, at least, attacked as the equivalent of a gerrymander, were not merely the earliest foundations of Athenian democracy, but they lasted through to its end. Gerry died in the highest regard, having been elected vice-president on the ticket with Madison. His particular electoral innovation did not survive, but it is thought that his memory still inspires some of his successors. At least he demonstrated the importance of paying attention to the grass roots.

There have been historians who have questioned Cleisthenes' motives, supposing that his aim was merely to pursue family rivalries more effectively and to establish the influence of his own house. The same accusations have been made against Disraeli, that his sensational widening of the franchise in 1867 was merely a device to outsmart his enemies or, as he put it, to "dish the Whigs." But

Disraeli did really have a belief in democracy, in addition to hopes that an enfranchised working class would favor the Conservatives. I think it is fair to ascribe some genuine ideals to Cleisthenes also. He may well have foreseen, as was realized by his collateral descendent, Pericles, that a democratic Athens would be more prosperous and effective.

Of course, the system he established was still, by our standards, imperfect. There were no votes for women. It is unfair to blame him for a failure so universal; no one can be expected to make an imaginative leap forward of more than two thousand years. No state in all antiquity conceded political rights to women, whose enfranchisement even in Western Europe and North America is only a life-span away. No thought was given to rights for slaves, but the "peculiar institution" of slavery was accepted without question even in civilized nations until just over a century ago and survived in some countries into the twentieth century. "Jacksonian democracy" is justly extolled by historians of the United States, and I shall have more to say of it later, but when Andrew Jackson was president after his second attempt in 1828, no one thought of giving the vote to either women or slaves. Cleisthenes was ahead of his time, but not by two-and-a-half millennia. He was, indeed, in many things conservative. Only the upper classes of citizens, determined by wealth, were eligible for office. The Areopagus, the traditional council of ex-magistrates, appointed for life, retained some of its powers, though vaguely and therefore vulnerably defined. But there is no point in underlining the negative. The fact remains that from 507 B.C. onwards, no legislation could be enacted in Athens without the consent of the people, acting through representatives chosen on a fair basis. Nowhere else in Greece was this true and in the millennia that have followed, it has been true only spasmodically and in few places.

I can picture my tutors at Oxford, where I graduated in Ancient History in 1936, raising their eyebrows at such a summary account of the great Cleisthenic reforms. "It is a thirty-mile speed limit," they would say, "and you've gone through it at ninety." I am unrepentant; only the most erudite among you will know the elaboration of detail I have spared you. All I was concerned with was to show that there was one man above all who can be credited with inventing the system which was described by Churchill as the worst form of government except all those other forms that have been tried from time to time.

It is not to be taken as a matter of surprise that democracy had a rocky ride in Greece and eventually petered out altogether. Democracy at Athens was overthrown at the end of the fifth century, restored again and suppressed at the end of the fourth century by the predominance of the Macedonian kings. It was not, I should add, the ideology of monarchy that triumphed, though there were some Greeks who fell for it, but rather the Macedonian army. Philosophically, democracy came under attack from the best minds in Athens. Plato, who so much influenced the development of political thought, was an aristocrat. He was one not only in the sense that he came from a rich, landed family; that may well have influenced his ideas on politics, but he genuinely believed that government should be in the hands best qualified for it. Stated in those terms the principle looks incontrovertible; but all experience shows that attempts to put it into practice come up against the unanswerable question: Who, in point of fact, are the best qualified? Plato regarded democracy as a degenerate form of government, only one degree above the worst, tyranny. Aristotle, the great inspirer of the next generation and of the Middle Ages, thought it a perversion.

After monarchy came back with Alexander, and the Roman Empire made it the ordinary form of government, democracy disappeared for many centuries. Some scholars and antiquarians were aware of it as something which had once existed and had been proved erroneous by Aristotle. During the Middle Ages, there were certain pockets of territory where peasant democracy of an old-fashioned type was practiced, notably in Iceland or in certain Swiss cantons. In principle, however, the leading intellectuals of the Middle Ages favored enlightened autocracy and kings and princes put it into practice, sometimes in an enlightened way and sometimes not. A few countries, notably England, preserved from primitive times quite effective means of bringing a measure of popular control to bear on their sovereigns, but they were uninfluenced by any theoretical ideas of democracy. They thought they were merely following the tradition of their ancestors when they made their kings swear, at their coronation, to govern "according to the good customs of the country" and, if they went too far in disregarding those customs, putting constraint on them or, sometimes, deposing them. Similarly the Cortes of Saragossa, in the sixteenth century, are reported as swearing allegiance to the King of Aragon in the following terms: "We who are as good as you swear to you, who are no better than we, to accept you as our King and Sovereign Lord, provided you observe all our liberties and laws; and if not, not." But this language, probably exaggerated in the report, reflected aristocratic pride and bourgeois self-confidence rather than democracy. The provocative formula was not repeated at the next accession.

The English Civil War of 1642 has long been regarded, certainly in Britain, as a democratic movement comparable to and completed by the American and the French Revolutions. Such was the view of Macaulay and his school in the nineteenth century. Since then we have had a Marxist interpretation, all in terms of the class war, supported by a venerable former Master of Balliol. But that seems to have crumbled, like the Berlin Wall. It was never easy to prop up. The current approach goes back to an earlier one and traces the origin of the war to differences about religion. At any rate, democratic ideas of the sort I have been considering had very little to do with it. There were indeed the Levellers and the Diggers, eccentric visionaries whose ideas have won favor with some modern politicians who run no danger of having to put them into practice, but Cromwell put them down by the sword and demolished their intellectual pretensions with the pungent epigram that democracy was the creed of all bad men and all poor men.

In the golden legend of democracy, the next stop is Philadelphia, for the consummation of the American Revolution. There is no doubt that the founding fathers created a great democracy, but they didn't intend to and didn't think they were creating one. Their aim, apart from maintaining American independence, which was their prime concern, was to produce an improved version of the British constitution. This was not only because they were mainly of British origin and, therefore, naturally conservative, even when engaged in rebellion. They could not help themselves because the whole intellectual world, and especially the French political philosophers who were their other great source of inspiration, was united in believing the British constitution to be the best in existence. It had also a respectable classical precedent. Polybius had maintained in the second century B.C. that the Roman constitution was the ideal one because it united the best elements of monarchy, aristocracy and democracy. These three elements were equally happily combined, according to a well known epigram by Voltaire, in the British constitution. They were represented there by the King, the House of Lords and the House of Commons and so the Americans would have their monarchical President, their aristocratic Senate and their popular House of Representatives. The fact that their monarch was not hereditary and ruled for a fixed term was of no importance, as Aristotle would have agreed.

In all this there is no hint of democracy. The word never occurs in the Constitution of the United States nor in any of the twenty-six Amendments. James Madison wrote on several occasions that the Constitution provides for a republican form of government and not a democratic one. He also wrote: "Democracies have ever been spectacles of turbulence and contention; have ever been found incompatible with personal security or the rights of property; and have in general been as short in their lives as they have been violent in their deaths." There was an aroma of mob-rule about the idea of democracy, inspiring fears of confiscation of property for the benefit of the poor. The landed gentry, the merchants, the comfortable people who made the revolution were not having that sort of thing.

The credit of democracy was not enhanced by the French Revolution. In his *Reflections,* Burke drew the conclusion that "a perfect democracy is therefore the most shameless thing in the world." The French in 1789, unlike the Americans thirteen years earlier, could not bring themselves to adapt an old and familiar constitution by degrees, so as to reform what they could and remove only what they could not reform. They were not pragmatic meliorists, like the Americans; they were idealists who desired to follow a wholly rational course. Unfortunately, what appeared to be just such a course had been expounded very recently in an entrancingly rhetorical style by Jean-Jacques Rousseau. The concept of "the general will" ruled all the constitutional discussions in Versailles and then in Paris. It should not have been surprising that, before long, the general will, a concept which Rousseau left undefined, to be embodied by anyone who should claim to do so, turned out to be the will of General Bonaparte. It had been a commonplace of Plato's theory of politics that democracy was liable to transmute into tyranny. The truth of the doctrine was driven home for political theorists of the early nineteenth century by the experience of the First French Empire.

In a recent lecture on democracy, Professor Lipson chose the years 1828-1835 as the turning point in the process of thought which was bringing democracy back into favor after centuries in which it was feared or, at least, suspected. Andrew Jackson was elected president in 1828, at his second attempt. He was the first to win that office under the political label of "democratic" and in his campaign he held himself out as a populist opponent of the old East Coast establishment. I am not suggesting he was not sincere in these claims and in his desire to ensure that as many citizens as possible participated in the political process. His supporters' tactics were typical of the early days of elective democracy. Last month, I came across a description of how, in one district of New York, "200 Irish voters were marched to the poll by one of the Jackson candidates who walked at the head with a cocked pistol in each hand and then, without leaving the polls, they voted three times apiece for the Jackson ticket." I was immediately reminded of the way citizens of Athens were persuaded to exercise their democratic rights in the period around 425 B.C. At the appointed hour, all exits from the Agora, which was both the market place and the common meeting place, were closed except the one leading to the place of assembly, and state slaves acting as policemen carried a rope dripping with red dye towards that exit. Anyone whose clothes were marked by the dye was fined.

The period 1828-1835 was also a turning point in politics in Britain. As

Chesterton used to say, the most important political event of the nineteenth century in Britain was the revolution which did not occur between 1829 and 1832. What occurred instead was the Reform Act of 1832. Lord Grey, an aristocrat like Cleisthenes, realized that permanent damage to the constitution could be averted only by a reorganization of the foundations of the system, the constituencies. Once the foundations were changed, as Cleisthenes found and Eldridge Gerry tried to copy, everything else had to follow; but because it was done pragmatically and not under any ideological guidance, it went gradually and was accepted with very few grumbles. Grey's measures, when first introduced, were thought drastic and excessive; later opinion considers them quite inadequate. It was indeed an example of a political rarity: precisely the right thing being done at precisely the right time. (Andrew Jackson's election was also assisted by earlier measures of franchise reform.) Since the heroic days of the nineteenth century, the redistribution of constituencies in Britain is now effected, less dramatically, by a completely neutral Redistribution Commission. It is confidently asserted that at the next election, the new electoral boundaries that will then be in force, made necessary by movement out of the cities and increased prosperity, will cost the Labour party some forty seats. There is, with all this, no hint of gerrymandering, except for the usual over-representation of Scotland.

By the middle of the century the new course was inevitable in all advanced civilized states. Carlisle, a thorough-going but glumly pessimistic Conservative, remarked in 1843: "To what extent Democracy has now reached, how it advances irresistible with ominous, ever-increasing speed, he that will open his eyes on any province of human affairs may discern. Democracy is everywhere the inexorable demand of these ages, swiftly fulfilling itself."

To turn to the present age is to see the fulfilment of Carlisle's prophecy. Two factors have reinforced it: the creation of parties, which has given discipline to the pursuit of particular interests, and of neutral and independent civil services, which has produced the machinery for ensuring continuity in administration. (Ancient Greek democracy had parties, but they were fluctuating factions with no consistent ideologies; there was no bureaucracy worthy of the name.) Of course, the actual practice of democracy is still restricted to a minority of states, but pretensions to it, and above all the mere name, are prized and flaunted all over the world. It is the fashion, and even those who do not understand it, and would dislike it if they did, are eager to pay it at least nominal honor.

How many countries there are which still proclaim themselves People's Democracies! The title was impertinently assumed by satellites of the late Soviet Union, which were in fact the most savage tyrannies, obedient servants of foreign masters; they nevertheless used the name as though it were a necessary guarantee of statehood. The same thing happened with many of the countries which were granted independence by their former imperialist rulers. Hypocrisy has been described as the tribute that vice pays to virtue, and perhaps it might be argued that some tribute, however disingenuous, is better than no tribute at all. The history of the gloomy, blood-stained dictatorships of Equatorial Guinea, or the People's Democratic Republic of Ethiopia or Myanmar, in happier days known as Burma, shows the extent of the crimes for which that hypocrisy is an ineffective cover.

It will not have escaped your notice that in all I have said so far about modern developments of democracy, I have been speaking of representative rather than participatory democracy. In the Athenian model the people in whose name government was conducted actually voted in person for every law or treaty or change in foreign policy. In modern times, originally because of the medieval tradition of remitting questions to representative delegations, but overwhelmingly on practical grounds, it is a very small proportion of the population, a representative one it is hoped, that deliberates and votes. The practical objections are very obvious: No modern state could conceivably assemble all its eligible citizens to deliberate and if even a tiny fraction of them were to assert their rights to speak no proceedings would ever end. An Athenian of the late sixth century would have thought it undemocratic to allow any restriction, but then he was used to an assembly of only some five or six thousand, and that on days when exceptionally interesting business was to be transacted. In Britain, each member of the House of Commons represents about 70,000 voters; in the United States, each Congressman represents on average 575,000. Both are likely to admit that they find it difficult to be sure of correctly interpreting the wishes of all their constituents.

In the late nineteenth century and for most of this century, vigorous attempts were made to remedy the dangers of what it is now fashionable to call such a failure of communications. There were public meetings on every scale, from the mass rally to the small group of the faithful in village school-rooms. Speeches by leading politicians were reported verbatim in the newspapers, which seventy years ago used not to flinch from filling several closely printed columns with rhetoric. Public meetings continue, but the press has found livelier and more frivolous topics. The radio had its vogue, especially with the famous "fireside chats" which President Roosevelt pioneered; in wartime Britain the radio carried to huge masses the spell of Hitler and the reassurances and encouragement of Churchill. But all these means of persuasion have been dwarfed and diminished by the further progress of the electronic revolution, and television reigns supreme.

Its effect on politics has been the same as on the arts or elsewhere: to trivialize. It has both revolutionized and reduced the dignity of politics. In choosing a candidate, great weight is given to his looks. As he progresses he becomes even more of a gift-wrapped parcel, furnished by film actors with advice on gestures and by speechwriters with smart epigrams of a brevity precisely calculated to match the public's span of attention. Nevertheless, the advance of technique could have its positive side. Television has given the chance to very high proportions - or one might almost say the whole – of the population to be present on great occasions, to listen to debates, to form an opinion on important questions. We are therefore returning to the situation of the Athenian citizen, who could hear the speeches and make up his mind on policy.

All that remains is for a technique to be developed whereby the listeners could respond. It is already within the scope of current science to arrange for everyone in the audience who so wishes to press one of a selection of buttons to record a valid vote. The totals could be produced instantaneously by computer. There are differences. Personal appearance had little influence in Athenian politics. Pericles' oddly shaped skull was much mocked by the comic poets, but he dominated politics for thirty years; in modern times an imperfect shave has, I believe, cast a shadow, in two senses, on a candidate's chances. More serious is the risk that hasty decisions might be taken on no more serious a basis than a fortunate display of rhetoric, and such a decision, being taken by the sovereign people itself, could only with the greatest difficulty be reversed. Thucydides gives tragic examples. It is legitimate, therefore, to feel doubts about taking such a revolutionary step into an uncertain future but it does produce a strange thrill to realize that, with a few appropriate technical arrangements, we could go back, at the touch of a button, to the Attic origins of open democracy.

Whatever the future may bring and in spite of the prevalence of spurious imitations, genuine democracy at the end of the twentieth century continues unchallenged and successful. In the new age brought into existence by the collapse of the Soviet Union, and especially in Europe, the truth of Churchill's epigram is becoming increasingly apparent. Democracy has triumphed over all competing systems of government. Its lenity and justice, its evident efficiency, have proved once more the superior virtues, in human terms, of the system first conceived by Cleisthenes two thousand five hundred years ago.

8

Democracy:
The First Twenty-Five Centuries

Leslie Lipson

The invention of a new form of government – new in the sense that it deviates from all the others in a fundamental feature – is a rare event in political history. But that was precisely what happened in Athens two and a half millennia before our time. The form of government to which I refer is, of course, democracy (*demokratia*, as it was known to ancient Greeks). The feature which makes it unique among political systems is in the location of ultimate power. All other systems place this in the government itself – at the apex, as it were, of the social pyramid – whence it trickles down to the people, who are viewed as the subjects of their rulers. Democracy, however, reverses that relationship. Here, the mass of the public is the source of power, and it is the people at large who entrust authority to designated officials. What is more, that authority is limited in function, circumscribed in time, revocable by those who conferred it. Thus, in a democratic regime the citizens retain in their own hands a residuary freedom which no other type of governance can parallel.

According to ancient legend, the goddess Athena was born, fully grown, from the head of Zeus. Athenian democracy, however, grew in more human fashion. It evolved over a century and a half in three stages, associated successively with the reforms of Solon (in 594 B.C.), of Cleisthenes (in 508 B.C.) and of Pericles and Ephialtes (in 462 B.C.). The work of Cleisthenes may appropriately be taken to mark the birth of democracy because his reorganization of Athens' political structure definitively altered its basic character, in kind and not merely in degree. He introduced two significant innovations. One was to construct the entire constitutional framework on the foundation of the *demes*, which were territorial subdivisions of government for local purposes. In substituting territory for the older principle of kinship, Cleisthenes radicalized the government. He opened the doors to direct participation in its processes not only to those whose citizenship was derived from birth, but also to those who were naturalized. The same purpose was evident in his other major reform: regrouping the *demes* into ten newly created tribes from which individuals would be picked at random to serve in the Council, which prepared the work of the all-powerful Assembly, and on the numerous committees, which supervised the administrative departments. Cleisthenes' achievement was to start bringing the facts of political life into conformity with what *demokratia* literally means: power (*kratos*) exercised in person by the people (*demos*). Before his time, Athenian governance was essentially aristocratic in spirit and tone; after him, it became democratic.

Democracy flourished in Athens for a century and a half, the continuity being briefly broken by the pro-Spartan oligarchy installed after Athens' loss in the Peloponnesian War. Only when Philip of Macedon expanded his empire to absorb the disunited city-states of Hellas did Athens finally see its democracy extinguished along with its independence.

I have called this system, as it evolved in ancient Athens, unique. In what respects was that the case? In what ways was democracy different? The answers consist in the values which democracy preferred and in the institutions of self-government which it devised. Athens was dedicated to three values: equality, freedom and citizen-participation. These were translated into practice by allowing anyone to speak in the Assembly, and selecting individuals by lot to serve in the Council and on the juries and commissions. Understandably, Pericles, when eulogizing democracy in his Funeral Oration, emphasized the aspect of the system which relied on the citizens themselves to undertake the work of governing. This was self-government with a vengeance.

So exceptional a system attracted attention and aroused much comment among historians, dramatists, and philosophers, most of whom had conservative values and therefore rendered a negative verdict. Thucydides criticized democracy for its errors in foreign policy, which had contributed to its defeat in the Peloponnesian War. Aristophanes – the George Bernard Shaw of his day – lampooned the institutions of democracy, as in *The Wasps*. Plato, when he listed the degenerate forms of government in the *Republic*, ranked democracy one above the lowest, tyranny. Aristotle classified it among the perversions. In modern idiom, democracy received a bad press.

Why such unfavorable judgments? The critics were men who either rejected democracy's fundamental values, or they argued that these had been applied in excess and with pernicious results. Plato, who worshiped order and hierarchy, could not accept the disorderly consequences of freedom. Both he and Aristotle condemned equality when equal rights and equal treatment were accorded to persons unequal in merit. All were distrustful of the rule of the many, since that spelled the enthronement of ignorance. Moreover, the objections to democracy from the right-wing were grounded in more than political factors. They had the overtones of distinctions based on social and economic classes. In a democracy, observed Aristotle, the many, who happen also to be the poor, plunder the few who are the wealthier – and that is destructive of good order. An important judgment, because it indicates that in its origins, as in our contemporary century, democracy's dimensions have always been economic and social as well as governmental.

A modern critic, too, would point to aspects of the Athenian reality which weakened, or even contradicted, its vaunted virtues. First, one should stress how small a proportion of the total population of Attica (perhaps one-tenth of the whole) enjoyed the privilege of participation as full citizens. Women were excluded, as were the resident aliens, and there were also the slaves who toiled for their public or private owners. Nor should one forget that at the height of its power Athens was unashamedly imperialist, forcing weaker city-states to submit to its naval forces. The *demos* that exercised authority was a broader segment of the whole than could be found anywhere else, but it was far from being all-inclusive.

Such was the legacy which Athens bequeathed to posterity. *Demokratia* had been an amazing invention, created without precedent from the past. It supplied the political context for some brilliant achievements: the defeat of the Persian invaders at Marathon and Salamis and the glorious flowering of intellect and the arts in the fifth and fourth centuries. But there were its failures, which dimmed the lustre of the positive. After all, had not the Athenian democracy finally succumbed to those efficient military machines in Sparta and Macedon? Had it not ostracized Aristeides, "the Just," and executed Socrates, whose questions so troubled his hearers? And were there not those damning verdicts recorded in the pages of Thucydides, Plato, and Aristotle? Democracy in Athens was an exceptional flash-in-the-pan, a premature happening, not soon to be repeated.

Not soon, indeed! In fact, not for two thousand years. For two millennia, Western civilization produced a number of regimes in succession: the Roman Republic and Empire, the Church, the feudal society, and the sovereign, centralized nation-state, all of them variations on the themes of autocracy, hierarchy and oligarchy. Northern Europe retained in a few isolated instances some residues of early Germanic folk-meetings and assemblies (Iceland's *Thing*, or the Swiss *Landsgemeinde*), but these were minor exceptions to the prevailing pattern.

And as long as the Roman tradition of *auctoritas* and *imperium* was dominant in Church and State, the mass of the people were relegated to the humble status of dutiful subjects. The Periclean vision of self-governing, participating citizens was not for them. *Demokratia* had been relegated to a literary memory.

History does not repeat itself, it has been said, historians do. True enough! But all the same, the reappearance at a later time of a set of conditions bearing some resemblance to a prior set may result in a comparable pattern of behavior. Such was the case with democracy. After an eclipse of twenty centuries there was a new dawning, and for understandable reasons. Where monarchy is the rule, and monarchs are all-powerful, one can be certain that several of them will turn out to be stupid and their stupidities will, of course, provoke rebellion. Similarly where aristocracies or oligarchies prevail, their ingrained arrogance and exclusiveness will eventually arouse an organized opposition. When, in addition, economic changes are creating novel forms of wealth, and new philosophies are challenging accepted verities, the ancestral order is unlikely to be taken for granted. People are then in the mood for something radically different. That was exactly what happened in the Atlantic region in the 17th and 18th centuries. Three major revolutions erupted between 1640 and 1789—in England, the United States, and France. Each singly, and all collectively, paved the way for a new mode of government. As a result, by the mid-nineteenth century modern democracy was born.

For this to happen, new institutions had to be created along with new thinking to supply their justification and rationale. The new thinking, which occurred primarily in England and France, was the work of political reformers with a speculative bent. In England, the egalitarianism of the Levellers, whose radical doctrines were a couple of centuries ahead of their time, was followed by the more moderate individualism of Locke. His emphasis on natural rights and the supremacy of the legislative branch buttressed his insistence that governments exist to protect those rights which individuals do not surrender in the original compact to create a civil society. Political power, so viewed, is a fiduciary trust granted under certain conditions and rightfully exercised as long as those limits are observed. When they are not, it is the people's right to rebel. So much for absolutism (whether papal or monarchical), the divine right of kings, "*l'etat, c'est moi*," etc., etc. The message of the Levellers and Locke was loud and clear. It is the individual who is truly sovereign. Individuals must think for themselves and assert themselves. Such ideas spelled the end of the established order, as had happened in England by 1688 and in its American colonies in 1776. When Thomas Jefferson set down in writing the eloquent opening phrases of the Declaration of

The First Twenty-Five Centuries

Independence, his concepts were Lockean both in sound and in substance.

Similarly in France, *les philosophes*, the intellectuals, set the stage for the drama which started to unfold in 1789. The thinkers of the Enlightenment and the writers of the *Encyclopédie* led an onslaught on the dogmas of the *ancien régime*. Louis XVI, like Charles I, lost throne and head – a portent to Hapsburgs, Romanovs, and Hohenzollerns. But these philosophical currents, which swirled in eighteenth-century France, differed in one significant respect from those of seventeenth-century England. Whereas Voltaire's doctrine was individualistic, Rousseau's was not. The citizen of Geneva was a collectivist, whose central concept—the general will, *volonté générale* – was ambiguous. It could be expressed by the majority – or by the few or by a single person who claims best to know the general interest. In those alternatives lay the fateful choice between democracy and the totalitarian extremes which have bedeviled the twentieth century. The intellectual ground for these was prepared by the confusion in Rousseau's troubled mind.

Besides generating some radical ideas, the three revolutions had another important consequence. They gave rise to institutions which, as earlier in the work of Cleisthenes, shifted the location of ultimate power. In England, the political result of the revolution was the supremacy of Parliament, which curbed the Crown and guaranteed the independence of the judiciary. The United States designed a new structure of government which enshrined the supremacy of the Constitution. Its central principle was to distribute powers in several places so that their holders would check one another in a balanced equilibrium. Part of this design was accomplished by the "separation of powers," a concept elaborated by Montesquieu. The rest was achieved through the federal system – an invention of the Founding Fathers which I consider the greatest American contribution to the art of government. The French, by contrast with the British and the Americans, failed utterly to devise a workable new framework. The consequent disorder was ended by Napoleon Bonaparte, under whose sway the General Will became the Will of the General. None of these innovations – neither the concepts nor the institutions – was presented by thinkers of the seventeenth or eighteenth centuries as signalling the arrival of democracy. The reason for that is clear in what Locke and Rousseau and Madison have to say on the subject. For all three the concept was defined within the terms and conditions which had obtained in ancient Athens. It signified a system where political power was wielded by the many, who themselves discharged the principal functions of government. Both Locke and Rousseau repeat the essentials of the Aristotelian classification – that governments differ according to whether one, few, or many are in command –

and, having mentioned democracy as one of the possible types, proceed to use other terminology to describe what they are advocating. Rousseau, in fact, dismisses democracy as an unattainable utopia: "Were there a people of gods, their government would be democratic. So perfect a government is not for men." In similar vein James Madison, writing in the *Federalist* to support the newly drafted Constitution of the United States, points out that it provides for a republican form of government, and several times draws the distinction between a republic and a democracy. A republic, for him as for others of his generation, was a system wherein people dispersed over a wide area could elect representatives from their districts to convene at some central point and there make decisions on behalf of the whole. That is why the terms "democracy" and "democratic" are nowhere to be found in the text of the U.S. Constitution, or in any of its twenty-seven Amendments. In addition, there was one further reason why the notion of democracy would have been unacceptable in 1787 to the majority of the delegates at the Philadelphia Convention. Those who had been educated in the Greek and Latin classics remembered well that a whiff of mob rule and confiscations of property hung around the concept. For merchants, lawyers, and gentlemen-farmers, this was a bit too radical. Their hearts were with Aristotle, the moderate conservative, not with the aristocratic populist, Pericles.

In political history, however, a generation is a long time, and attitudes towards democracy - to the term and all that it signified – were markedly different after 1830 from what they were before 1790. Britain was by then exploring its new frontier of the industrial revolution, whose social and economic changes brought their political dividends. The United States, fully confident, secure and expansionist was extending its own frontiers and luxuriating in a climate of individualism and egalitarianism. France, settling down after a quarter of a century of revolution and empire, was seeking a constitutional consensus through a succession of short-lived regimes. Innovation, in other words, was the spirit of the age. With it came a new interest in democracy. Once again in the history of Western civilization, this was an idea whose time had come.

If one were to pinpoint the exact years which marked the turning point, I would select the period from 1828 to 1835. In 1828, Andrew Jackson, a populist, was elected President of the United States, the first to win that office under the political label of "Democratic." In 1830, revolutions occurred in several European capitals, resulting in the installation of more liberal regimes. In 1832, after two years of intense conflict, the British Parliament adopted the first Reform Act, which began the process of extending the franchise for elections to the House of Commons and of redistributing constituencies more in conformity with the spread of population. In 1835, de Tocqueville published the first volumes of *De la Démocratie en Amérique*, based on his observations during his visit in 1831-32 – the first opportunity anyone had had since ancient Athens to analyze a functioning democracy.

Democracy, in the consensus of political observers, was the wave of the future. "The organization and establishment of democracy among Christians," wrote de Tocqueville, "is the great political problem of our time." That indeed was his reason for voyaging to the United States. "I avow that in America I have seen more than America; I have looked there for an image of democracy itself." A decade and a half later his compatriot, Guizot, offered similar testimony to the new attitudes:

[Democracy] is the banner for all the hopes, for all the social ambitions of humanity, be they pure or impure, noble or base, sensible or insane, practicable or utopian. . . . The word 'democracy' is now spoken every day, at every hour, in every place. Everywhere, and constantly, it is heard by everyone.

And further confirmation comes from an opponent and critic – that crusty conservative, Thomas Carlyle. "To what extent Democracy has now reached," he lamented in 1843, "how it advances irresistible with ominous, ever-increasing speed, he that will open his eyes on any province of human affairs may discern. Democracy is everywhere the inexorable demand of these ages, swiftly fulfilling itself."

For the concept to have become generally acceptable was a notable, indeed, an extraordinary, change; for it to operate successfully in practice, something else was required. That was the invention of new institutions to supplement those inherited from earlier centuries, as occurred in the nineteenth century. A trio of novelties was then introduced, all being essential to the operation of a democratic state. These were: the grant to all adults of the right to vote, a party system of two or more sharing office in turns, and a civil service of life-time employees recruited through merit.

The extension of the suffrage was a fundamental necessity if genuine meaning was to be attached to the requirement that the authority to govern must be derived from the consent of the governed. If any group was denied the right to vote, the state would be less than democratic to the extent of that denial. True democracy, therefore, could not be said to exist until voting rights on an equal basis were granted universally to all adult citizens. Even for countries such as Great Britain, which had long been holding elections to one branch of the legislature, the change now accomplished was one of kind, not merely of degree. In 1830, less than three percent of the population of England and Wales could vote in elections to the House of Commons. Not until 1884 were virtually all the adult males enfranchised. Forty-four years later, women were treated the same as men. In terms of the ballot box, Britain has been a full democracy only since 1928.

The United States leaped ahead of Britain in this respect, early in the nineteenth century, by rapidly reducing, and then removing, the barriers which prevented the less wealthy and the propertyless from voting. But other barriers remained. Sexual discrimination was abolished by the Nineteenth Amendment in 1919. Racial discrimination was another matter. It was banned in federal elections by the Fifteenth Amendment, adopted after the Civil War. Nevertheless, blacks were inhibited or intimidated by extra-legal means, especially in the states of the old Confederacy, where they were more numerous. It required a social and political revolution as recently as the nineteen-sixties to ensure that the ballot box would henceforth be color-blind. As far as depends on the right to vote, and effective opportunities to practice that right, democracy in the United States is barely twenty years old. On the European continent, adult males were generally enfranchised before World War I or in the nineteen-twenties. Women had to wait longer, especially in Catholic countries where they received the vote only after World War II. The last democracy to enfranchise its women was Switzerland, not altogether surprising for an isolationist people which thus far has not even wanted to join the United Nations!

The effect of mass enfranchisement is, of course, to redraw the parameters of democracy. The traditional definition, which restricted it to direct government by the people themselves, was still being employed by Rousseau and Madison late in the eighteenth century. What happened after 1815 was the removal of the restriction. Citizen-participation was still a prerequisite, but this could be satisfied by participation at the ballot box. Representative democracy was no longer a contradiction in terms. It had at last become an acceptable concept.

Now, with millions registered as voters and with several candidates competing for their votes, some organization was necessary or the electoral system would degenerate into chaos. That was where the political parties evolved to fill a need. Before the nineteenth century there had been groupings within the body politic which opposed one another over issues of principle or because they were tied to specific interests. Britain had its Whigs and Tories; the United States, its Federalists and Democratic-Republicans. But outside of Parliament or Congress these were not organized, and in any case they were often characterized in a derogatory sense as "factions," a term associated historically with conspiracy and division.

The party became respectable, as did democracy, because it was needed. As the franchise was extended to embrace, first, hundreds of thousands and then millions, it was necessary to have organizations which would encourage citizens to register and vote and would forge links between the electorate and the elected. Moreover, in no other way could coherent and stable majorities be sent to the legislatures for the conduct of public business. Out of these requirements was born the party system. It guaranteed that essential feature of democracy: freedom of choice among a variety of programs and candidates, and the alternation in power of rival groups. Without the political parties, modern democracy would have been unworkable.

To make it work efficiently, however, something else was required, and this was the third major innovation of the nineteenth century. The democratic state was then being called upon to provide more services for its citizens, especially for the newly enfranchised. This meant an expansion of the numbers of public employees who had to supply continuous and expert administration. As a result, the traditional system which had filled the departmental offices by patronage, and the practice of giving out jobs as rewards for political support (the "spoils system"), were replaced by the career civil service recruited through open competition – an ancient Chinese invention rediscovered in the West a little more than a century ago.

Thus was the modern democratic state equipped to navigate that sea of troubles whereon we have voyaged in this turbulent twentieth century. Two World Wars, a worldwide economic depression, the challenges of the totalitarian dictatorships, Fascist, Nazi and Communist, and of Japanese militarism, such mortal threats did the democracies confront and overcome between 1914 and 1990. Indeed, those were tests which would assuredly have destroyed a weaker system. Yes, the democracies succeeded in surviving the ordeals, albeit at a price. Hence in this last decade of the second millennium A.D., when humanity stands poised at a turning point in history, now is the appropriate moment to take stock, to assess the record, and speculate about the prospect. The experience of these last two centuries warrants certain conclusions about democracy, and these are now possible from a perspective which no previous generation can match.

My first comment is that the ancient Greek thinkers were correct in their insight that democracy is not only a unique form of government, but that its dimensions extend to the social and economic. What that means is that its basic values – freedom and equality – cannot be achieved at the level of government unless they also permeate the social order and the economy. Or, to state the same point in another way, if the structure of the economy or the spirit of social institutions is undemocratic, in the sense of being antithetical to equality and freedom, then democracy will be nullified in the political sphere. How true that is! How amply is it confirmed by modern experience!

Great Britain is a country which has achieved full equality for all in the right to vote, and participation in elections is very high. But its social order is still colored by the traditional class system whose premise is inequality of status accorded by accident of birth, without relation to the merits of the individual. The United States, similarly, has now ensured that, as far as the Constitution and the laws can provide, all its citizens are equally entitled to vote. But the equality which the political system enshrines is negated by the grossly unequal distribution of wealth and incomes. Where an oligarchy rules the economy, democracy cannot rule in politics. Germany, likewise, had an educational system that, until World War II, crammed knowledge into students' heads with a strict discipline, but authoritarian teachers discouraged independent or critical thinking – as the experience of young Albert Einstein at the Luitpold Gymnasium can illustrate. This militates against democracy, which requires of its citizens that they be prepared always to question authority. Similar obstacles have been presented by the power of religious organizations. Modern democracy is essentially secular and humanist. Its spirit and outlook owe much to the Enlightenment. Any society where one religion predominates, and that one staffed by a powerful clergy, will find a conflict between the uncritical acceptance of dogma through faith and the search for truth through reason. Openness of mind and a tolerance of diversity are the intellectual prerequisites of democracy.

The point I am making here, that democracy is much more than a mode of governance, that it is indeed a whole social order, is particularly pertinent now that several countries are undergoing a transition since the collapse of regimes which Communist parties controlled for four decades. Constantly nowadays in the mass media and the more sophisticated journals, one hears and reads descriptions of the governments in eastern Europe as "the new democracies." The same is regularly repeated in the American media about contemporary regimes in Central and South America. Such statements, in my judgment, are wishful thinking at their best and sheer nonsense at their worst. Holding two or three elections is not enough to constitute a democracy. These are only the beginning of a long process, which will take at least two generations to be successful, of transforming the basic institutions of a whole culture and the values to which their people attach priority. In order eventually to become democratic, the people of eastern Europe will need to reorganize their economies, revitalize their education, restrict the power of their churches, and exorcise the authoritarian traditions of Communist, Fascist and monarchical regimes. The Czechs are the ones with the best prospects of succeeding; I am less hopeful of the rest. And in Latin America, it is meaningless to speak of democracy in any genuine sense until the present gross inequities in land ownership have been abolished, until the wings of the financial oligarchies are clipped and until those armies whose guns and tanks exist to protect the privileges of the very wealthy are transformed in purpose and effectively subordinated to civilian authority.

Underlying what I have just said is a question of fundamental importance which must be squarely faced. It is a historical fact that democracy was invented within the Western civilization, and it is in this one civilization that its most conspicuous examples are to be found. However, the ideals, the values, the vision of humanity, which democracy expresses are not parochial. Their scope is truly universal. Can this system be successfully transplanted to other civilizations and there take root? Can the civilizations of Asia, the Sinic, Hindu, and Islamic, containing the great majority of human beings, adapt this Western import to their traditions and conditions? Can Africa and the hybrid cultures of Latin America do the same?

My own answer to these queries is not a simple, unequivocal "yes" or "no," but rather a "yes, but". With hope I am saying "yes" because of what I believe to be democracy's greatest strengths: its emphasis on the worth and dignity of the individual and its universality. Democracy's values have no place for supermen or submen. They transcend the physical distinctions of sex and race and the man-made divisions of language, status and religion. For a democracy, there is only one classification: the human being. As such, in principle this doctrine would seem, *prima facie*, to have the best chance of being universally accepted. The appeal of democracy is nowhere so strong as when its emphasis is placed on human rights – the same for all persons everywhere. That is the basis for believing that this system, which started in the Athenian *polis*, could one day embrace the cosmopolis.

There is, however, a qualifying "but" to be attached to this optimistic "yes." Democracy was not easily achieved in the West, either in ancient times or modern. It was the result of struggle. To speak more exactly, it originated in revolution. What was accomplished in Athens was revolution, and revolutions were the achievement of English, French and Americans in the seventeenth and eighteenth centuries. Enough of the people were aroused in opposition to the autocracies which stifled them to take power into their own hands and then institute procedures by which they retained the residuary power. Most of the world has yet to undergo this kind of revolution. It will, I believe, occur eventually in Latin America, and when it does I trust that its spirit will be Jeffersonian. In China,

Sun Yatsen and Mao Zedong began the revolutionary process, but no democracy resulted from their efforts; a further stage in China's evolving revolution has yet to take place. In India, the British introduction of self-government, along with education in the English language, were the most significant parts of the imperial legacy. Self-government has continued, albeit in the face of serious difficulties, and India can truly boast of containing the world's largest electorate. But the problems of appalling poverty and of religious fanaticism remain endemic. No one would confidently predict that India in the foreseeable future will become both harmonious and prosperous.

As for Islam, I regard this as the least hopeful of the world's major civilizations for the next half century. This proud civilization, whose achievements were considerably ahead of Europe's in the Dark and early Middle Ages, went into a decline after the flowering of the Safavids, Moghuls and Ottomans, from which it has never yet recovered. For peoples whose world has been shaped by what they believe to be a religious revelation written into a text which is the word of Allah, to adapt to an altered world is indeed a challenge – intellectually and spiritually, as well socially. In its essential character Islam is dogmatic because its truths come from a divine source; it is, therefore, intolerant of those who deny its truths. That was not always the case, however, for Cordoba under the Moors was tolerant of both its Jews and Christians. But today, having been outstripped by the West, Islamic leaders, Sunni and Shiite alike, react by reaffirming their fundamental ancient precepts. The resulting regimes, as in Saudi Arabia and Iran, are the negations of what Western democracy embodies. Their crisis will come in the future when their oil wells run dry.

If the West is to succeed in persuading other branches of humanity to reconstitute their societies along democratic lines, two requirements must be fulfilled. First, we should be clear in our own minds about what democracy means. Otherwise we shall sound confused and therefore be unpersuasive when we are recommending that others follow our example. Second, if others are to imitate us, we had better be sure that we practice what we preach. Our advice abroad will be disregarded if we are seen to act differently at home.

I emphasize that we should clarify our conception of democracy because currently our principles appear to me a muddle of potential contradictions. If one inquires, "what is the theory of democracy?" the honest answer is that at present we have none. What we do have is a medley of ideals, principles and concepts, for each of which, taken singly, a strong case can be made, but which, assembled together, cancel one another out. For example, we insist that freedom and equality are the two basic values of democracy. Fine, but what do these terms mean?

Each can be understood in one of two ways. Freedom may be defined as freedom from restraint or as freedom to act. When we use our freedom affirmatively we often affect the freedoms of others, sometimes to their disadvantage. If so, should not our freedom be restrained? And what about equality? That can be interpreted in the uniform, identical sense. Or it can be viewed as proportionate and, if so, proportionate to what? To merit? To need? To wealth? Then there is the problem of reconciling freedom and its two meanings with equality and its two. Whereas freedom is an individualistic concept, equality denotes a social relationship. When individuals exercise their freedom without restraint, inequalities always ensue. When equality is enforced, however, some liberties have to be restricted. Where, how, can the twain be harmonized?

The same holds for other doctrines to which we ascribe. We assert the requirement of majority rule, but at the same time we emphasize the rights of minorities. Where does the rule end and where do the rights begin? We talk about individual initiative and creativity, while we emphasize social responsibility and the public interest. We affirm our respect for the rule of law. Yet, when the law's content is unjust or unethical, as does happen, we admire those rare individuals who courageously disobey it on grounds of conscience. In other words, we doff our hats both to Creon and to Antigone. But, can we have it both ways? The democratic philosophy has become an amalgam of fine-sounding opposites and inconsistencies, and no one has yet sorted out its confusions. How can we be persuasive to others when our own minds are unclear?

The same question applies, *a fortiori*, when we turn the searchlight upon ourselves and ask in all honesty how closely our practices conform to our professions. How far has democracy reached when half of the citizens of voting age do not trouble to vote? How much equality is there in cities where homeless people are begging and sleeping in the streets? What kind of social justice is it when the elderly cannot walk safely in the streets at night, when millions cannot pay for medical care and do not receive it from the state, when young unemployed people become brutalized and join criminal gangs or kill other spectators at sporting contests, when hoodlums attack strangers who migrated from another part of their country or even – perish the thought! – from some foreign land, when wealthy speculators break the law in order to accumulate more wealth, when individuals fear or hate other persons whose skin is a different color or who worship a different deity or who speak some other language?

The modern democracies have come a long way when these same countries are compared with the state they were in two centuries ago. There is vastly more popular participation, there is more social justice, the sphere of basic human rights has been enlarged and procedures exist nowadays to bring wrong-doers (both public and private) to justice. What is more, the democracies have by now liquidated the empires which they, like Athens of old, had acquired. No democracy is yet perfect, but some are better than others. Relatively speaking, I would judge the best at this point in time to be the Scandinavian countries and the Netherlands, plus Australia and New Zealand. All these, you will be thinking, have much in common. Their populations are fairly small and are generally homogeneous, and their military security is principally provided by others. Quite true! Small is beautiful, in government as elsewhere in life, and a militarized society will too often sanction deviations from democracy (witness Israel). As for homogeneity, I recall the dictum of Aristotle that the *polis* should be composed as far as possible of equals and similars, and can only remark how easy government would be if that were generally the case. Unfortunately, it is not. The task of statesmanship is to discover a *modus vivendi* amid diversities. Tolerance is the supreme virtue of a democracy, and this is manifested only by those who feel secure enough to live and let live.

In the course of two thousand five hundred years, we have come a long way in the direction to which Cleisthenes pointed us, but there is still a distance to be traveled. Gandhi, when asked by a journalist what he thought of Western civilization, is said to have replied: "I think it would be a good idea." We could say the same of democracy. This too would be a good idea. The remedy for the incomplete democracies we now observe is surely to have more democracy.

A great challenge awaits the next two generations as a new millennium dawns. It is for them to complete our unfinished task. The vision is noble and inspiring. Democracy, when truly applied, is superior to all other forms of government because it most accords with the dignity and worth of every individual on Planet Earth. It is the form of government which is the truest expression of our humanity.

9

Citizenship as a Form of Psycho–Social Identity

Eli Sagan

In this paper, I would like to elaborate on the concept of citizenship as a form of psycho-social identity. Under ordinary circumstances, I entertain an abhorrence of jargonized hyphenated expressions such as "psycho-social," and for some time now I have been attempting to find a better phrase for the concept under discussion, but without success. "Psycho-social" seems to say it exactly, if unimaginatively. By "psycho" I mean to say that there is a universal human need, existing to a greater or lesser degree in all people, to establish a sense of identity. This identity, however, can be rendered only by society. This is a crucially fundamental circumstance for the nature of society, for human history and for social evolution. It is not enough to say: "I am the son of so-and-so, the brother of so-and-so, the spouse and father of so-and-so." One is also impelled to insist: "I am a member of the buffalo clan." The buffalo clan is a social phenomenon, outside the boundary of the individual psyche, and yet it is essential to the psyche's existence. It is fascinating and revealing to talk with someone who lived with the Bushmen of the Kalahari Desert when they were still hunters and gatherers, existing essentially in small groups of only 30 to 50 people, and to learn how complex was the kinship system that defined their existence, that determined their psycho-social identity. One is inclined to ask why they needed the system in such a simple society? Kinship, clearly, is not enough for human beings; the kinship system, in all its ramifications and without which there is no psycho-social identity, is an essential human need.

From the point of view of individual psychology, one may speculate on what great need the establishment of psycho-social identity satisfies. It allows the individual to get out from under, to go beyond the restricted and conflicted world of the nuclear family. It creates a new world that, in many ways, is hierarchically superior to family life. It makes it possible for the child to grow up and become an adult. Talcott Parsons has commented that if the child has to deal only with his father, or with her mother, there is no way out of certain psychological conflicts. The child can never really conceive of replacing the parent and becoming an adult itself. Such a world is one where there is only one father and one mother. The way out of this dilemma, Parsons argues, is the creation of the concept of fatherhood or motherhood, for in such a world there are many fathers and mothers and I too could become one. The world of many parents, of fatherhood and motherhood, can only be created by going beyond the nuclear family. Only within society do these generalizations exist; in the buffalo clan there are many fathers and many mothers.

Taking a leaf from Durkheim, we may say that the kinship system is the elementary form of psycho-social identity. All evolved forms of such identity represent transformed modes of kinship, and a certain primitive feeling of kinship pervades all more developed forms, whether we are talking about religious identity, nationalism, ethnic identification or citizenship. Although we may never know the true answer, we nevertheless like to speculate about what it was in ancient Greek and Roman cultures that made their conceptions of citizenship so profoundly different. The answer may lie precisely in the fundamental differences in the respective kinship-systems that these two peoples brought with them into the Mediterranean world.

Nationalism as we understand the term, which I will address at greater length later, cannot be said to have existed in the ancient world; it seems to be a modern phenomenon. But citizenship of various kinds was powerfully important, and the conflicts and tensions (and their partial resolutions) between kinship and citizenship define much of the politics of the ancient world. In 1993, we celebrated the 2500th year of the reforms of Cleisthenes. Since we do not know what exactly was the political role played by the "tribes" before those reforms, we cannot know exactly what opposition Cleisthenes had to overcome, but it seems clear that what he did was to replace kinship forms of social cohesion and psycho-social identity with forms of citizenship.

The great struggle for democracy in the ancient world may have contained an important dimension beyond that which is usually addressed, of the relative political power of the *demos* and the aristocracy. Possibly there was something in the spirit of society that significantly affected the outcome of that struggle, something connected with psycho-social identity and the forms of social cohesion. The question is often raised of how came it that, comparing the Greek

Citizenship as a Form of Psycho-Social Identity   149

polis with Rome, even though the social systems were remarkably similar, democracy was born within the Greek *polis* and never really came close to existence in Rome. One answer that is frequently given is "clientage." The *demos* in Rome was psychologically incapable of challenging the aristocracy and seizing significant political power because the system of clientage destroyed its capacity for independent action. We may, however, push the question back further: Why did the people in Rome feel the necessity of clientage and those in the Greek *polis* did not? Could it be that the Roman people were incapable, within themselves, of transforming kinship forms of psycho-social identity into citizenship and that, for them, the anxiety of leaving the kin was so great that it could only be endured by huddling under the protection of the aristocracy? The great invention and achievement of the Greek *polis* was the ideal conception, and the living reality, that when the kinship system was abandoned or transformed, citizenship – and ultimately democratic citizenship – could serve the needs of psycho-social identity and social cohesion.

Touching upon the notion of the forms of social cohesion brings us to another crucially important function that psycho-social identity serves: It holds society together. In Durkheim's phrase about religion, it unites disparate individuals "into one single moral community." What is it, after all, that unites me into one community with someone in Arizona whom I have never met? In the modern democratic world, two things serve that function: citizenship and nationalism. On the one hand, we both live under the Constitution, respect each other's rights and have the prerogative of participating in political life. On the other hand, we both celebrate the fact that we are still number one because we beat up on Grenada and wiped the shame of Vietnam off our faces in the Persian Gulf.

All of which brings us to an extraordinarily important question for any society: What is it that people are ready to die for? The answer differs profoundly from one society to another, from one stage of social development to another. Thucydides/Pericles' great funeral oration is a powerful statement of what one may call the *paideia* of dying. It seeks to educate the Athenian citizenry about what it is that is worthy of giving one's life for.

A few years ago, when we all saw on television the lone Chinese student slowly and majestically walking in front of the tank in Tienanmin Square, when we observed the huge rallies in Prague, when we became cognizant of Gorbachev risking his life to reform Soviet society, most of us, I assume, felt that if the Soviet Union were to disintegrate, most people who were willing to die for something would do so in the struggle for democracy against authoritarianism. Not so, we discovered to our amazement. Some, indeed, were willing to engage in that struggle, but most would only lay their lives on the line for Slovakia, the Ukrainian Republic or Serbia. Most funeral orations were to be given in celebration of the ethnic state and not democratic citizenship.

Despite great social diversity, one generalization seems valid, nonetheless: People are willing to die for the preservation of their psycho-social identity. Most of us were ignorant of how powerful ethnic nationalism still was in eastern Europe and how weak democratic citizenship was in the construction of that identity. We may begin to have a sense of how intimately related are the fashioning of psycho-social identity, the forms of social cohesion, and the killing of other human beings. And the role citizenship may play in this very complex relationship belongs at the very center of this rumination.

Returning to the Durkheimian concept that kinship and the kinship system are the elementary forms of psycho-social identity, it is important to try to understand what happens to this identity as it gets further and further from kinship. Nationalism and citizenship, for instance, are forms of kinship, but they are not kinship and not based on the kinship system. They are highly developed, intricately evolved, complicatedly transformed, deeply sublimated forms of kinship identity and cohesion. The problem for human society is that, as these forms separate more and more from their original kinship basis, they become increasingly attenuated, increasingly vulnerable, subject even to the possibility of collapse. More and more they become dependent upon "external," if you will, modes of support. Human society, as it develops, can get over-extended, when old forms of identity have been abandoned and new forms are not yet adequate to provide psychic stability. In the modern world we have discovered names for that disquieting state: "*anomie*," "cultural despair," "the age of anxiety."

Under these circumstances, ritual that reaffirms social identity becomes enormously important. Professor Connor's discussion of the elaborate rituals of citizenship in Athens illuminates this configuration. When he declares that one may "identify a strand of thought that implied that the *polis* should, ideally, achieve a perpetual festival-like state for its citizens," one may wonder what particular anxiety this fantasy response was intended to defend against. My reading of social and political life in Athens in the fifth and fourth centuries is that there was an underlying anxiety that citizenship would not hold, that by itself it could not provide the powerful satisfaction of social identity and cohesion that kinship and subservience to aristocracy had provided previously. Rituals of citizenship, which reaffirmed over and over again its power to make society cohere, were one answer to that anxiety. It is much more difficult to preserve a society based on the transformed-kinship of citizenship than a society based upon the kinship system itself. And that is one significant reason why democratic societies, both ancient and modern, are so vulnerable and so fragile.

At the risk of contradicting myself, possibly in the interests of a dialectical truth, it is probably more accurate to say that all systems of psycho-social identity are vulnerable and fragile, that all such systems require constant, repetitive ritual to reaffirm their effectiveness. All ritual is either an attempt to defend against anxiety or an attempt to reconcile a basic contradiction and ambivalence. And even in the very beginning of human society, we encounter rituals which reaffirm and legitimize the kinship system. It reminds me of Malinowski's great reponse to the questions of why so-called primitive peoples surrounded birth and sexuality and marriage with elaborate ritual. You want to know, Malinowski asserted, why they acted as if such occasions and practices were dangerous. The answer is, he went on, they *are* dangerous. And leaving the nuclear family, even to go no farther than the buffalo clan, is a journey fraught with danger and requires ritual protection. Yet, we have no choice but to go. Perceiving such a fundamental contradiction, we may begin to see why history has had such a tragic dimension. How many societies in all of human history have there been that we can admire with the enthusiasm with which we revere ancient Athens?

And when we come to the modern world, the problems concerning psycho-social identity and the catastrophes that have resulted from the failures to resolve these conflicts are prodigious. "Modernity," Zygmunt Bauman writes, "makes all being *contingent,* and thus a 'problem,' a 'project,' a 'task'." The forlorn attempt to restore a fractured psycho-social identity that the modern world has produced in trying to close the terrible chasm that opened up when the Enlightenment declared, in essence, that *das Volk* could no longer serve as an instrument of social cohesion, has produced social regressions that range from religious fundamentalism to fascism to genocide. Years ago, perceiving the beginnings of the modern world, Tocqueville warned us that the old form of psycho-social identity of being a subject to a divine, supposedly benevolent king would no longer hold in the future. Either democracy will prevail or else all power will be concentrated in the hands of one man, and "we will see things that our fathers never saw." The modern world leaves us with only this choice: citizenship or catastrophe. Every day the news from eastern Europe and many other parts of the world brings us the truth of this proposition.

Modernity, however, is only the latest version of the problem with psycho-social identity that has existed from its very beginning. From its origin, that rose was sick; there has always been a canker within its bloom. To illustrate what I wish to say, I need to relate a small anecdote. My wife teaches literature to high school seniors. Teaching *Crime and Punishment*, she was explaining to her class that Dostoevsky was a devout Christian and a Russian and therefore believed deeply in the redemptive power of suffering. She explained that, for Dostoevsky, Sonya, who had suffered most, becomes the most understanding, compassionate person in the novel. And yet, she went on, Svidrigailov had also suffered greatly, though he responded to his suffering by bringing evil. At which point one of her students interrupted. "Mrs. Sagan," she said, "you don't understand. There are two kinds of suffering: clean suffering and dirty suffering." And we may, with justice, describe the whole of Dostoevsky's work as seeking to make clear to us the difference between clean and dirty suffering.

And so it is with all forms of psycho-social identity. There is a clean nationalism and a dirty nationalism – and a clean citizenship and a dirty citizenship. Citizenship, the most highly developed, most morally complex form of social cohesion ever seen, has still been compatible with jingoistic warfare, imperialism, and, in the case of Athens itself, with genocide.

No one has yet been able to tell us why this has been so. In part, but only in part, the answer lies in the fact that identity and social cohesion take their power from the assertion of a great negative: We are who we are because we are not them. "Them" are those who live outside the borders of the kin, those who reside beyond the boundaries of justice. (Listen to the Athenians addressing the Melians.) In itself, this differentiation does not necessarily have to be a problem, but the human drives of destruction inevitably become part of the picture. "Them" are always legitimate objects of aggression: They can be killed without fault or guilt. I have no answer to this great question. Perhaps the conflicts, the contradictions, the anxieties that arose when we first left the immediate family for the buffalo clan still inform the politics of our most modern of worlds. That we become "us" by negating "them" is understandable, but why we are then entitled, possibly even driven, to dominate them or take their lives, this even the great Thucydides, though demonstrating it over and over again, could not really explain.

Liah Greenfeld, in her recent important book on the rise of nationalism, brilliantly demonstrates that we can only understand this phenomenon if we comprehend its clean and its dirty dimensions, though she does not use such colloquial terms. In England and in France, civic nationalism was a remarkably progressive force. In France, most particularly, one can trace the evolution of what I am calling here psycho-social identity. First, being a Christian, a devotee of an omnipotent and omniscient God; second, a subject of a semi-divine monarch; and third, a *citizen* of a partly divine nation. In the movement from

Citizenship as a Form of Psycho-Social Identity 153

monarchy to nation, both citizenship and the sovereignty of *le peuple* were born; democracy on a scale that was impossible in the *polis* became a real prospect. Without nationalism, Greenfeld argues, modernity and modern democracy would not have been possible.

For Europe that was only half the story. There were also those countries that refused to be dragged into the modern world except on their own terms. For them, nationalism became a regressive force: an ethnic, not a civic nationalism, a collectivist-authoritarian nationalism, not an individualistic-libertarian one. And ethnicity can come dangerously close to race and racism. Writing of this particular form of nationalism, Bauman asserts that nationalism became "the racism of the intellectuals, and racism – the nationalism of the masses." We can all write the tragic twentieth-century conclusion to that story.

It may prove of interest and of value to apply these general theoretical ruminations to a specific historical phenomenon, and to see what insight they might bring. I would like to talk about a time in history as far back as the eye can see, the time when human beings ceased living in tribal kinship societies and established the first states. Depending upon what estimate one takes for the length of time that the species *homo* has roamed the planet, it is accurate to say that the human species existed for a million or a million and a half years without the benefit of state institutions.

During that time, the only forms of social existence were tribal kinship societies. Before approximately 10,000 to 8,000 B.C. there were no kings, tax-collectors or standing armies anywhere in the world. The forms of social cohesion in these societies were all kinship forms. So pervasive and all-consuming is the kinship system in such societies that it is no exaggeration to say that the social system and the kinship system are equivalent. One is born, educated, initiated, married, labors productively, engages in ritual, makes war on enemies, gives birth to chidren, marries them off, dies and is buried all within the boundaries of the kinship system, all within the rules of kinship-system custom. All psycho-social identity was kinship-based.

Those kinship societies which survived into the nineteenth and twentieth centuries – Nuer, Dinka, Hopi, Kwakiutl – became the main area of study and observation by the new field of anthropology. In such societies there was no government as we understand the term: no police, no courts, no jails, no governors, no kings, no tax-collectors. They lacked schools, standing armies, an organized priesthood and any extensive division of labor. They exhibited no social classes, no stratification of society. There was no political tyranny. There was no state.

At some point, some to 10 to 12 thousand years ago, the first great social revolutions occurred. In certain places, people transformed tribal kinship societies into states ruled by authoritarian monarchs. What did those early states look like? We have only very slight archaeological evidence for the earliest of these, but we do have a remarkably huge quantity of data about certain forms of society that existed into the eighteenth and nineteenth centuries. It is a more than reasonable hypothesis that these societies were similar to the very earliest forms of the state. Let me describe a little these early states, or what I like to call Complex Societies.

When John Hanning Speke, in 1862, and Henry Morton Stanley, in 1875, entered the ancient kingdom of Buganda at the northwest corner of Lake Victoria in East Africa, each found what he had been looking for. Speke correctly conjectured, and Stanley confirmed, that Lake Victoria was the source of the Nile. What they also found there, eight hundred miles inside "darkest Africa," was an extraordinary and fascinating society that had evolved independently of more advanced cultures into a complex, sophisticated kingdom. Lacking any written language, which for us is the hallmark of civilization, Buganda had nevertheless developed an amazing variety of social and cultural institutions that we are accustomed to regard as compatible only with a culture capable of the written word. An authoritarian monarch, heading an aristocratic social structure of governors, subgovernors, sub-subgovernors and thousands of petty bureaucrats, ruled a million people. Politics was sophisticated and complex. A complete legal system, consisting of a hierarchy of courts to which one could appeal, was in place. Specialization of labor had proceeded to the extent that many people no longer worked the land but made their living as tax collectors, army officers, bards, drummers, fishermen, house builders and executioners of the thousands sent each year to their deaths as human sacrifices. This economic and political stratification went far enough to result in the creation of social classes. The contrast between this ancient kingdom and the tribal kinship societies that Stanley and Speke had passed through on their way to Buganda was palpable.

As sharply contrasted as it was to tribal society, the ancient kingdom of Buganda was not at the stage of social and political development that had been exhibited in the great Archaic Civilizations of the past: ancient Mesopotamia, ancient Egypt, the Minoan world, or the Archaic Civilizations of China and India. The kingdom of Buganda represented a crucial stage in social evolution, one that succeeded tribal kinship society and preceded Archaic Civilization. It is, in fact, a more than reasonable hypothesis that exactly such early states or Complex

Societies preceded, and then were transformed into, the great civilizations of Egypt and Mesopotamia. The creation of Archaic Civilization required the invention of certain instruments and institutions that Complex Societies lacked: writing, a benevolent as well as a terrifying conception of monarchy, an organized and bureaucratic priesthood and nurturing as well as terrible gods.

What is remarkable to discover is that half way around the globe, in the middle of the Pacific Ocean at the end of the nineteenth century, societies existed in exactly the same stage of development and exhibited the same fundamental social characteristics as the kingdom of Buganda. The great Polynesian kingdoms on Hawaii, Tahiti and Tonga – which were "discovered" and explored by Bougainville, Cook and Bligh – were, with their own inevitable individual variations, other versions of the same non-literate, authoritarian, tyrannical, centralized state form. From Africa, we also have extensive evidence from other societies at this stage of development when they were first contacted by European civilization: Benin, Dahomey, Zulu, Bunryoro, Ankole and so forth. It is fascinating to discover what the first non-tribal, non-kinship human societies looked like. The peoples themselves were some of the most attractive, from the human point of view, of any who have graced the earth. When one reads descriptions of those who lived in ancient Buganda or ancient Polynesia, images of the Italian Renaissance or fifth-century Athens come to mind in the attempt to find a people as energetic, expansive, as full of new possibilities and complexities of human existence. From Captain Cook in the Pacific to Stanley in Africa, many of the first Europeans to visit these societies were, for good reason, enchanted by the people they found there.

The peoples who inhabited these Complex Societies in the distant past invented the individualism that we prize so highly, a form that did not exist in kinship society. They created epic poetry, fairy tales, professional bards and the theater. They were the first to construct an accurate calendar, to practice medicine, navigation and astronomy. Many of the important "civilized" and "civilization" inventions that we think began in the great Archaic Civilizations of Egypt or Mesopotamia, actually had their genesis in the Complex Societies that preceded these Archaic Civilizations. Living in a remarkable culture, the people were deserving of Miranda's great cry of delight: "O, brave new world, that has such people in't!"

And yet, as exhilirating and as life-enhancing as all of this is, the tragic nature of human existence results from the fact that a radical transformation of the modes of psycho-social identity creates enormous psychic problems: a quantum leap of anxiety and a corresponding need to defend against that anxiety. A remarkable fact is that *every* early state, every Complex Society – without exception – exhibited three significant psychological and sociological forms. First, in every such society the kinship system was being transformed and destroyed to make way for state politics. Second, each of these societies practiced human sacrifice on a massive scale. We are not talking here about the illustrative stories of Abraham and Isaac or Iphigeneia in Aulis, but of thousands slaughtered every year. Third, all of these societies were ruled by a tyrannical, authoritarian monarch. There was no aristocratic, democratic, communitarian, priestly road to state formation. Only a tyrannical and charismatic king had the capacity to smash the kinship system.

In order to create a state, society must simultaneously create non-kinship forms of social cohesion. The kinship system must be partially destroyed and transformed. Though the king is clearly, from the psychological point of view, a father, loyalty to the king and fear of his power are far different things than conforming to kinship-system mores. Kinship-system forms of cohesion continue to operate in society; they exist even within our advanced society, but nobody would claim that twentieth-century societies are held together primarily by kinship. Nor were the first early states. The breakdown and transformation of the kinship system gave birth to the state, to politics as we know the term and to tyrannical kingship.

This initial breakdown and transformation of the kinship system was one of the most difficult, one of the most exhilirating and at the same time, one of the most anxiety-provoking acts that human beings have ever undertaken. The leaving of the kin – albeit to huddle under the power of an omnipotent monarch – was one of the most frightening tasks humankind set for itself. And what happens when such a social revolution takes place is that the old forms of psycho-social identity come under attack, resulting in a quantum leap of anxiety. And this anxiety has to be defended against. In early states, two institutional forms were created to contain that anxiety: tyrannical kingship and human sacrifice. Nothing in the world is more important to an individual, or to society, than the preservation of psycho-social identity. In that task, resort may even be made to some extreme, anti-human forms of defense.

Let me elaborate somewhat on the ritual of human sacrifice, since it seems to be intimately connected with the attempt to preserve psycho-social identity. When looking over the data we have, it quickly becomes apparent that human sacrifice was never performed except under circumstances that provoked particular anxiety: the death of the king, the inauguration of a new king, the erection of a new temple, going to war. It is remarkable to note that on the very day he marched into Poland, Hitler ordered the execution of inmates in insane asylums (Jews and Gentiles alike), an obvious human sacrifice to facilitate the winning of the war. And many incidents of the French Revolution can be understood better if we keep the notion of human-sacrifice-as-a-defense-against-anxiety in mind: the Great Fear, the September massacres, the Terror itself.

There was a remarkable correlation between human sacrifice and the rise of early states. With almost no exceptions, it is accurate to say that there was no human sacrifice in tribal kinship societies. It begins with the beginning of Complex Societies and comes to an orgiastic climax in the most advanced Complex Societies. We have data, for instance, for twenty or so traditional Polynesian societies. In regard to political development, they range from kinship-system societies to complex centralized states. If one ranks them in a progressive order, reflecting the degree of centralized statehood as one moves from bottom to top, human sacrifice becomes increasingly important. At the very top of this political scale, in the centralized kindgoms of Tahiti, Hawaii and Tonga, human sacrifice existed on a massive scale.

When Complex Society gives way to Archaic Civilization, when the intense anxiety of the breakdown of the kinship system is somehow handled in a more productive, more "civilized" way, human sacrifice ceases. We have evidence for it in first-dynasty Egypt and then it disappears. The same with the pre-dynastic tombs replete with sacrificed people that Wooley uncovered in Sumeria. And the exact situation existed in early China. The beginnings of Archaic Civilization continue the practice inherited from early states, but it is then discontinued. With certain few but inevitable exceptions, it is accurate to say that human sacrifice correlates with early states and with no other stage of social evolution.

By looking back to the very beginnings of history, we may learn how fragile and vulnerable is psycho-social identity, how subject human beings are to panic when it becomes destabilized, and what terrible acts they have recourse to in the attempt to preserve that indentity intact. All this may help us understand some of the catastrophes of our tragic century.

In conclusion, since the theory of social evolution is central to all my theoretical work, I would like to ruminate, in a much too cursory manner, on the possibility of setting the forms of psycho-social identity into an evolutionary sequence. Some aspects of this endeavor seem quite clear to me; others can only remain tentative and open to all kinds of argument. To begin with, it does seem that kinship and the kinship system are the elementary forms of identity. When the kinship system breaks down and is transformed, and the early state is established, an authoritarian, omnipotent, tyrannical king becomes, in almost every case (if not every case), the ruler of society. At that stage of society, for the elite (and there is now an elite), being a subject of such a monarch is the state of psycho-social identity. Archaic Civilizations (Egypt, Sumeria, Minoa) ameliorate the harshness of that kingship, but psycho-social identity remains at the stage of being a subject of the king and of the state.

At some point in the early archaic ancient world, monarchy gives way to aristocracy, a crucial social revolution because now citizenship is possible and psycho-social identity may become one with citizenship. I am not a subject, but a Spartan or an Athenian or a Roman. Citizenship is possible even where the aristocracy still rules, that is, even when there is no democratic citizenship. Most Greek *poleis* and Rome, it seems to me, demonstrate that. In a few rare and precious places, as we all know, citizenship gets transformed into democratic citizenship and a new form of psycho-social identity is established.

I wish to argue, contrary to generally accepted opinion, that in the ancient world psycho-social identity, even in a democratic *polis*, remains, in many crucial ways, tribal. There is no universality of rights or citizenship, the latter being conceived in a highly restricted, tribal manner. The direct democracy of the *ecclesia*, though admired by us as a "true" democracy, has an eerie resemblance to the tribal assembly of migrating barbaric tribes. Though we now know that the society was not so nearly a face-to-face one, as was once assumed, still the ethos of the polity, the *mentalité*, was that we are all Athenians here, that in essence we are all known to each other, that strangers have no place. Representative democracy was not only not desirable, but was psychologically impossible. Again, a kinship *Weltanschauung*. And even in warfare, Max Weber asserts that the ancient city-state was of the structured type of a war-band; the whole citizen-body was the fighting force, exactly as in kinship society.

A modern, national democracy that could embrace one hundred million people was impossible as long as such an ethos prevailed. In the western world, it was Christianity, at this critical point, which provided the evolutionary force. Leaving aside the question of the role played by the universalism of Roman citizenship, which I cannot adequately address, it was Roman Catholicism which created a universal conception of membership. One could join the Church regardless of one's ethnic situation, one's place of birth or residence, or one's political situation. Psycho-social identity could become voluntary, not inexorably given by society. And, subsequently, it was reformed Catholicism (Calvinism) that made civic virtue into a calling and sent believers out into the real world, ultimately to transform it.

As a result of this evolution in culture and society, in the sixteenth century we see

Citizenship as a Form of Psycho-Social Identity

the beginnings of nationalism, the beginnings of national citizenship, the beginnings of the sovereignty of the *demos* on a huge scale. And so, modernity brought its own highly evolved form of psycho-social identity, but one still inadequate to human needs. There remains too much dirty suffering in the world. Hopefully, history, as it has in the past, may yet bring us further transformations.

10

The Role of Cyprus in the Ancient Mediterranean and the Origins of Its Hellenization

Vassos Karageorghis

Today we can grasp the reality of our entire planet and even of other galaxies, but our remote ancestors confined themselves to the Mediterranean world, which was the hub of their economic, political and cultural life. Favorable climatic conditions encouraged sea travel from an early period all along the Mediterranean littoral, initially from the more culturally advanced East to the West. As an island, Cyprus of necessity forged contacts with the outside world more than her continental neighbors, a characteristic shared with all other Mediterranean islands which were involved with sea transport from the dawn of their history.

The first major commodity to be traded across the sea was obsidian, a volcanic glass used mainly for producing sharp cutting blades. It was imported to the Greek mainland from the island of Melos and to Cyprus from southern Anatolia by the 7th millennium B.C. With the construction of better ships, trade in other commodities, such as copper, foodstuffs and luxury goods, became easier, and a more complicated maritime network became possible. The three main navigation circuits in the Mediterranean involving Cyprus were conditioned by prevailing winds as well as by economic, political and other factors. They did not, however, start operating at the same time. The first route embraced the Aegean, the Libyan and Egyptian coasts, Cyprus and the Syro-Palestinian coast, the southern coast of Cyprus and the Dodecanese. The second circuit included Cyprus, the Aegean and the Central Mediterranean, and the third also embraced the West Mediterranean. Cyprus held an extremely advantageous geographical position for the development of external trade and its valuable deposits of copper sulphide ores provided the basis for exports and imports.

Figure 1. Clay tablet from Enkomi, *c.* 1500 B.C. Cyprus Museum, Nicosia. The script in which it is inscribed is called Cypro-Minoan; it is still undeciphered.

Of the four largest Mediterranean islands, Cyprus became most active in pursuing inter-Mediterranean connections. Easily accessible from the Levantine and southern Anatolian coasts, it soon became the stepping-stone for the westward journeys of Near Eastern seafarers and a safe outpost for Aegean seamen in their approach to the Levantine coast. The relatively small distance between Cyprus and the southern coast of Anatolia made it an obvious refuge for Anatolian visitors who introduced goods and industrial skills to the island.

Though the island's proximity to Anatolia and Western Asia was frequently the cause of its political vulnerability, occasionally with disastrous consequences, its insular character generally provided a protective shield, especially as regards cultural affairs. Cyprus developed its own culture, often influenced and enriched from outside, but to a lesser degree than other islands, such as Sicily and Sardinia, which ultimately became satellites of the nearby Italian peninsula. Crete is the only other Mediterranean island which can claim cultural independence, but only before the middle of the second millennium B.C.

Several factors kept Cyprus at the center of international relations, allowing it to play an important role in the area. In this brief survey, the foreign contacts and cultural development of Cyprus within the broader Mediterranean context will be outlined.

The first humans may have landed on Cyprus from the neighboring coasts some time before c. 8000 B.C., probably as seasonal hunters of pygmy hippopotami and pygmy elephants[1]. Steady habitation, however, occurred from c. 7500 B.C., when the first permanent Neolithic settlers arrived from southern Anatolia and the Syro-Palestinian coast.[2] Cyprus then entered the East Mediterranean cultural sphere. A period of relative isolation of some 4,000 years ensued and it was not until the mid-third millennium B.C. that real contacts were initiated with Western Asia, following the construction of larger and more seaworthy ships. Not only were foreign commodities and cultural ideas introduced, but so was the ox, which was to play such an important role in the economic, social and religious life of the Cypriots. Such changes may have been caused by the influx, probably

Figure 2. Mycenaean krater of the pictorial style from Pyla-Verghi, early 14th century B.C. It is decorated with two chariot groups on each side.

The Role of Cyprus   163

164   *Vassos Karageorghis*

from Anatolia, of a new population component which was ultimately also responsible for the introduction of metallurgical activities to the island;[3] these, however, became apparent from c. 2,000 B.C.

The systematic exploitation of the rich copper sulphide deposits initiated the emergence of a factor in the island's history which predestined its subsequent fortunes and misfortunes, since it created the interest and envy of Cyprus' neighbors. If we accept the equation Alasia=Cyprus, then by the 17th century B.C. the island had become known as a copper-producing country as far east as Mesopotamia. The island's commercial and cultural bonds with Western Asia continued, though some exchanges of goods may indicate indirect relations with the Aegean.

These relations became closer c. 1500 B.C. The Minoan Cretans travelled by sea to the East Mediterranean quite early and trade with the cosmopolitan town of Ugarit on the Syrian coast opposite Cyprus is well attested. By c. 1500 B.C., the Cypriots had adopted a system of writing which was borrowed from Crete. It is possible that the Cretans had begun to show an interest in the island's copper, but this has not yet been fully documented by archaeological evidence.[4]

The expulsion of the Hyksos from Egypt c. 1555 B.C. and the establishment of peaceful conditions in the East Mediterranean encouraged trade and interconnections. The Cypriots took full advantage of this new situation to develop commercial relations with their neighbors. Written documents from Egypt, namely the tablets of Tell el Amarna, describe the exchange of royal gifts and tributes which preceded real trade.[5] The growth of the island's economy brought about the establishment of urban centers, especially along the eastern and southern coasts. When the Mycenaeans succeeded the Minoans as the dominant power in the Aegean, Cyprus was one of the first places to which they were attracted in their eastward expansion. They became frequent visitors to the island's harbor towns where they brought prosperity by exchanging their goods for Cypriot copper. Recently discovered cargo vessels bear eloquent witness to such Aegean-Cypriot commercial dealings.[6] At the same time the Mycenaeans gradually introduced Aegean artistic styles, as well as enriching their own repertory. During the 14th and 13th centuries B.C., the island attained the apogee of its economic and cultural development and acquired a cosmopolitan character through contacts with the East and West.[7]

There is substantial evidence for the export of considerable quantities of copper to the Aegean and also as far west as the central Mediterranean area. It was, perhaps, Cypriot copper that enhanced relations between the Aegean and the central Mediterranean. In recent years, several sites in southern Italy, Sicily and

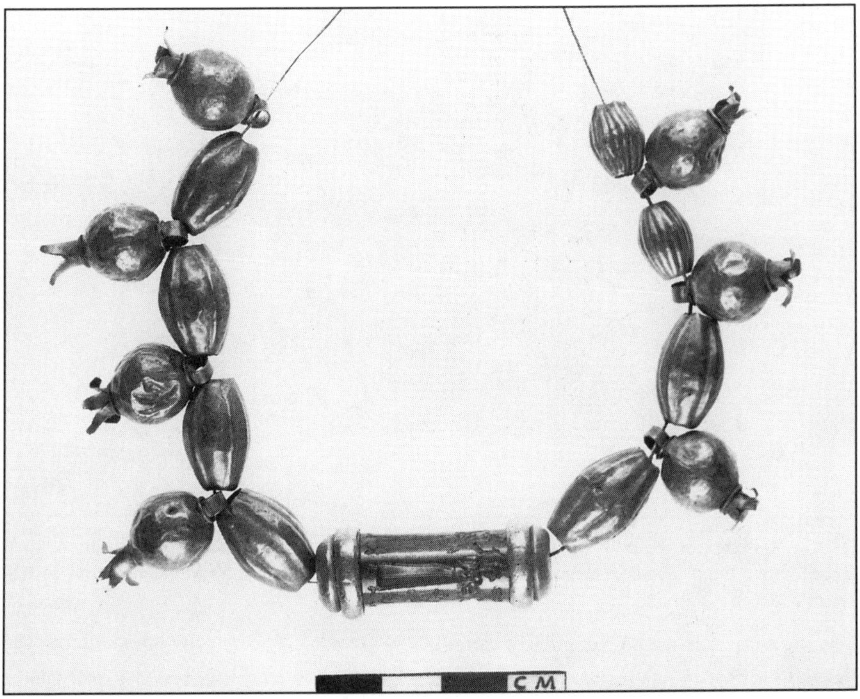

The Role of Cyprus

Figure 3. Necklace from Ayios Iakovos, 14th century B.C. It consists of beads in the form of pomegranates and dates and has a pendant in the form of a Babylonian seal.

Sardinia have yielded Mycenaean material, always in association with Cypriot objects. Whether this new trade circuit was in the hands of Mycenaeans or whether Cypriots were also involved is not easy to determine, but the imitation of Cypriot pottery shapes in Sicily during the 13th century B.C. speaks in favor of a Cypriot presence there.[8]

The bonds of familiarity and collaboration which were forged between the Cypriots and the Mycenaeans as a result of trade prepared the ground for the second stage in this relationship, when Mycenaeans settled on the island following the collapse of the Mycenaean "empire" c. 1200 B.C. A long and complicated process of relations ensued, culminating in the Hellenization of Cyprus, a phenomenon which became apparent in the 11th century B.C.[9]

In a discussion published recently on the political and cultural changes which characterized Cyprus in the 11th century B.C. we read of the "growth and enhancement of a conscious sense of ethnic identity among certain groups on Cyprus," i.e. the Greek element among the population of the island, which

Figure 4. Copper ingot in the form of an ox-hide, weighing 86 pounds, six ounces. Such ingots have been found in large numbers in recently excavated shipwrecks near the south-west coast of Anatolia.

resulted in "an archaeologically detectable Greek-Cypriot ethnogenesis on the island."[10] For the first time in the island's history, we may discern the embryo of some of the elements which constituted Greekness, according to Thucydides, that is common blood, language and religion. Such phenomena do not occur overnight. In the case of Cyprus, the process lasted about one hundred years.

The complex character of this "ethnogenesis" cannot be discussed in detail within the limits of this short paper, but it is important to underline the fact that, for the first time in history, a Greek outpost was established in the east Mediterranean, 800 kilometers from Athens, which is paradoxical. The reasons may be found in the interest of the Mycenaeans in Cypriot copper, in the favorable conditions for interrelations in the East Mediterranean and in the strategic position of Cyprus.

Other areas in the east Mediterranean, namely Syria and Palestine, also received Mycenaean refugees c. 1200 B.C. and might have experienced events similar to those in Cyprus, but the intensity and time span of the process was not so pronounced and the Greek elements were soon absorbed and had vanished by the 11th century B.C.[11]

The establishment of a Greek outpost in the east Mediterranean had far-reaching consequences, not only for the political and cultural development of Cyprus

Figure 5. Skyphos from Sinda imitating the style of Mycenaean ceramics on the Greek mainland of the early 12th century B.C. Made in Cyprus from local clay.

but also for the whole of the east Mediterranean and the Aegean. The island became the point where two great cultures of the Old World, those of the Aegean and the Near East, met and intermingled. Once the seed was sown, it was not easy to eradicate, as is evident from the subsequent political and cultural history of the island. It is also clear from the study of Greek culture, which was freed from relative isolation and broadened its horizons as a result of contacts with the wisdom and exuberance of the East.

When the Phoenicians began their westward expansion from the Levantine coast at the end of the 9th century B.C., their primary landfall was Cyprus, where they established their first outpost. Though initially commercial, it nevertheless affected the political and cultural life of the island. If Phoenician art does exist, then it is better known in Cyprus than anywhere else in the Phoenician world.[12] Eastern and western artistic styles met and influenced one another, creating new fashions which in turn brought about the emergence in the Aegean of one of the most robust aspects of Greek art, the so-called "Orientalizing" style.

Cyprus continued to exploit the copper resources which were doubtless of inter-

Figure 6. The promontory of Maa-Palaeokastro, on the west coast of Cyprus (north of Paphos), where some of the Aegean immigrants established a military outpost c. 1200 B.C.

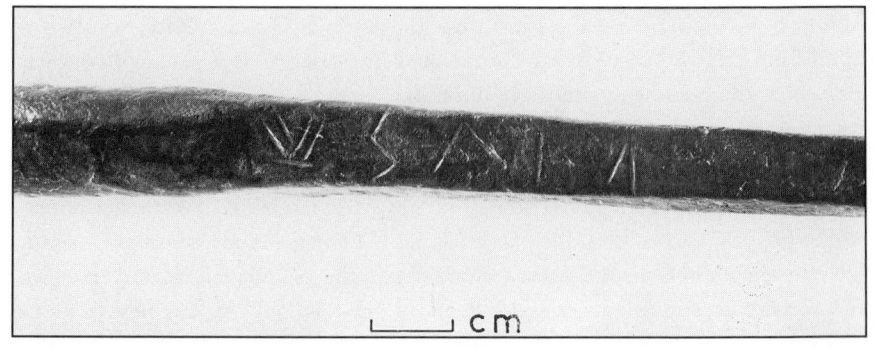

Figure 7. Inscription in the Cypriot syllabary engraved on a bronze *obelos* found in an 11th century B.C. Palaepaphos. It mentions a Greek proper name. This is the earliest evidence so far for the use of the Greek language in Cyprus.

Figure 8. Limestone head of a youth, imitating the styles of late Archaic Greek sculpture. From Salamis, c. 500 B.C. Famagusta District Museum.

est to the commercially minded Phoenicians. The information given by Eusebius that the island was one of the *"thalassocracies"* of the 8th century B.C. may be an exaggeration, but it is archaeologically suggested that both Cypriots and Phoenicians found their way as far west as the Atlantic coast of Spain,[13] probably exchanging Cypriot copper for silver, following the same trade circuit as the Mycenaeans and Cypriots some 600 years earlier. Once again, Cyprus became a bridge for East-West interconnections. In the 8th century B.C., the Greeks of Euboea started founding colonies on the southern coast of Asia Minor and on the Levantine coast. Cypriots may have been directly involved, to judge from the abundance of Cypriot material found at towns like Tarsus in Cilicia and Posideion in Syria. During the same period, direct commercial and other relations between Cyprus and the Aegean were renewed, especially after the establishment of the Greek colony at Naucratis in Egypt.[14]

Cyprus has been identified here as a bridge for interconnections in the Mediterranean, but unfortunately for the Cypriots it was also an easy prey for all those Eastern empires which aimed to dominate the east Mediterranean and beyond: the Assyrians, the Egyptians and the Persians. The latter dominated

Figure 9. Mosaic pavement of the third century A.D. depicting the myth of Theseus, Ariadne and the Minotaur. The names of the various persons are shown in Greek capital letters. From the "Villa of Theseus," Paphos.

Cyprus for over two centuries when the Cypriots shared a fate similar to that of the Ionian Greeks, who also suffered under the Persians. This is an interesting period for the student of Greek-Cypriot relations. Common struggles against a common enemy strengthened the Greek consciousness of the Cypriots and in turn the Greeks realized that they had a responsibility for the political fate of Cyprus. Even if the speech of the Greek general before the battle of Salamis at the beginning of the Ionian revolt is a Herodotean invention, one cannot fail to be moved by his declaration of a common ethnic identity which urged an overall effort for freedom.

The Persians, like other imperial powers two and a half thousand years later, discovered the great weakness of the Greeks and exercised a "divide and rule" policy. They sowed political discord among the Cypriot kingdoms the same way they did among the Greeks of Greece proper, and Greek freedom as envisaged by the Ionian general never materialized. During this period, Cyprus produced one of the greatest political leaders of the Greek world, Evagoras, king of Salamis, whose political vision was the unification of all the Hellenes against the Persians under the leadership of the Athenians. This goal was to remain an unfulfilled dream.[15]

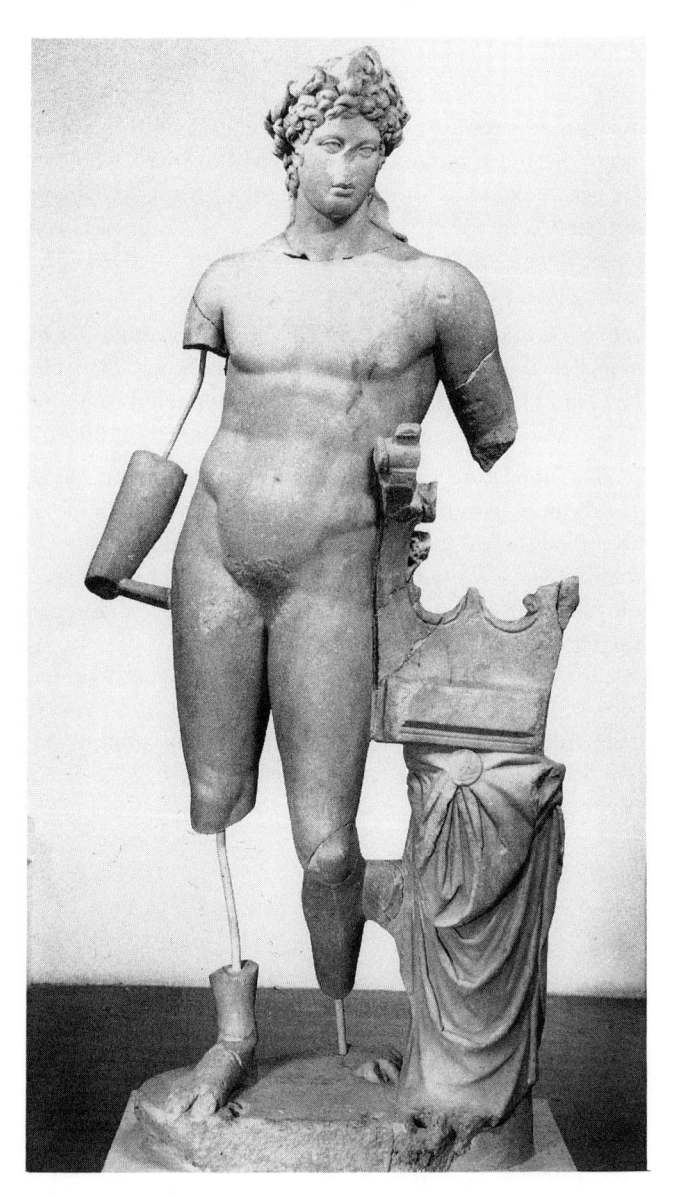

10. Over life-size marble statue of Apollo the Lyre-Player, from the Gymnasium of Salamis, second century A.D.

With Alexander the Great and his successors, Cyprus became a center for the development of Hellenistic culture in all its aspects and of Greek political institutions. Unlike the rest of the Hellenistic empire, where this culture was shared by the Greek settlers, in Cyprus it was adopted by the entire Greek population. The fact that the island belonged to the kingdom of the Ptolemies, whose cultural and political center was Alexandria, meant that many elements of Egyptian art and religion penetrated Cyprus, enriching the original culture. The first public schools offering Greek education were established on the island, thereby strengthening the island's Greek traditions.

When the Romans occupied Cyprus, the Greek cultural tradition had already grown so strong that they imposed little of their own other than their political authority. The island's language and culture were not altered. With the advent of Christianity, Cyprus again shared the experiences of the rest of the Greek world.

This short sketch of the island's political and cultural evolution has covered the period from the dawn of its appearance in the Mediterranean arena to the end of antiquity. This period shaped the ethnic and cultural identity of the Cypriots and predestined their future down to the present day. This evolution may seem paradoxical without some familiarity with the historical background against which it occurred. Having been for some six thousand years within the orbit of the Orient, at the end of the second millennium B.C. the island became part of the Hellenic world. This, in a nutshell, is the background of Cypriot Hellenism, which may help us to understand all its peculiarities as well as its vigor and resilient powers.

The Role of Cyprus

NOTES

[1] A.H. Simmons, "Humans, Island Colonization and Pleistocene Extinctions in the Mediterranean: The View from Akrotiri *Aetokremnos*, Cyprus". *Antiquity* 65 (1991), 857-869.

[2] For a recent general survey, see I.A. Todd, "Early Prehistoric Society: A View from the Vasilikos Valley," in E. Peltenburg, *Early Society in Cyprus* (Edinburgh, 1989), 2-13.

[3] Cf. E. Peltenburg, "Kissonerga-Mosphilia: A Major Chalcolithic Site in Cyprus," in *Chalcolithic Cyprus* (J. Paul Getty Symposium, 1991) 17-35; M. J. Mellink, "Anatolian Contacts with Chalcolithic Cyprus," *ibid.* 167-175.

[4] For a general account and references on the relations between Cyprus and Crete in the Late Bronze Age, see G. Cadogan, "Cyprus and Crete *c*. 2000-500 B.C." (Nicosia, 1979), 63-68; V. Karageorghis, *Cyprus, from the Stone Age to the Romans* (London, 1982), 61-67; for recent evidence, see L.V. Watrous, (Edit.), *Kommos III. The Late Bronze Age Pottery* (Princeton N.J. 1992), 172, 174.

[5] Cf. E. Peltenburg, "Greeting Gifts and Luxury Faience: A Context for Orientalizing Trends in Late Mycenaean Greece," in N. H. Gale (Edit.), *Bronze Age Trade in the Mediterranean* (*SIMA* XL, Göteborg 1991), 163-179; for recent evidence confirming the exchange of goods as described in the Tell el Amarna tablets see G. F. Bass, "A Bronze Age Shipwreck at Ulu Burun (Kas): 1984 Campaign," *American Journal of Archaeology* 90 (1986), 269-296; Cenal Pulak *et. al.*, "The Shipwreck at Ulu Burun, Turkey: 1992 Excavation Campaign," *The INA Quarterly*, 19 (1992), 11, 21.

[6] See note 5 above. To these one may add the evidence from an as yet unexcavated shipwreck found in the Gulf of the Argolid; several large storage jars *(pithoi)* and other Cypriot vessels have been collected from the surface of the wreck.

[7] For a general survey of the Late Bronze Age in Cyprus during the 14th and 13th centuries B.C., see V. Karageorghis, *op.cit.*, 61-86.

[8] R. R. Holloway, *Italy and the Aegean, 3000-700 B.C.* (Louvain-la-Neuve and Providence, Rhode Island, 1981), 83-87; L. Vagnetti and F. Lo Schiavo, "Late Bronze Age Long-Distance Trade in the Mediterranean: The Role of Cyprus," in E. Peltenburg (edit.), *Early Society in Cyprus*, 217-243.

[9] For a concise examination of the 12th and 11th centuries in Cyprus, the Aegean and the Levant, see V. Karageorghis, *The End of the Late Bronze Age in Cyprus* (Nicosia, 1990); idem. (edit.) *Proceedings of an International Symposium, "The Civilizations of the Aegean and their Diffusion in Cyprus and the Eastern Mediterranean, 2000-600 B.C.*, (Nicosia, 1991).

[10] E. S. Sherratt, "Immigration and Archaeology: Some Indirect Reflections," in *Acta Cypria. Acts of an International Congress on Cypriot Archaeology Held in Göteborg on 22-24 August 1991*, Part 2, Edit. P. Aström, (Jonsered, 1992), 338.

[11] See note 9, above.

[12] For the role of the Phoenicians in Cyprus and a general bibliography, see Karageorghis, *Cyprus, from the Stone Age to the Romans*, 123-127; idem. "Cyprus," in *The Phoenicians*, S. Moscati (edit.) (Milano, 1988), 152-165.

[13] J. P. Garrido Roiz and E.M. Orta Garciá, *Excavaciones en la Necropolis de "La Joya" Huelva* (Madrid, n.d.).

[14] For a survey of this period, see J. Boardman, *The Greeks Overseas* (new edit. London, 1980).

[15] A detailed account of this period appeared recently, by P. J. Stylianou, "The Age of the Kingdoms. A Political History of Cyprus in the Archaic and Classical Periods," in Μελέται και Υπομνήματα II. (Κέντρο Επιστημονικών Ερευνών, Λευκωσία 1989), 375-530.

List of illustrations

(Unless otherwise noted, all photos supplied by the Cyprus Museum, Nicosia)

1. Clay tablet from Enkomi, c. 1500 B.C. Cyprus Museum, Nicosia. The script in which it is inscribed is called Cypro-Minoan; it is still undeciphered.

2. Mycenaean krater of the pictorial style from Pyla-Verghi, early 14th century B.C. It is decorated with two chariot groups on each side.

3. Necklace from Ayios Iakovos, 14th century B.C. It consists of beads in the form of pomegranates and dates and has a pendant in the form of a Babylonian seal.

4. Copper ingot in the form of an ox-hide, weighing 86 pounds, six ounces. Such ingots have been found in large numbers in recently excavated shipwrecks near the southwest coast of Anatolia.

5. Skyphos from Sinda imitating the style of Mycenaean ceramics on the Greek mainland of the early 12th century B.C. Made in Cyprus from local clay.

6. The promontory of Maa-Palaeokastro, on the west coast of Cyprus (north of Paphos), where some of the Aegean immigrants established a military outpost c. 1200 B.C.

7. Inscription in the Cypriot syllabary engraved on a bronze *obelos* found in an 11th century B.C. Palaepaphos. It mentions a Greek proper name. This is the earliest evidence so far for the use of the Greek language in Cyprus.

8. Limestone head of a youth, imitating the styles of late Archaic Greek sculpture. From Salamis, c. 500 B.C. Famagusta District Museum.

9. Mosaic pavement of the third century A.D. depicting the myth of Theseus, Ariadne and the Minotaur. The names of the various persons are shown in Greek capital letters. From the "Villa of Theseus," Paphos.

10. Over life-size marble statue of Apollo the Lyre-Player, from the Gymnasium of Salamis, second century A.D.

Appendices

Appendix A
Constitutional Development of Athens: Key Terms and Dates

Archon:	Highest official, literally "ruler," successor to the kings at Athens.
Basileus:	King, later title of one of the three principal Archons of Athens.
Oligarchy:	The rule of a few wealthy property owners.
Aristocracy:	System of government where power was concentrated in the hands of a small group of ruling nobles.
Tyrant:	Autocrat who usurped power, often from an aristocracy and sometimes with the backing of a broader section of the citizen body.
683/2 B.C.:	Traditional date for the first annual Archons at Athens.
620:	First written Athenian lawcode attributed to Draco.
594/3:	Solon's reforms at Athens: debts cancelled, debt bondage outlawed, officials to be elected on basis of landed wealth, not noble birth. Citizens without property allowed to elect officials, attend Assembly and (perhaps) sit as court of appeal. Solon's laws assert principle that the law should be above the individual or group of individuals.
546/28:	Tyranny of Pisistratus in Athens.
514:	Harmodius and Aristogiton attempt to end tyranny of

Appendices

	Pisistratus' sons, Hippias and Hipparchus; the latter is assassinated.
510:	Hippias expelled from Athens.
508/7:	Cleisthenes' democratic reforms: a Boule or Council of 500 chosen annually by the citizen body was set up, to act as a steering committee for the Assembly. Citizenship now based on residence, through inscription on register of a local deme (village, ward).
462/1:	Ephialtes' reforms, with the assistance of Pericles, limit power of the Areopagus or Council of ex-Archons, consolidate extension of administrative and judicial power to Council of 500, and establish new People's Court chosen by lot.
429:	Death of Pericles.
411-10:	*Coup d'etat* in Athens abolishes most of the democratic constitution; rule of the Four Hundred; eventual restoration of constitution.
404:	Spartans install tyranny of The Thirty in Athens.
403-400:	Democracy restored; revised lawcode drawn up and published on stone; Periclean citizenship law re-enacted.
399:	Trial and execution of Socrates.
384:	Birth of Demosthenes and Aristotle; founding of Plato's Academy.
338:	Defeat of Athens at Chaeronea gives Philip II of Macedon control of all Greece.
336:	Accession of Alexander the Great of Macedon.
323:	Death of Alexander.
322:	Defeat of Athenian rebellion against Macedon. Death of Demosthenes and Aristotle. Macedon terminates Athenian democracy. *

* Hansen, M., "Kleisthenes and the Icons of Democracy", *History Today*, Volume 44(1), (January 1994) 15.

Appendix B
Pericles, "Funeral Oration"
Thucydides (460-400 B.C.)

Pericles . . . was chosen to give the funeral oration for the first who had fallen. When the proper time arrived, he advanced from the tomb . . . and spoke as follows:

"I shall begin with our ancestors . . . . They dwelt in this country without interruption from generation to generation, and handed it down to the present time by their bravery . . . .

"Our constitution does not copy the laws of neighboring states; we are rather a model for others than imitators ourselves. Its administration favors the many instead of the few; this is why it is called a democracy. If we look at the laws, they afford equal justice to all in settling private differences. As for prestige, advancement in public life goes to men with reputations for ability: class considerations are not allowed to interfere with merit, nor again does poverty bar the way. If a man is able to serve the state, he is not hindered by obscure origins or poverty. The freedom we enjoy in our government extends also to our private life. There... we do not feel called upon to be angry with our neighbor for doing what he likes, or even to indulge in those injurious looks which cannot fail to be offensive, although they inflict no actual harm. But all this ease in our private relations does not make us lawless as citizens . . . . We obey the magistrates and the laws, particularly those for the protection of the injured whether they are actually on the statute book, or belong to that code which, although unwritten, yet cannot be broken without acknowledged disgrace.

"Further, we provide plenty of means for the mind to refresh itself from business. We celebrate games and sacrifices all the year round and the elegance of our private establishments forms a daily source of pleasure and helps to banish our cares. Then, too, the magnitude of our city draws the produce of the world into our harbor, so that to the Athenian the products of other countries are as familiar a luxury as those of his own.

"If we turn to our military policy, there also we differ from our antagonists. We throw open our city to the world, and never pass laws to exclude foreigners from any opportunity of learning or observing, although the eyes of the enemy may occasionally profit from our liberality. We rely less on secrecy than on the native spirit of our citizens. In education, where our rivals from their very cradles seek after manliness through a very painful discipline, at Athens we live as we please, and yet are just as ready to encounter every legitimate danger . . . . And yet if with habits not of labor but of ease, and with courage which is not artificial but real, we are still willing to encounter danger, we have the double advantage of escaping the experience of hardships in anticipation and of facing them in the hour of need as fearlessly as those who are never free from them.

"We cultivate refinement without extravagance and knowledge without effeminacy; wealth we employ more for use than for show, and place the real disgrace of poverty not in admitting the fact of it but in declining the struggle against it. Our public men have, besides politics, their private affairs to tend to, and ordinary citizens, though occupied with the pursuits of industry, are still fair judges of public matters. Unlike any other nation, we regard a man who takes no part in these duties not as unambitious but as useless . . . . Instead of looking on discussion as a stumbling block in the way of action, we Athenians consider it an indispensable preliminary to any wise action at all.

"In generosity we are equally singular, acquiring our friends by conferring, not receiving, favors. Yet, of course, the doer of the favor is the firmer friend of the two, in order by continued kindness to keep the recipient in his debt; while the debtor feels less keenly from the very consciousness that the return he makes will be a repayment, not a free gift, and it is only the Athenians who, fearless of consequences, confer their benefits not from calculations of expediency, but in the confidence of liberality.

"In short, I say that as a city we are the school of Hellas; while I doubt if the world can produce a man who is equal to so many emergencies where he has only himself to depend upon, and who is graced by so happy a versatility as the Athenian.... For Athens alone of her contemporaries is found, when tested, to be greater than her reputation and alone gives no occasion to her assailants to blush at the antagonist by whom they have been worsted, or to her subjects to question her title by merit to rule. Rather, the admiration of the present and succeeding ages will be ours, since we have not left our power without witness, but have shown it by mighty proofs; and far from needing a Homer for our panegyrist, or another poet whose verses might charm for the moment only for the impression which they gave, to melt at the touch of fact, we have forced every sea and land to be the highway of our daring, and everywhere, whether for evil or for good, have left imperishable monuments behind us. Such is the Athens for which these men, in the assertion of their resolve not to lose her, nobly fought and died; and well may every one of their survivors be ready to suffer in her cause.

"If I have dwelt at some length upon the character of our country, it has been to show that our stake in the struggle is not the same as theirs who have no such blessings to lose, and also that the praise of the men over whom I am now speaking might be confirmed by definite proofs. My speech is now largely complete; for the Athens that I have celebrated is only what the heroism of these and others like them have made her, men whose fame, unlike that of most Hellenes, will be found to be only proportionate to what they deserve. And if a test of worth be wanted, it is to be found in their last scene, and this not only in the cases in which it set the final seal upon their merit, but also in those in which it gave the first intimation of their having any. For there is justice in the claim that steadfastness in his country's battles should be as a cloak to cover a man's other imperfections, since the good more than outweighed his demerits as an individual . . And while committing to hope the uncertainty of final success, in the business before them they thought fit to act boldly and trust in themselves. Thus choosing to die resisting, rather than to live submitting.

"So died these men as became Athenians. You, their survivors, must be determined to have as unfaltering a resolution in the field, though you may pray that it may have a happier outcome . . . . You must yourselves realize the power of Athens, and feed your eyes upon her from day to day, till the love of her fills your hearts; and then when all her greatness shall break upon you, you must reflect that it was by courage, sense of duty, and a keen feeling of honor in action that men were enabled to win all this, and that no personal failure in an enterprise could make them consent to deprive their country of their bravery except as a sacrifice of the most serious contribution they could offer. For this offering of their lives made in common by them all, each of them individually receives that renown which never grows old, and for a tomb, not so much that in which their bones have been deposited, but that noblest of shrines wherein their glory is laid up to be eternally remembered upon every occasion on which deed or story shall call for its commemoration . . . . Take these as your model, and recognize that happiness comes from freedom and freedom comes from courage; never decline the dangers of war. For it is not the miserable who have the most reason to risk their lives; they have nothing to hope for: instead, it is they to whom continued life may bring reverses as yet unknown, and to whom a fall, if it came, would be most tremendous in its consequences. Surely, to a man of spirit, the degradation of cowardice must be immeasurably more grievous than the unfelt death which strikes him in the midst of his strength and patriotism.

"Comfort, therefore, not condolence, is what I have to offer to the parents of the dead who may be here. Numberless are the chances to which, as they know, the life of man is subject; but fortunate indeed are they who draw their lot a death so glorious as that which has caused your mourning, and to whom life has been so exactly measured as to terminate in the happiness in which it has been passed . . . My task is now finished. I have performed it to the best of my ability, and in words at least the requirements of the law are now satisfied. If deeds be in question, those who are here interred have received part of their honors already, and for the rest, their children will be brought up till manhood at the public expense: thus the state offers a valuable prize as the garland of victory in this race of valor, for the reward both of those who have fallen and their survivors. And where the rewards for merit are greatest, there the best citizens are found.

"And now that you have brought to a close your lamentations for your relatives, you may depart."

[From Thucydides, *Peloponnesian War*, trans. Richard Crawley (London: J. M. Dent & Co., 1903), Vol. I, pp. 120-28, Vol. II, pp. 59-67; language modernized.]

Appendix Γ
Politics VI, ii
Aristotle (384- 322 B.C.)

... A basic principle of the democratic constitution is liberty. People constantly make this statement, implying that only in this constitution do men share in liberty; for every democracy, they say, has liberty for its aim "Ruling and being ruled in turn" is one element in liberty, and the democratic idea of justice is in fact numerical equality, not equality based on merit; and when this idea of what is just prevails, the multitude must be sovereign, and whatever the majority decides is final and constitutes justice. For, they say, there must be equality for each of the citizens. The result is that in democracies the poor have more sovereign power than the rich; for they are more numerous, and the decisions of the majority are sovereign. So this is one mark of liberty, one which all democrats make a definitive principle of their constitution. Another is to live as you like. For this, they say, is a function of being free, since its opposite, living not as you like, is the function of one enslaved. This is the second defining principle of democracy, and from it has come the ideal of "not being ruled", not by anyone at all if possible, or at least only in alternation. This is a contribution towards that liberty which is based on equality ...

Appendix Δ
Law for the Protection of Democracy (337-336 B.C.)

In the archonship of Phrynichus, in the ninth *prytany* of Leontis for which Chairestratos, son of Ameinias, of Acharnai, was secretary; Menestratos of Aixone, of the *proedroi*, put the question to a vote.

Eukrates, son of Aristotimos, of Peiraieus, made the motion: with Good Fortune of the *Demos* of the Athenians, be it resolved by the *Nomothetai*: If anyone rise up against the *Demos* for tyranny or join in establishing the tyranny or overthrow the *Demos* of the Athenians or the democracy in Athens, whoever kills him who does any of these things shall be blameless. It shall not be permitted for anyone of the Councillors of the Council from the Areopagus – if the *Demos* or the democracy in Athens has been overthrown – to go up into the Areopagus or sit in the Council or deliberate about anything. If anyone – the *Demos* or the democracy in Athens overthrown – of the Councillors of the Areopagus goes up into the Areopagus or sits in the Council or deliberates about anything, both he and his progeny shall be deprived of civil rights and his substance shall be confiscated and a tenth given to the Goddess. The secretary of the Council shall inscribe this law on two *stelai* of stone and set one of them by the entrance into the Areopagus, that entrance, namely, near where one goes into the Bouleuterion, and the other in the Ekklesia.

For the inscribing of the *stelai* the treasurer of the *Demos* shall give 20 *drachmai* from the moneys expendable by the *Demos* according to decrees.

The Contributors to this Volume

John Boardman was educated at Chigwell School and Magdalene College, Cambridge where he received a B.A. degree in 1948 and M.A. in 1951. He has been Lincoln Professor of Classical Archaeology and Art, and Fellow of Lincoln College, University of Oxford, since 1978. He was Reader in Classical Archaeology, University of Oxford, 1959-78, and Fellow of Merton College, Oxford, 1963-78. He has been Professor of Ancient History, Royal Academy, since 1989. Member of the British Academy since 1969, he was knighted in 1989. From 1958 to 1965, he served as editor of the Journal of Hellenic Studies. His many publications include *The Cretan Collection in Oxford, Greek Art, Excavations at Toora, Archaic Greek Gems, Greek Burial Customs, The Parthenon and Its Sculptures, The Oxford History of the Classical World,* and *Athenian Red Figure Vases, Classical Period.*

Robert Browning, Professor Emeritus of Classics, Birkbeck College, University of London, was educated at the Kelvinside Academy, Glasgow, Glasgow University, and Balliol College, Oxford. From 1939-46 he served in the army in the Middle East, Italy and the Balkans. He is a member of the British Academy and Corresponding Member of the Academy of Athens. His numerous publications include, *Medieval and Modern Greek, Justinian and Theodora, Byzantium and Bulgaria, The Byzantine Empire, The Emperor Julian, The Greek World: Classical Byzantine and Modern,* and *History, Language and Literacy in the Byzantine World.*

Robin James Lane Fox was educated at Eton and Magdalen College, Oxford. He is a Fellow of New College and University Reader and Tutor in Ancient History. His publications include, *Search for Alexander, Pagans and Christians, Alexander the Great,* and *Better Gardening.* He is weekly gardening correspondent for the *Financial Times.*

David Hunt was educated at St. Lawrence College, and Wadham College, Oxford, where he studied Classics. He was a Fellow of Magdalen College, Oxford, and an archaeologist before 1939. After, he was Private Secretary to Attlee and Churchill as Prime Ministers and subsequently High Commissioner in Uganda, Cyprus and Nigeria and Ambassador to Brazil. He was President of the Society for the Promotion of Hellenic Studies (1986-1990). His many honors and decorations include the Bronze Star of the United States and the Grand Cross, Order of the Southern Cross, Brazil. His publications include, *A Don at War, On the Spot, Footprints in Cyprus, Gothic Art and the Renaissance in Cyprus* (Edited with Iro Hunt), and *Caterina Cornaro: Oueen of Cyprus*. Sir David writes as well for several scholarly journals.

Vassos Karageorghis was educated at the Pancyprian Gymnasium, Nicosia, and at the University College, London where he obtained his PhD degree in 1957. His knowledge of practical archaeology was acquired at the University of London under Sir Mortimer Wheeler. He is the leading authority on the art and archaeology of Cyprus. From 1963 until recently he served as the Director of the Department of Antiquities of Cyprus. He is a member of the Royal Swedish Academy, Corresponding Fellow of the Academy of Athens, as well as the British Academy, and honorary member of the Society for the Promotion of Hellenic Studies. He is recipient of the Chevalier de la Légion d'Honneur (France) and the Order of Merit First Class, Federal Republic of Germany. He is the author of more than 20 books and publications on the archaeology of Cyprus, including, *The Civilization of Prehistoric Cyprus, Excavations in the Necropolis of Salamis I-IV, Excavations at Kition: The Tombs, Ancient Cyprus: 7000 Years of Art and Archaeology,* and *Cyprus from the Stone Age to the Romans*.

Anthony Kenny was educated at the Gregorian University in Rome and at St. Bent's Hall, Oxford where he obtained a D.Phil. in 1961. Formerly Master of Balliol College, he is Warden of Rhodes House, Oxford and Secretary of the Rhodes Trust. Sir Anthony was President of the British Academy. His numerous publications include, *Anatomy of the Soul, Will Freedom and Power, The Aristotelian Ethics, Freewill and Responsibility, Faith and Reason, Reason and Religion, The Heritage of Wisdom, The Metaphysics of Mind* and *What Is Faith?*. His latest publication is *Mountains: An Anthology*.

John A. Koumoulides was educated in the United States at Montclair State College and the University of Maryland and at Fitzwilliam College, University of Cambridge, in England. He is Professor of History at Ball State University in Muncie, Indiana. He is honorary member of the Society for the Promotion of

The Contributors

Hellenic Studies, and Corresponding Member of the Academy of Athens. He has written and edited numerous books on Greece and Cyprus, his latest being the *History and Treasures of the Monastery of Tatarna* (jointly with Mr. Lazaros Deriziotis and Mrs. Roula Sdrolia).

Leslie Lipson was educated in the United Kingdom and the United States. He came to the United States as a Commonwealth Fund Fellow from Balliol College, Oxford University, where he was a senior scholar, and took his doctorate in political science at the University of Chicago. He taught for 33 years at the University of California, Berkeley, as Professor of Political Science. His publications include *The Great Issues of Politics, The Democratic Civilization* and others. He is the author of *The Ethical Crises of Civilization: Moral Meltdown of Advance?* published in 1993.

Oswyn Murray, Balliol College, Oxford, has written and edited numerous books on Greece, his latest being, *The Greek City from Homer to Alexander, Early Greece,* and *Latin Poetry and Classical Traditions: Essays in Medieval and Renaissance Literature* (with Peter Godman, Editors).

Andrew Colin Renfrew, Baron Renfrew of Kaimsthorn, was educated at St. Albans School and at St. John's College, Cambridge, where he received his B.A. degree First Class Honors in Archaeology, and is Disney Professor of Archaeology, University of Cambridge, and Master of Jesus College, Cambridge. He is a Fellow of the British Academy. His many publications include, *The Emergence of Civilization, Before Civilization, Problems in European Prehistory, The Archaeology of Cult, Archaeology and Language,* and *The Cycladic Spirit.* He is a member of the House of Lords.

Eli Sagan is on the graduate faculty of the New School for Social Research in New York. His publications include, *At the Dawn of Tyranny: The Origins of Individualism, Political Oppression and the State,* and *The Honey and the Hemlock: Democracy and Paranoia in Ancient Athens and Modern America.*

Index

Africa, civilizations in, 154
Agamemnon, 22
Aghia Irini temple, 16-7
Agora, 81
Akrotiri on Thera, 17
Alcibiades, 34, 63
Alcmaeonidae family, 1
Alexander the Great, 46
Aliens, in early democracy, 2
Altar of the Twleve Gods, 81
Ameinias of Acharnai, 182
American Revolution, 69, 127, 136; liberty and, 38
Ammerman, A.J., 12
Amorgos, 8
Anatolians, language origins of, 13-14
Andrewes, John, 87-88
Andros, 8
Antigone, 46
Aphrodite, 19, 31
"Apollo the Lyre-Player," 171
Apollon, 19
Archaic Civilization, Sagan's concept, 154-158
Archon, definition of, 175
Areopagus, Council of, 60
Areopagus court, 122

Ares, 19
Aristocracy, definition of, 175 and early democratic forms, 58-62; word origin, 120
Aristophanes, 134
Aristotimos of Peiraieus, 182
Aristotle, 47, 58, 60, 63, 79, 95-116, 181; ethical writings, 95-116; Eudemian and Nicomachaean positions compared, 98-102; views on democracy, 126
Arius Didymus, 99
Art, under early tyrants, 81
Artemis, 19
Assembly, in early democracy, 61, 83-90, 134-135
Assembly of five hundred, 123
Athena Nike temple, 29
Athene (Athena), 19, 30
Athenian democracy, See Greek democracy
Athenian Empire, definition of, 66
Athens, early forms of democracy in, 57-69; tyranical rule in, 1

Attica, 16
Auden, W.H., 97
Augustus, 83
"Autobahn" theory, 82
Autonomia, 44-45, 77
Ayios Iakovos, necklace from, 165

Ball State University, Greek Studies Programme, 3
Basileus, definition of, 175
Bauman, Zygmunt, 151
Beloch, K.J., 91
Berlin, Isaiah, 37, 41, 49
Boule (citizens' council), 2
Bremner, Rory, 34
Bronze age, 8-12; obsidian in, 14 religions of, 16-19
Burke, Edmund, 128

Carlyle, Thomas, 139
Carter, Laurence, 47
Case, Thomas, 99-100
Casson, Sir Stanley, 2
Cavalli-Sforza, L.L., 12
Celts, 22
Centralization, 82
Chadwick, John, 12, 15

Chairestratos, 182
Charles I, King of England, 137
Chesterton, G.K., 129
Chios, 75-76
Christianity, 51-52
Cicero, 98
Citizenship, in early Athens, 57-66; and psycho-social identity, 147-159
Classes, in democratic society, 63-64
Cleisthenes, 58-59, 61, 120, 148; exile years, 77; family background, 122-123; governmental reform under, 123; governmental reforms under, 71-91; lot first used by, 73; and origins of democracy, 1-2, 36, 44, 133-144; political restructuring under, 124
Coinage, first efforts at, 81
Complex Societies, Sagan's views of, 154-158
Constant, Benjamin, 39-41, 48-50, 52
Constitutions, Constitution of Athens (Aristotle), 79; Spartan constitution, 74
Contemplation, in Aristotelian philosophy, 95-98
Copper deposits, in Cyprus, 164, 167-68
Corinth, 90; early government forms, 57
Council of 500, 59, 72, 79-80
Council of the Areopagus, 60, 123
Crete, early religions of, 16-19
Crime and Punishment (Dostoevsky), 152
Critias, 46
Croce, Benedetto, 50
Cyclades, early religions of, 16
Cyprus, 161-174; conquests of, 169-172; early culture of, 162-164; first settlers, 163-164; navigational circuits, 161-162; Roman occupation, 172

Dark Ages, 8, 10-11
De Sanctis, Gaetano, 50
Declaration of Independence, 136
Delos (Artemision deposit), 18
Delphi, 18, 20 , 77
Demarchs, 75
Demes, definition of, 79
Demeter, 19
Demiurgoi, 75
Democracy, attitudes toward, 138-139; Cleisthenes and, 1-2, 36, 44, 58-59, 61; in early Athens, 57-69; in early drama, 134; efficiency of as system, 121-122; eleutheria and, 43-44; in France, 137-138; freedom of speech and, 44-45; invention of, 133-135; laws for protection of, 182; liberty and, 34-43; lot used in, 72-73; modern views of, 36-43; modern vs. ancient, 35-36; modernity and, 151-152; in nineteenth century, 128-130; origins of, 1-3, 33-34, 120-126; political reform and, 136-137; public property in, 73; roots of, 120-124; in United States, 137-138; word origins of, 34-36, 43-45
Demokratia, 75-79
Dhaskaleio Kavos, 16
Diagoras of Melos, 46
Diogenes the Cynic, 45-46
Diogenes Laertius, 99
Dionysos, 19
Diophantus, 120
Disraeli, Benjamin, 124-25
Dodona, 20
Dorian invasions, 10

Double axes, significance of, 16
Dumézil, Georges, 18-19
Durkheim, Emil, 148-50
Dynasty, word origin, 120

Egypt, Cyprus and, 164
Einstein, Alfred, 142
Ekklesia (citizens' assembly), formation of, 1-2
Eleutheria ("freedom" or "liberty," 43-45
The Emergence of Greek Democracy (Forrest), 57-58
England, suffrage movement in, 139-140
English Civil War, 126-27
Enkomi, clay tablet from, 162
Enlightenment, liberty and, 38
Ephialtes, 36, 133
Ethics, Aristotelian, 95-116
Ethnicity, of Greek people, 20-23; influences of, 9-10; meaning of, 8
Ethnogenesis, Greek-Cypriot, 166
Euboea, 16, 169
Euclid, 120
Eudaimonia, 95, 98-101, 112-114
Eudemian Ethics (Aristotle), 96-115
Eudoxus, 120
Eukrates, 182
Eunomia, 36, 77
Eupatrid, 89
Eusebius, 169
Euthyphro (Plato), 111
Evagoras, 170
Evans, Sir Arthur, 7

Favorinus of Arles, 99
Finley, Moses, 65
First Palace period, 16
Forrest, George, 57-58

Index

Franchthi Cave, 14
Franco, Francisco, 80
Freedom, as element of democracy, 36-45; limitations of in early Athens, 46-49; of speech, 44-45, 47; types of, 40-43; see also Democracy
Freedom in the Making of Western Culture (Patterson), 42-43
Freeman, Edward Augustus, 64
French Revolution, 38-39, 52, 128, 136

Gellner, Ernest, 9
Genetic unity, 12
Genetics, Greek-Cypriot ethnogenesis, 166
Gillies, John, 69
Greek civilization, customs of, 14-15 ethnicity and, 8-10; land and, 11-12; religions of, 15-20; self-identity of, 20-23; tyranny as form of rule, 80-85; see also Democracy
Greek democracy, in ancient Athens, 57-69; freedom of opinion in, 46-47; limitations of, 62-65; linguistic factors and, 34-36, 43-45; modern democracy compared to, 36-43; modern views of, 134-141; origins of, 34-36; ostracism in, 40, 61-62, 86; Spartan constitution, 74; see also Democracy
Greek language, democracy expressed through, 34-36, 43-45, 75-78, origins of, 10, 12-14
Greek people, ethnicity of, 20-23, genetic unity and, 12, origins of, 7-8
Grey, Lord, 129

Hall, Edith, 23
Hansen, M.H., 48
Hansen, Mogens Herman, 42
Hegel, on history, 120
Hellene, as ethnonym for Greek people, 21-22
Hephaistos, 19
Hera, 19
Hermes, 19
Herodotus, 1, 21, 73, 76, 78, 89-90, 123
Hesiod, 30
History, purposes of, 34, 71; value of, 119-120
Homer, 22
Hyskos, 164

Identity, of Greeks as people, 20-22; personal vs. national, 9; psycho-social, 147-159
Individual psychology, 147-148
Indo-European languages, 12-13, 19
Isagoras, 78, 123
Isegoria, 44-45
Isokratia, 77
Isomoiria, 77
Isonomia, 36, 76, 78, 123

Jackson, Andrew, 128
Jefferson, Thomas, 136
Jeffery, L.H., 90

Kalokagathia, in Aristotle, 103-107, 110
Kamares, 16
Kato Syme, 18
Kea figures, 16-17
Keros, 16
Kinship, as social structure, 153-54
Kirsten, Ernst, 11
Knossos, occupation of, 15
Kouros, 11

Kronos, 19

Language. See Greek language
Lefkandi centaur, 18
Lerna IV, 10
Levellers, 136
Lewis, D.M., 86
Liberty, as element of democracy, 36-45; limitations of, 46-49; types of, 37-38; see also Democracy
Locke, John, 37, 136
Lot, in early democracy, 72-73
Louis XVI, King of France, 137
Lycurgus, 57

Maa-Palaeokastro promontory, 168
Macedonian occupation, 58
Madison, James, 127, 138
Maeandrius, 76
Malinowski, B., 151
Maps, early forms of, 11
Marathon, Persian defeat at, 135
Massilia, 77
Menestratos of Aixone, 182
Metallurgy, development of, 14
Miletus, 77
Mill, John Stuart, 37-41, 51-52, 64
"Minoan Goddess with Upraised Arms," 17
Minoans, 8, 14-15; Cyprus and, 164-65; religions of, 15-17
Minyan ware, 10
Modernity, views of, 151-152
Momigliano, Arnaldo, 50-52
Monarchy, word origin, 120
Moghuls, 144
Montesquieu, 137
Morris, Ian, 10
Mossé, Claude, 67

Mycenaeans, 8, 11, 14-5; Cyprus and, 164-67; language origins of, 13-14; religions of, 15-19
Mykale, 66
Myres, Sir John, 7
Mytilene, revolt in, 65

Nationalism, 148, 152-154
Naxos, 8
Neolithic period, farmers in, 18; religions of, 16
Nicolaus of Damascus, 99
Nicomachaen Ethics (Aristotle), 95-116
Nilsson, Martin, 8, 15
Nussbaum, M.C., 96

Obsidian, in early culture, 14; trade of, 161
Oligarchy, definition of, 175; word origin, 120
Olympia, 18, 20; Parthenon and, 29-31
Olympic games, 22
"On the Liberty of Ancients...." (Constant), 39-41
On Representative Government (Mill), 64
Ostracism, 40, 61-62, 86
Ottomans, 144

Palaces, Minoan, 16-17
Palaepaphos, 168
Palestine, 166
Pandora, 30-31
Panhellenic movement, 22
Paros, 77
Parrhesia, 45-46
Parsons, Talcott, 148
Parthenon, 29-31, 81
Partial virtues, in Aristotle, 102
Parva Naturalia, 100
Patterson, Orlando, 42-43, 49
Pausanias, 30

Peisistratus family, 122-123
Peloponnesian War, 46, 67
"People," early meaning of term, 73; power of, 77
Periander, 57
Pericles, 2-3, 29, 36, 48, 64, 133; "Funeral Oration," 134, 149, 177-180
Persephone, 31
Persians, Cyprus and, 169-172
Phaistos, 17
Phaselis decree, 85
Phi and Psi figurines, 17
Philip of Macedon, 134
Philo of Alexandria, 99
Phocaea, exiles from, 77; public meeting in, 73
Phoenicians, Cyprus and, 167-168
Phratries, 79, 82
Phrynichus, 182
Phylakopi, shrine at, 17-18
Pisistratus, 1, 80-84
Pittacus, 73
Plataea, 66
Plato, 38, 63, 65, 134; views on democracy, 126
Pliny, 30
Polis, Greek and Roman compared, 148-49
Political rights, in early democracy, 74
Politics (Aristotle), 47, 181
Polybius, 127
Proto-Indo-European languages, 12-13, 19
Prytaneis, of Cleisthenes, 85
Prytany (standing committee), 63
Psycho-social identity, 147-159
Public property, early concept of, 73
Pyla-Verghi, 163

Reflections (Burke), 128
Reform Act (of 1832), 129

Religion
 and democracy, 51-52, 158
 in early Greek civilization, 15-20, 82-83
 "Minoan Goddess with Upraised Arms," 17
 Parthenon decoration and, 29-31
Rhetrai, 75
Roosevelt, Franklin Delano, 130-131
Rousseau, Jean Jacques, 38-40, 138
Rousseau, J.J., 128

Safavids, 144
Salamis, 66, 169
 Persian defeat at, 135
Samos, 18, 76-77
Science, in Aristotelian theory, 113-14
Sculpture, early forms, 81
Second Palace period, 16-17
Self government. See Autonomia
Self-identity, personal vs. national, 9
Sinda, skyphos from, 167
Slavery, 41
 in early democracy, 2, 49-50, 62
 eleutheria and, 43-44
"Smiting god," 17
Snodgrass, Anthony, 8
Social Contract (Rousseau), 38
Socrates, trial of, 46
Solon, 57, 75-76, 80, 133
Sophocles, 46, 59
Sovereignal freedom, 42
Spain, democracy in, 80
Sparta, 36, 78, 123
 constitution of, 74
 early government forms, 57
Speech, freedom of, 44-45
Speke, John, 154

Index

Stanley, Henry Morton, 154
State coinage, first efforts at, 81
Stuart, Gilbert, 123
Suffrage movement, 139-140
Suppliants (Aeschylus), 77
Syria, 166

Tell el Amarna tablets, 164
Terracotta, as clue to religious development, 16
Theophrastus, 98
Thessaly, and language origins, 13
Thucydides, 21, 44, 59, 64, 149
Tienanmin Square, 149

Trade, democratic influences of, 57; under early tyrants, 81-82
Trojan War, 22
"Two Concepts of Liberty" (Berlin), 37
Tyranny, under Pisistratus, 80-85; word origin, 120
Tyrant, definition of, 175

United States, suffrage movement in, 140
Uranos, 19

Ventris, M., 15
Villages (demes), 79

Voltaire, 127, 137-138

War, effects on democracy, 67
The Wasps (Aristophanes), 134
Wealth, in Aristotelian ethics, 105-106
Women, in early Athens, 49-50, 62; in early democracy, 2; suffrage movement, 139-140

Xenarchus, 98

Zagora, 8
Zeus, 19, 31, 133
Zimmer, Stefan, 18